T0038036

BACKPACKING ON VANCOUVER ISLAND

BACKPACKING
ON VANCOUVER ISLAND

The Essential Guide to the Best Multi-Day Trips and Day Hikes

TARYN EYTON

Foreword by Məlidas (Steven Recalma)

GREYSTONE BOOKS
Vancouver/Berkeley/London

Copyright © 2024 by Taryn Eyton
Foreword copyright © 2024 by Məlidas (Steven Recalma)

24 25 26 27 28   5 4 3 2 1

All rights reserved. No part of this book may be reproduced, stored in a retrieval system or transmitted, in any form or by any means, without the prior written consent of the publisher or a licence from The Canadian Copyright Licensing Agency (Access Copyright). For a copyright licence, visit accesscopyright.ca or call toll free to 1-800-893-5777.

Greystone Books Ltd.
greystonebooks.com

Cataloguing data available from Library and Archives Canada
ISBN 978-1-77840-010-0 (pbk.)
ISBN 978-1-77840-011-7 (epub)

Editing by Lucy Kenward
Copy editing by Merrie-Ellen Wilcox
Proofreading by Alison Strobel
Indexing by Stephen Ullstrom
Cover and text design by Fiona Siu
Cover photograph by EB Adventure Photography/Shutterstock.com
Interior photographs by Taryn Eyton, except where credited otherwise
Cartography by Steve Chapman, Canadian Map Makers

Printed and bound in Malaysia on FSC® certified paper at Papercraft. The FSC® label means that materials used for the product have been responsibly sourced.

Greystone Books thanks the Canada Council for the Arts, the British Columbia Arts Council, the Province of British Columbia through the Book Publishing Tax Credit, and the Government of Canada for supporting our publishing activities.

Canadä

Greystone Books gratefully acknowledges the xʷməθkʷəy̓əm (Musqueam), Sḵwx̱wú7mesh (Squamish), and səlilwətaɬ (Tsleil-Waututh) peoples on whose land our Vancouver head office is located.

PREVIOUS SPREAD: *Castlecrag Mountain as seen from the trail to Kwai Lake (Trip 18).*
Photo: Reid Holmes

CONTENTS

Safety Notice ... 7
Foreword by Məlidas (Steven Recalma) ... 9
Introduction ... 11
Backpacking Basics ... 13
    Trip Planning ... 13
    Safety ... 17
    Wilderness Ethics and Leave No Trace ... 24
How to Use This Book ... 29
Key to Map Symbols ... 31
Overview Map ... 32
Trips at a Glance ... 34

SOUTHWEST COAST TRIPS ... 39
    1. Narvaez Bay ... 42
    2. East Sooke Coast Trail ... 46
    3. Juan de Fuca Marine Trail ... 51
    4. Kludahk Trail ... 60
    5. T'l'oqwxwat (Avatar Grove) ... 71
    6. West Coast Trail ... 75
    7. Carmanah Valley ... 90
    8. Keeha Beach ... 95

PORT ALBERNI AND TOFINO TRIPS ... 101
    9. Mount Arrowsmith (Judge's Route) ... 103
    10. Della Falls ... 107
    11. Hišimy̓awiƛ Hut and 5040 Peak ... 115
    12. Wild Pacific Trail ... 120
    13. Big Tree Trail ... 125
    14. Wild Side Trail ... 128

COURTENAY-COMOX TRIPS 135
    15. Helliwell Loop 138
    16. Cumberland Community Forest 142
    17. Forbidden Plateau Traverse 146
    18. Helen Mackenzie and Kwai Lakes Loop 154
    19. Circlet Lake and Mount Albert Edward 164
    20. Augerpoint Traverse 168

CAMPBELL RIVER TRIPS 179
    21. Ripple Rock 182
    22. Flower Ridge 185
    23. Bedwell and Cream Lakes 191
    24. Upper Myra Falls 197
    25. Arnica Lake and Phillips Ridge 202
    26. Elk River and Landslide Lake 206
    27. Crest Mountain 213

NORTHWEST COAST TRIPS 217
    28. Upana Caves 220
    29. Nootka Trail 225
    30. Tatchu Peninsula 239
    31. North Coast Trail 247
    32. Cape Scott 257
    33. San Josef Bay 264
    34. Raft Cove 268
    35. Grant Bay 272

Acknowledgements 277
Index 279
About the Author 288

SAFETY NOTICE

HIKING, SCRAMBLING, BACKPACKING, camping, and all forms of outdoor recreation involve inherent risks and an element of unpredictability. Many of the trips in this guidebook are not for novices and may not be safe for your party. There are dangers on every road, trail, beach, and route, and conditions can change at any time. While every effort has been made to ensure accuracy, this book may contain errors. You assume full responsibility for your safety and health in the backcountry. The author, publisher, and distributors accept no liability for any loss, damage, injury, or death arising from the use of this book. Check current conditions, carry the Ten Essentials, exercise caution, and stay within your limits.

FOREWORD

MY TRADITIONAL GIVEN NAME is Məlidas. My borrowed English name is Steven Recalma. I am a member of the Qualicum First Nation, with matrilineal ties to the Musqueam Indian Band through my Grandmother as well as many relatives spanning different nations in what are now known as Canada, the United States, and other territories around the world. My life has been informed, influenced, and shaped by my experiences and relationships with many of the forests, trails, oceans, lakes, and natural locations in this book.

Having received the gifts offered by my traditional lands and waters, and as a member of one of the host nations of the territories discussed within these pages, it is both my honour and my responsibility to raise my hands in welcome to you. My ancestors have welcomed adventurers, writers, and other guests to our territories for thousands of years. They have shared their deep knowledge of these places, knowledge gained as caretakers of the lands and waters we call home. I must also acknowledge that not all the territories discussed within these pages are mine to welcome you to. Indeed, other Indigenous nations hold those rights and responsibilities as stewards of the vast and sprawling forests, mountains, and waters that have been their gathering places for thousands of years.

When we serve as hosts and guests, our role is to protect the community and territory, and to nurture and affirm our collective identity as qayəwmıxʷ (human beings) through respectful conduct. As hosts, Indigenous Peoples have a responsibility to remind our guests that we expect them to uphold the same respect for and reciprocal relationship with the natural world that we have held since time immemorial. In Qualicum territory, we remind our guests that the right to access these lands and waters—and experience them fully—comes with a responsibility: to approach with an open heart, an open mind, and open eyes. That means taking the time and care to disconnect in order to reconnect with yourself and the world around you, and to acknowledge the interconnectedness between us all and the living sense of being in every element of nature around us.

The principles that guide our relationship with the natural world are based in reciprocity and sustainability. They ensure that we take only what we need and leave behind enough for those who come after us, and that we leave these territories better than when we found them. I am therefore honoured to write this foreword to remind those who make use of our territories and the knowledge of them gained in this book, to carry forward and pass down the responsibilities my ancestors have maintained for thousands of years—to our forests, waters, and mountains.

Welcome, readers, to a glimpse into the spiritual, mental, and emotional nourishment our territories have to offer. While backpacking across what is now known as Vancouver Island, travel well and with a good heart and mind.

Məlidas (Steven Recalma) is from the Qualicum First Nation on Vancouver Island with matrilineal links to the Musqueam. He was born and raised in Qualicum traditional territory and is passing on the knowledge he's learned from his Elders about being a steward of the lands and waters and the gifts they offer. He is a member of the Vancouver Island Indigenous snowboard team, an ambassador for NativesOutdoors, and associated with the Indigenous Life Sport Academy. He and his partner and their two kids are active in the outdoors, including hiking and backpacking.

INTRODUCTION

BACKPACKING ON VANCOUVER ISLAND covers multi-day hiking destinations across Vancouver Island, as well as on neighbouring islands in the traditional territories of the Coast Salish, Pacheedaht, Ditidaht, Nuu-chah-nulth, and Kwakwaka'wakw. It also includes destination-worthy day hikes in each region. The 35 trips include 650 kilometres (404 miles) of trail to 84 back-country campgrounds, with the option to add over 150 more km (93 mi) by extending your trip or day hiking from a base camp.

Two decades ago, I went on my first backpacking trip. It was a baptism by sand, mud, and fog on the West Coast Trail. While that trip was very challenging, I was hooked, both on backpacking and on Vancouver Island. Since then, I've returned to its coast dozens of times to walk through the rainforest and camp on isolated beaches. I also ventured inland to discover the wonder of the Island alpine: jagged peaks of volcanic rock crowned with lingering snow, tenacious wildflowers, and deep blue tarns nestled into rocky hollows.

When I first started visiting Vancouver Island, I had trouble finding information about backpacking trips. I could find details about day hiking, but little information about where to camp or how to explore farther than you could walk in a day. I've created this book to be the guide I've been looking for all these years.

This book is for people who want to go beyond day hiking to camp under the stars, enjoy the solitude of sunrise, and explore remote areas. Since parts of Vancouver Island are so isolated, I've also included a few stand-out day hikes across the island so you can extend your stay. Each trip highlights a different backcountry destination and gives you all the information you need to get there, what facilities you can expect at camp, and where you can hike from your campsite. I've hiked all of the trails in this guide, as well as a few that didn't make the cut.

This guidebook contains trips that range from easy to difficult, to suit hikers and backpackers of various levels of experience. While most people hike and backpack in the summer months on Vancouver Island, this book also includes low-elevation trails that you can hike year-round, provided you are prepared for wet weather and messy trail conditions. I've made sure to include the must-see locations that most hikers have heard of, and a handful of off-the-beaten-path trips for those seeking solitude or adventure.

When choosing which backpacking trips to include in this book, I kept a few guiding principles in mind. The trips must be:

- on Vancouver Island or one of the surrounding islands
- accessible by 2WD vehicles
- worth dedicating your time to
- extendable, where possible, by adding day hikes from a backcountry base camp, or your choice of multiple campgrounds
- located in an area with a land manager, such as a park, hiking club, or government agency

The last point is very important to me. As a certified Leave No Trace Master Educator, I am passionate about outdoor ethics education. When a location is featured in a guidebook, increased traffic usually results. I wanted to ensure that, where possible, this book has mitigated the impact that increased traffic can bring. By including only areas with a land manager, I know that a regulatory framework is already in place to make trail maintenance plans and install infrastructure like outhouses and food caches.

This guide also includes sections on Leave No Trace best practices, trip planning, and safety. Prepared hikers are more likely to have a smaller impact on the land and to be able to self-rescue in an emergency. They also have more fun. And having fun is the main reason we go backpacking.

BACKPACKING BASICS

TRIP PLANNING

1. WEATHER AND SEASONS

While the weather on Vancouver Island's southeast coast is often mild, it is usually colder, wetter, and windier on the rest of the island. Be prepared for cold and wet weather in any season. City weather forecasts are useless. Instead, use algorithmic forecasts, like SpotWx, or mountain-forecast.com, for precise locations. Use caution in periods of high rainfall or snowmelt. All that extra water can cause flooding and landslides that wash out bridges and trails.

On Vancouver Island, July and August are the driest and warmest months, and therefore the best time to plan a backpacking trip, especially in the mountains. May, June, and September can also be nice, but the weather is a bit colder and more variable. If you get a window of good weather, backpacking in April and October is a possibility if you're prepared for chillier temperatures.

Unless you have snowshoes, winter clothing, and avalanche training, backpacking in the mountains during the winter months is unpleasant and even dangerous. With a good weather forecast, you can backpack some of the coastal trails in winter. However, be prepared for lots of mud, high tides, rushing creeks, windy weather, and washouts.

In this guide, you'll find a recommendation for the best months to hike each trail. All the trips are snow-free from mid-July to mid-September. But lots of trips at lower elevations are also snow-free in spring and fall or even year-round. The snow melts at different rates each year, so check trail conditions before you go.

2. FITNESS

Hikers of any age can enjoy backpacking as long as they are in good health. However, backpacking is more challenging than hiking, due to the extra weight of camping gear, so it's best to ease into it. When choosing a trip, consider the fitness of each hiker in your group. Vancouver Island has some very technical trails that are rocky and rooty underfoot and/or very steep. New backpackers should start with the trips rated "easy" before tackling more challenging trails.

Each person hikes at their own pace. However, a good way to estimate hiking times for backpackers is 3 to 4 km (1.9 to 2.5 mi) per hour, plus 15 minutes for every 100 metres (328 feet) of elevation gain. This formula assumes average fitness, short breaks, and non-technical terrain. While some of Vancouver Island's coastal trails are flat, the terrain is very technical, so expect travel times slower than this formula.

3. TRAIL CONDITIONS

Mother Nature changes our trails every year. Fallen trees, lingering snow, missing markers, overgrown sections, mud, and washed-out bridges are common, especially outside of summer. On Vancouver Island, volunteers or understaffed park rangers maintain our trails, and some trails may go years without maintenance. The Further Resources section for each trip contains links to help you get an idea of current trail conditions.

4. NAVIGATION

Most trails in this guide are easy to follow, but a few require navigation skills. The maps in this guide are for reference only. For navigation, invest in a topographic map, compass, and/or GPS device or app. In the Further Resources section for each hike, you'll find listings for recommended trail maps and National Topographic System (NTS) map sheets.

Hiking on Vancouver Island can test your navigation skills. Fog, unexpected snowstorms, thick forests, overgrown trails, and confusing networks of logging roads can easily disorient you. Watch for trail markers as you hike. If you think you're off track, don't keep going. Turn around and head back to the last trail marker, then try again.

5. BACKROAD DRIVING

Many of the trips in this guide involve driving on gravel forest service roads (FSRs). While most are 2WD accessible, you may encounter potholes, steep hills, bumpy sections, unbridged creeks, and deep cross-ditches. On Vancouver Island, road conditions change each year as rain, snow, and logging operations reshape the landscape. All road descriptions were current at the time of writing.

Drive slowly, and get out of the car to evaluate hazards before continuing. Bring a spare tire, a shovel, and a saw to assist with self-rescue. Most of these roads have no cell service and navigation can be challenging. Use a GPS device or app with a backroad map layer, or bring a backroad map book, to stay on track. You will share the roads with logging trucks, industrial traffic, and ATVs. Always drive with your headlights on and go slowly around curves. Pull over to let faster traffic pass. In central and southern Vancouver Island, some logging roads are gated and open to the public on weekends only. Refer to the Getting There section of each trip for advice on specific roads.

6. WATER TAXIS, FLOATPLANES, AND SHUTTLE BUSES

Getting to the trailhead can be an adventure. Several trips in this book are inaccessible by road, so you will need to book a water taxi or floatplane to get to and from the trailhead. A few of the point-to-point trips are accessible by shuttle bus.

The Getting There section of each trip includes information on service providers and tips for booking. Availability can be limited, so make reservations well in advance.

Depending on tides, conditions, and vessel type, water taxis and floatplanes may drop off at docks, on coastal rocks, or on the beach. Be prepared to step directly into the water or onto slippery rocks. In some weather and wind conditions, water taxis or floatplanes may not operate, so you may need to delay the start of your trip or wait an extra day or two for pickup. Some

A water taxi leaving Yellow Bluff Bay on the Tatchu Peninsula (Trip 30)

water taxis have enclosed passenger cabins, whereas others leave you and your backpack exposed to the elements during your ride. For specific advice, inquire when booking.

7. FEES AND RESERVATIONS FOR CAMPING AND HUTS

Backpackers impact the wilderness more than day hikers do. Camping fees are used to create and maintain tent pads, food lockers, and outhouses to minimize these impacts, as well as to maintain the trails. You can find information on whether fees are required and how to pay them in the details for each trip.

Although most hikes in this guide are first-come, first-served, at the time of writing, four trips require reservations: Narvaez Bay, West Coast Trail, Keeha Beach, and Hišimỵawiƛ Hut. Links with information on reservation opening dates can be found in the Further Resources section for each trip. Available spots get booked, so make reservations as far ahead as possible.

8. REGULATIONS

In many areas, fires, smoking, cannabis, dogs, bikes, swimming, and drones are regulated to minimize environmental impact and create a welcoming space for everyone. If you choose to fish, obtain the appropriate licence (B.C. Recreational Freshwater Fishing Licence for lakes and rivers, Tidal Waters Sport Fishing licence for the ocean). Be a responsible backcountry citizen and check the regulations before you go.

9. BACKPACKING GEAR

Having the right gear can be the difference between a trip that is safe and fun and one that isn't. When selecting backpacking gear, choose lightweight items appropriate for the conditions. Bring only the essentials and try to carry less than 25% of your body weight. For clothing, go with wool or synthetics, not cotton, which holds moisture and makes you cold. For more advice on choosing backpacking gear, see my website, happiestoutdoors.ca, or get advice from staff at an outdoor store that specializes in backcountry camping and hiking.

The Ten Essentials

You should carry the Ten Essentials on every trip to ensure you have what you need in case of an accident or emergency.

1. Illumination (headlamp or flashlight with extra batteries)
2. Nutrition and hydration (extra food and water)
3. Insulation (extra clothing)
4. Navigation (map, compass, and GPS)
5. Fire starter
6. First aid kit

7. Emergency shelter (tent, tarp, or space blanket)
8. Sun protection (hat, sunscreen, sunglasses, and long sleeves)
9. Knife
10. Communication (whistle, mirror, phone, personal locator beacon, or satellite messenger)

But you'll need a lot more than the Ten Essentials to be comfortable on a backpacking trip. For a complete summer backpacking gear checklist, see my website: happiestoutdoors.ca/backpacking-checklist. Make sure everything fits well and you know how to use it before your trip. You don't want to be hours into the backcountry and discover your boots are uncomfortable or you don't know how to use your stove.

10. FOOD PLANNING

It can take a bit of practice to figure out a backpacking meal plan that works for you. In general, keep food lightweight, compact, easy to cook, and calorie-dense. You might burn more calories than usual, so you may want to bring more food than you'd eat at home.

Dehydrated and freeze-dried meals made with rice, pasta, and oatmeal are ideal. You can dehydrate your own, buy dried ingredients at the grocery store, or purchase pre-packaged backpacking meals at an outdoor store. For protein, cured meats, nuts, and hard cheeses are good options. Don't forget ready-to-eat snacks like energy bars, candy, dried fruit, and trail mix. Hot liquids like tea, coffee, hot chocolate, and soup are also nice in cold weather. Avoid canned and bottled food. For backpacking food tips, see my website, happiestoutdoors.ca/tag/camping-food.

SAFETY

1. FIRST AID

Backpacking trips take you far from medical help. Always carry a well-stocked first aid kit and know how to use everything in it. Check it before every trip to restock frequently used items like Band-Aids, blister dressings, and painkillers. Consider taking a wilderness first aid course to learn how to treat common injuries in the field.

2. TRIP PLAN

If you don't come home on time because you are lost or hurt, will anyone know where to look for you? Leave a detailed trip plan with a friend or family member, with instructions to call search and rescue if you aren't back on schedule. Use the trip planning form on the AdventureSmart app or website, or create your own. The plan should include names and contact information for all group members, details about your planned route, what kind of gear and supplies you have with you, and when you expect to be back. When you get home, don't forget to follow up with a call to those who have your trip plan.

3. HAZARDS

Hypothermia

Wet and cold weather is the most dangerous thing backpackers can encounter, and it's common on Vancouver Island. Hypothermia occurs when a person's core body temperature drops below 35°C (95°F). Mild symptoms include uncontrolled shivering, slurred speech, and loss of balance. Without treatment, hypothermia patients stop shivering, have shallow breathing and a weak pulse, and may lose consciousness.

Prevent hypothermia by packing warm, dry wool or synthetic clothing to change into. If the weather gets bad and you have not reached your destination, pitch your tent instead of pressing on. Change into dry clothing and get into a dry sleeping bag. Eat and drink warm foods and fluids.

Getting Lost

It can be surprisingly easy to get lost while hiking. You can miss a junction, accidentally turn onto an unmarked trail, or get off track in overgrown areas. To avoid getting lost, carry a copy of the trail description, a trail map, and a compass or GPS, and check them frequently to make sure you're on the right track.

If you aren't sure you are on the correct trail, don't just keep hiking. Ask other hikers for help. Backtrack to the last junction or trail marker and try again. If you do become truly lost, stay put. If possible, call for help and wait. (See the How to Get Help section below for more information.) If you keep moving, it will be difficult for rescuers to find you. Do not hike downhill, hoping it will lead you to a road or the coast. This strategy can lead you into dangerous terrain with cliffs and waterfalls that can make rescue more difficult and has led to fatal falls.

Drinking Water and Hygiene

Although it might be nice to think that water in the backcountry is clean and pure, you never really know if humans and animals have pooped (or died) upstream. Lakes and streams can contain bacteria, viruses, and protozoa that can make you sick. Use a backcountry water filter or purifying drops or tablets to treat your water.

On coastal trips, water is often tea-coloured thanks to the tannins in the nearby swamps and bogs. In some cases, the water is just an off-putting colour, but in others, it tastes unpleasant. The fine particles also clog water filters, so you may want to pre-filter your drinking water through a clean

Wading a creek on the Tatchu Peninsula (Trip 30)

bandana or coffee filter. Be sure you know how to clean your water filter in the field. If the taste or colour bothers you, juice or electrolyte powder can help.

Poor hygiene, rather than contaminated water, is often the cause of gastrointestinal issues in backpackers. Take care to wash your hands or use hand sanitizer after going to the bathroom and before eating.

Creek Crossings

Some trails in this book cross unbridged creeks. In summer, you can hop from rock to rock across many of these creeks without removing your boots, while others may require a knee-deep wade. However, after periods of high rainfall or snowmelt, some creeks rise dangerously. As well, some coastal streams are best waded at low tides. Assess a creek carefully before crossing. If your itinerary takes you back across the same creek, remember that it may rise further, cutting off your route to the trailhead.

Wider parts of a creek tend to be shallower, with a slower current, and therefore safer for wading. Cross downstream from logs, waterfalls, boulders, and other hazards that could trap you underwater if you slip. Consider waiting for water levels to subside or the tide to go out before crossing.

Cross streams wearing your hiking boots or other securely fitting footwear. Going barefoot or wearing flimsy footwear often leads to falls or injured feet. Unbuckle your backpack so it won't drag you down if you fall. Use trekking poles or a sturdy stick to help you keep your balance. Face upstream, shuffle across sideways, and maintain three points of contact with the ground, moving one foot or pole at a time.

Snow and Ice

In the early season or high in the mountains, it is common to encounter snow on the trails. A simple slip and fall on a steep snow slope can result in injury or death. Melting snow can conceal hidden holes or creeks. Drowning, ankle injuries, and hypothermia are common when hikers fall through broken snow.

Check trail conditions before you go to know how much snow to expect. Leave high-elevation hikes until late in the summer when they are more likely to be snow-free. When encountering snow, use extra caution. Bring microspikes or crampons and an ice axe for better traction. Be prepared to turn back if snow conditions are more than your group can handle.

If you choose to backpack in the mountains of Vancouver Island, especially in winter or spring, know that many of the trips in this book are in serious avalanche terrain. Take an avalanche course to learn how to recognize and avoid avalanche-prone terrain and to conduct a rescue if an avalanche strikes.

Tides and Coastal Travel

Some routes in this guide follow the shoreline instead of a trail. It is important to know the predicted tides so that you can safely pass cliffs that may be inundated with water at high tide. As well, many campgrounds are on the beach, so you will need to be careful to pitch your tent above the high-tide line.

Carry a tide table on all coastal hikes. Look for information on the relevant tide table in the Further Resources section. I recommend printing out the predicted hourly heights section as well as the highs and lows.

Use caution on coastal hikes where your route is on the beach instead of a trail. You may need to clamber over or under logs. Expect surfaces to be slippery with algae and seaweed. Use care where you must scramble over rocks and headlands.

Watch carefully for buoys hanging in trees. These mark places where your route leaves the beach and heads into the forest on a trail. In many cases, remaining on the beach will lead you into impassable or dangerous terrain. Each trip description includes details about important beach exit routes.

Cable Cars, Ladders, Ropes, and Crumbling Infrastructure

Some trails use cable cars to cross creeks. These small carts hold one or two hikers and their packs. They are attached to a cable with pulleys at either end like a clothesline. Be careful around cable cars and on elevated platforms. Keep gear, hands, and hair away from the pulleys.

A few trails in this book use ladders or fixed ropes on cliffs and steep slopes. Always maintain three points of contact on ladders. Watch for missing

A cable car across Camper Creek on the West Coast Trail (Trip 6). Photo: Reid Holmes

or damaged rungs. Test ropes before putting your weight on them—many have been exposed to the elements for years. Ensure that only one hiker is using the rope at a time.

Some hikers like to wear gloves to protect their hands when using cable cars, ladders, and ropes. I recommend inexpensive work gloves from the hardware store. If you use hiking poles, collapse them at these points and attach them to your pack. If you let them dangle from your wrist they can swing around and impede your progress, which can be dangerous.

Use caution on any wooden infrastructure, such as boardwalks, bridges, and stairs; slipping and sliding are common. Step carefully to avoid holes, broken planks, and nails on unrepaired wooden infrastructure, the result of decades of underfunding for our parks.

Trailhead Security

Unfortunately, car break-ins and vandalism are common at some of the trailheads in this guide, especially along Highway 14. The only foolproof way to avoid this problem is to use a shuttle bus service or get dropped off and picked up at the trailhead. If you do leave your car parked at a trailhead overnight, do not leave anything in your vehicle. Consider leaving the glove box and console open to show thieves you aren't hiding anything from view.

4. WILDLIFE

Insects

More a nuisance than a danger, mosquitos and blackflies can be bad on Vancouver Island, especially in May, June, and early July in wet areas. Insect repellent, a head net, and clothing that covers your arms and legs can be helpful. If you are sensitive to bites, bring a topical anti-itch cream and antihistamine tablets.

Wasps with trailside underground nests can be an issue, particularly during warm and dry summers. If you are stung, wash the area with soap and water to remove as much venom as possible. Ibuprofen and antihistamine tablets can help with the pain and swelling. Hikers with wasp allergies should always carry their EpiPen.

Ticks can carry Lyme disease, which is becoming more prevalent locally. Use caution on the Gulf Islands, southeastern Vancouver Island, and lower-elevation trails in dry climates. Ticks seek exposed skin where they can bite, then burrow into your flesh. Wear long pants and long sleeves. Check yourself frequently for ticks. At camp, remove your clothing and do a thorough check, paying particular attention to the areas at the edges of your clothing and your hairline. If you discover a tick, remove it carefully with tweezers. When you get home, talk to your doctor about Lyme disease testing and treatment.

Bears

Black bears live throughout Vancouver Island. Bears will usually run away when they see people. They are more likely to bluff charge or attack if they are surprised, have cubs with them, or are defending food.

To avoid surprising a bear, talk or sing as you hike, especially in dense vegetation like berry bushes. Travel in a group and keep your dog on a leash. If you come across a dead animal, leave the area immediately. To avoid attracting a bear to your campsite, follow the tips in the Food Storage section below.

If you see a bear, give it lots of space. Stay still and talk calmly to the bear while avoiding eye contact. Don't run. If you are attacked or bluff charged, use bear spray at close range if you have it. If that doesn't work, lie down and play dead. A territorial bear will leave you alone. However, if the bear keeps attacking after you play dead, fight back, because the bear is predatory. If you have a negative encounter and the bear poses a danger to public safety, report it to the B.C. Conservation Officer Service by calling 1-877-952-7277 (RAPP).

Cougars
While cougar sightings are infrequent, the Vancouver Island cougar population is large. It is very rare for cougars to attack adults, but they will sometimes attack children and dogs. If you see a cougar, don't run. Back away slowly. Gather together in a group, pick up small children, and leash your dog. Try to look big by waving your arms over your head. If the cougar doesn't retreat, shout at it and throw things. If it attacks, fight back.

Wolves
Wolves are common on coastal trails on Vancouver Island, especially on northern Vancouver Island. You are far more likely to see wolf tracks than to spot the canines. However, your odds of a negative wolf encounter are very high if you are travelling with a dog. Wolves are very territorial and have attacked and killed dogs on coastal trails.

In some areas, wolves have also become habituated to eating human food and feces. Keep a clean camp and use the tips in the Food Storage section below to avoid attracting wolves. Use outhouses whenever possible.

If you see a wolf approaching, make noise and wave your arms over your head. Throw sticks and rocks to deter it from coming closer. Gather your group close and act in unison. If a wolf is aggressive, back away slowly. Use bear spray and fight back if a wolf attacks.

Food Storage and Backcountry Cooking: Protecting Your Food From Animals
In many backcountry campgrounds, animals have realized that humans carry food.

To avoid attracting mice, squirrels, and birds as well as larger, more dangerous animals like bears and wolves to your campsite, always cook 100 m (328 ft) away from your tent. Clean up all food scraps after eating. Never burn food scraps in a fire; this can attract animals. Store all food, cooking equipment, and scented items—such as toiletries and sunscreen—in a food locker, bear hang, or bear canister. Any clothing that is smelly from food or toiletries should be cached as well. Never leave these items in your tent or backpack.

Many of the backcountry campgrounds in this guide have food storage lockers. Others have food hanging poles or wires to suspend your food out of reach of bears. Protect your food from the elements and clever birds or rodents by placing it in a weather- and chew-resistant bag like a lightweight dry bag.

In campgrounds without provided food storage, you can construct a food hang with a rope and carabiner to protect your food from bears. Suspend your food from a tree branch at least 1.5 m (5 feet) from the branch and the tree trunk and 4 m (12 feet) off the ground. This technique takes a lot of practice to get right, and finding trees with suitable branches can be very difficult or impossible, especially at high elevations.

Consider investing in a bear canister, a crush-proof plastic container that requires tools and thumbs to open. Thankfully bears have neither. Bear canisters hold less food, and are heavier and more expensive than building a food hang. However, they are much easier to use. Another alternative is an Ursack, a lightweight bag made of durable Spectra fabric that is designed to be tied securely to the trunk of a tree. Ursacks can resist being chewed or clawed by bears and other animals. However, they are not odour-proof, waterproof, or crush-proof, so the manufacturer recommends lining them with a specially designed odour-proof bag and an aluminum sleeve.

5. HOW TO GET HELP

No one plans to get injured or lost on a hike, but it happens to even the most prepared people. If you need to call for help, remember that search and rescue is completely free in B.C. If you have cell service, call 911. The dispatcher will help coordinate search and rescue.

Many of the trails in this guide do not have cell service. Consider carrying a satellite messaging device like a Garmin inReach to call for emergency help. Blow a whistle, which carries farther than the human voice, to alert other hikers in the area or help rescuers locate you. A mirror, flares, and matches to make a signal fire can also help rescuers see you from the air. If you can't call for help, your trip plan is your lifeline. Your emergency contact will call 911 to trigger a rescue if you do not return on time.

WILDERNESS ETHICS AND LEAVE NO TRACE

As more and more people go into the wilderness, we must all do our part to keep our wild places wild. The seven principles of Leave No Trace guide wilderness users to minimize their impact on the environment. I am a certified Leave No Trace Master Educator and a former member of the Board of Directors of Leave No Trace Canada, and have been volunteering with Leave No Trace Canada since 2006. To learn more about Leave No Trace, visit leavenotrace.ca.

Whether you are new to backpacking or not, familiarize yourself with the Leave No Trace principles below.

1. PLAN AHEAD AND PREPARE

Check the weather forecast, trail conditions, and park regulations before your hike. This step ensures that you will have a safe and fun hike, while also

Tent platforms at Circlet Lake (Trip 19)

minimizing your impact on nature. Leave a trip plan and pack a first aid kit and the Ten Essentials (page 16) in case something goes wrong. Portion and package food at home to reduce the chance of leaving garbage on the trail.

2. TRAVEL AND CAMP ON DURABLE SURFACES

Hike and camp on durable surfaces like rocks, gravel, bare soil, and snow. Avoid alpine meadows, marshes, and other sensitive surfaces where the vegetation can take years to grow. Stay on the trail. Cutting switchbacks or walking off-trail to avoid mud causes erosion and tramples vegetation. If there is no trail, have your group spread out to avoid creating a new one.

If possible, camp in a designated or previously used campsite, preferably on a wooden tent platform or earthen tent pad. If there are no designated or previously used campsites, pitch your tent on sand, gravel, bare dirt, snow, or dry grass to minimize your impact. Try to camp 70 m (230 ft) away from water sources to protect fragile vegetation and give animals uninterrupted access routes to water. Most of the trips in this guide have established campsites. The hikes without established campsites each have recommendations on the most low-impact place to camp.

A boardwalk protects sensitive shoreline at the viewpoint on Battleship Lake (Trip 18)

3. DISPOSE OF WASTE PROPERLY

Be responsible when disposing of trash, human waste, and soap in the wilderness. These can pollute water, making it unsafe to drink or killing plants and fish. Animals who learn to eat human food or waste may stop eating their natural food. It can also make them sick. Plus, garbage and poop on the trails look disgusting!

Bring a plastic bag to pack out all of your trash, including food waste like fruit peels and eggshells. They can take months to biodegrade and, in the meantime, they attract animals. A good rule is "If it didn't grow here, it doesn't go here." Never burn your trash. It doesn't burn well, so it leaves a mess and can attract animals.

When washing dishes or yourself, try just using a warm, wet cloth. If you do use soap, choose the biodegradable kind. Don't wash directly in a river or lake: use a pot as a dish basin instead. Strain out any large particles, then dump the dirty water 70 m (230 ft) away from water sources. Biodegradable soap needs to filter through the soil to break down, so don't dump it directly in a lake or stream. When camping on the beach, you can dump your dishwater into the ocean or well below the high-tide line.

A dip in a wilderness lake is a fun way to cool off, but it can harm fragile ecosystems. Before you jump in, head 70 m (230 ft) away from the shore and use water and a cloth to wash bug spray and sunscreen off your skin. The chemicals kill plants and fish. If the lake is tiny and is the only water source for a nearby campground, consider skipping the swim. Most campers don't want to drink someone else's swimming water, even if it is filtered or purified.

Use a toilet for human waste whenever possible. If there is no outhouse, pick a spot 70 m (230 ft) away from trails, campsites, and water sources. Pee on bare ground, soil, or rocks to avoid damaging vegetation. If you have to poop, use a small trowel, stick, or tent peg to dig a hole 15 cm (6 in) deep. Poop into the hole, then bury it. On coastal trips, you can also dig a hole well below the high-tide line. The best practice is to bring a resealable plastic bag to pack out your toilet paper, but you can also bury it with your poop. Don't burn it, since you can accidentally start a forest fire.

Pack out used menstrual supplies in a resealable plastic bag, as they don't biodegrade. Don't dump them in outhouses. Securely store the bag along with your food and toiletries at night to avoid attracting animals. If you use a menstrual cup, bury the fluid in a cat hole or pour it into an outhouse. For more information on backpacking while menstruating, see happiestoutdoors.ca/camp-and-hike-on-your-period.

If you are backpacking with a dog, pack out their poop or bury it as you would human poop. Dog poop contains bacteria and parasites that aren't normally found in the backcountry. Leaving it in the wilderness can make wildlife sick.

4. LEAVE WHAT YOU FIND

Leave the wilderness as you found it to keep ecosystems intact and let other hikers enjoy them too. If we all picked flowers or brought home rocks or historical items, there wouldn't be any left. Take a photo instead.

Good campsites are found, not made. Don't build structures, cut down trees, or dig trenches. When you leave your camp, it should look like you were never there. Please don't leave graffiti or "art" like inukshuks. Other hikers may mistake your rock art for trail marker cairns, and can be led astray. As well, many animals and insects live under rocks. When you move the rocks, you destroy their homes.

5. MINIMIZE CAMPFIRE IMPACTS

Careless campers accidentally start many forest fires. Campfires can also scorch soil or lead to dead branches being overharvested from the forest. It can take ecosystems decades to recover. Plan to cook on a stove, not a fire. It's quicker and more fuel-efficient, and has a smaller impact on the wilderness. Consider forgoing a fire and gathering around a small lantern instead.

If you do have a fire, learn to minimize your impact. Before you go, find out if fires are permitted in the park or the region. All non-beach trips in this guide have year-round fire bans to protect sensitive ecosystems with fragile soils, short growing seasons, and a lack of firewood. Use an existing fire ring and avoid building new ones. On coastal trips, build your campfire below the high-tide line. Ensure that the soil under the fire is protected with gravel, rocks, or ash to avoid scorching soil or burning tree roots. When gathering firewood, stick to the "Four Ds": dead, down, dinky, and distant. Dead and down wood burns best: never cut live trees. Dinky branches help keep your fire small and mean you don't need to carry an axe. Gather your firewood from a place distant from your camp to avoid overharvesting.

Most importantly, make sure your fire is completely out when you leave it. Bring a collapsible bucket or water container and make campfire soup: douse the fire, stir up the ashes, test to see if it feels warm, then repeat until it's cool to the touch.

6. RESPECT WILDLIFE

Always treat wildlife with respect. Never feed animals, either intentionally or by leaving your food unattended. Human food can make them sick. If they develop a taste for it, they may lose their ability to find food on their own. They may also attack people in the hope of getting food.

Wild animals need space to maintain their natural behaviour. Observe from a distance using binoculars or the zoom lens on your camera. If an animal changes its behaviour, you are too close. Keep your dog on a leash and under control so it doesn't harass wildlife. Off-leash dogs can also be dangerous if they chase after a predator and then the predator follows the dog back to you. While dogs are permitted on many trips in this book, they are not recommended in areas with high wolf activity.

7. BE CONSIDERATE OF OTHERS

We all share the trails, huts, and campsites. Respect the way other people wish to experience nature, and do not let your behaviour negatively impact someone else's experience. Learn and follow basic backcountry etiquette. Yield to others on the trail. Step off the trail to take breaks so you aren't in someone's way. Give other groups space at viewpoints, popular photo spots, or in camp. Keep your voice low and avoid yelling. Leave the music at home: most campers want to enjoy the sounds of nature. Backpack in small groups of fewer than 10 people to minimize your impact on the environment and others. But above all else, be kind. Being nice goes a long way when you're sharing space.

HOW TO USE THIS BOOK

THE TRIPS IN this book are divided into geographic regions. Each region includes an overview of the area and its Indigenous context, as well as practical information for visitors, including how to get there, where to buy supplies, and where to stay. Each hike includes a map, photo, statistics, ratings, driving directions, trail description, camping details, information on how to extend your trip, and a list of further resources. (Please note: The trail and road information is written for summer conditions.)

Below are definitions for the statistics and ratings used in this book:

★: While all of the trips in this book are worthwhile, a select few are truly spectacular.

Difficulty: A subjective assessment of how challenging each trip will be.

● *Easy:* Trips that are short and flat.

■ *Moderate:* Trips are longer, with more than 200 m (656 ft) of elevation gain or include more technical terrain.

◆ *Challenging:* Trips that are long and have lots of technical terrain and/or more than 500 m (1640 ft) of elevation gain.

◆◆ *Very challenging:* Trips with lots of very technical terrain and/or route-finding.

Duration: For backpacking trips, the recommended number of days you should allow to complete the trip. This includes your hike to the campground and back, as well as day hikes from a backcountry base camp. For day hikes, the estimated number of hours it will take to complete the described trail.

Distance: The distance you'll cover on the hike. For round-trip or loop hikes, this is the distance from the trailhead to the campground, then back to the trailhead. If the hike is typically completed as a point-to-point traverse, the distance will be listed as "one way." Trips with multiple options are expressed as a range, with the precise distance to each location noted in the description. This statistic does not include day hikes from a backcountry base camp.

Elevation Gain: The difference between the highest and lowest points on the trip. Trips with multiple route options show elevation gain as a range, with statistics for each option noted in the trail description. Where your route climbs straight up a mountain, this statistic is straightforward. However, on cross-country routes, the elevation gain statistic does not encompass all of the small ups and downs you will encounter.

High Point: The highest elevation you'll reach on the trip. For trips with multiple routes, this is the highest point on any described route. Use this statistic along with the best months recommendation to pick the best time to hike each trail.

Best Months: The best months of the year to hike each trail without encountering significant snow, freezing temperatures, seasonal trail closures, or stormy weather that can impact trail conditions.

Fees and Reservations: Any user fees and/or reservations that must be paid online or at trailheads in advance.

Regulations: Any restrictions on fires, smoking, cannabis, dogs, bikes, swimming, and drones.

Caution: Any unique hazards, such as challenging navigation, exposed terrain, wildlife, shared trails with mountain bikes, or extreme weather, that you might encounter.

KEY TO MAP SYMBOLS

P Parking

4WD 4-Wheel-Drive Road

Bus Stop

Toilet

Car Camping

Designated Camping

Informal Camping
(no facilities)

Food Storage

Waterfall

Viewpoint

Car Ferry Dock

Water Taxi Landing

Float Plane Landing

Backcountry Hut

Backcountry Shelter

Hand-Operated Cable Car

Lighthouse

⚠ Warning/Hazard

▲ Mountain Peak

Direction of Travel

→ Off-Map Destination

Road

Track

Trail

Described Trail

Described Route (off trail/on beach)

Alternative Trail

Alternative Route (off trail/on beach)

800 Major Contour Line (100 m/328 ft)

Minor Contour Line (20 m/65 ft)

Stream/Creek

Parks

Ocean, Lake, Major River/Creek

Wetland

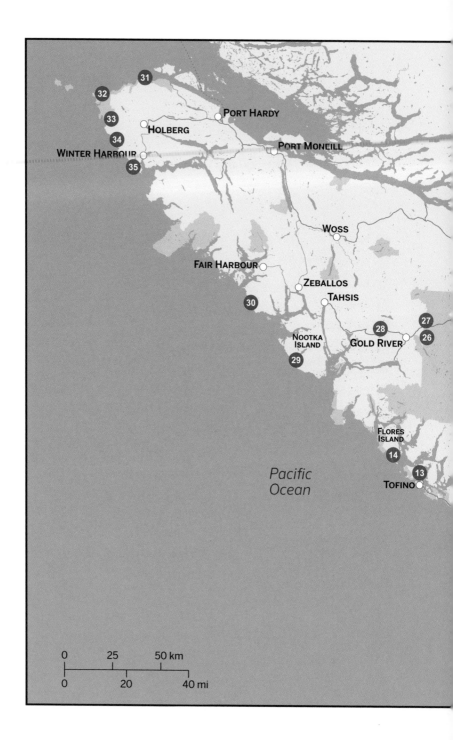

OVERVIEW MAP

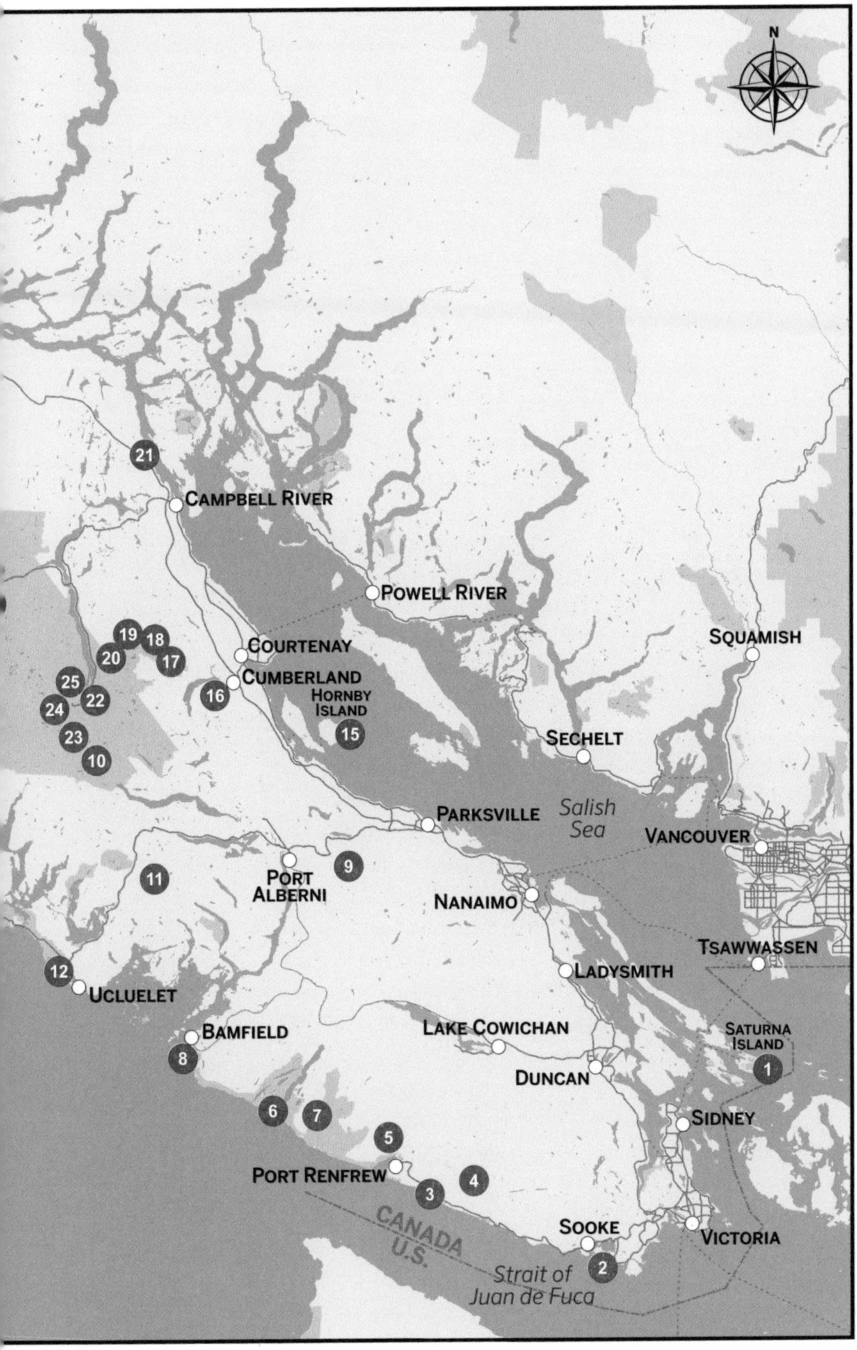

Trip	Difficulty	Duration	Distance	Elevation Gain	High Point
1 Narvaez Bay	●	2 days	2 km (1.2 mi) round trip	50 m (164 ft)	80 m (262 ft)
2 East Sooke Coast Trail	◆	5.5–8 hours	12.3 km (7.6 mi) one way	65 m (213 ft)	65 m (213 ft)
3 Juan de Fuca Marine Trail	◆	3–5 days	47 km (29.2 mi) one way	195 m (640 ft)	195 m (640 ft)
4 Kludahk Trail	■	2–4 days	40 km (24.9 mi) one way	350 m (1148 ft)	1100 m (3609 ft)
5 T'l'oqwxwat (Avatar Grove)	●	1 hour	1.25 km (0.8 mi) round trip	110 m (361 ft)	180 m (591 ft)
6 West Coast Trail ★	◆	6–8 days	75 km (46.6 mi) one way	213 m (699 ft)	213 m (699 ft)
7 Carmanah Valley	●	2 days	7 km (4.3 mi) round trip	90 m (295 ft)	240 m (787 ft)
8 Keeha Beach	■	2 days	8 km (5.6 mi) round trip	50 m (164 ft)	50 m (164 ft)
9 Mount Arrowsmith (Judge's Route)	◆◆	5–7 hours	6.2 km (3.9 mi) round trip	1060 m (3478 ft)	1817 m (5961 ft)
10 Della Falls	■	2–4 days	32 km (19.9 mi) round trip	545 m (1788 ft)	625 m (2051 ft)
11 Hišimy̓awiƛ Hut and 5040 Peak ★	◆	2–3 days	6 km (3.7 mi) round trip	700 m (2297 ft)	1320 m (4331 ft)
12 Wild Pacific Trail	●	1–3 hours	3–10 km (1.9–6.2 mi) round trip	40–80 m (131–262 ft)	40–80 m (131–262 ft)
13 Big Tree Trail	●	2 hours	3.5 km (2.2 mi) loop	10 m (32 ft)	10 m (32 ft)
14 Wild Side Trail ★	■	2 days	22 km (13.7 mi) round trip	5 m (16 ft)	5 m (16 ft)
15 Helliwell Loop	●	1.5 hours	4 km (2.5 mi) loop	50 m (164 ft)	50 m (164 ft)
16 Cumberland Community Forest	●	1.5–2 hours	5 km (3.1 mi) loop	75 m (246 ft)	225 m (738 ft)
17 Forbidden Plateau Traverse	■	2–3 days	24 km (14.9 mi) one way	150 m (492 ft)	1240 m (4068 ft)
18 Helen Mackenzie and Kwai Lakes Loop	●	2–3 days	8.3–15.4 km (5.2–9.6 mi) loop	190 m (623 ft)	1270 m (4167 ft)
19 Circlet Lake and Mount Albert Edward ★	■	2–3 days	22.6 km (14 mi) round trip	195 m (640 ft)	1230 m (4035 ft)

Best Months	Fees	Reservations	Dogs Allowed	Food Storage	Toilet(s)	Water Taxi/ Floatplane Required
Year-round	Y	Y (summer only)	Y on leash	Y	Y	N
Year-round	N	N	Y	n/a	Y	N
May to October	Y	N	Y on leash but not recommended	Y	Y	N
June to October	N	N	Y	N	Y	N
Year-round	N	N	Y	n/a	N	N
May to September	Y	Y	N	Y	Y	N
April to October	Y	N	Y on leash	N	Y	N
May to September	Y	Y	N	Y	Y	N
July to September	N	N	Y but not recommended	n/a	N	N
June to October	N	N	Y on leash	Y	Y	Y
July to September	Y for hut only	Y for hut only	Y but not in the hut	Y	Y at the hut only	N
Year-round	N	N	Y on leash	n/a	Y	N
Year-round	Y	N	N	n/a	Y	Y
May to September	Y	N	Y but not recommended	Y	Y	Y
Year-round	N	N	Y on leash	n/a	Y	N
Year-round	N	N	Y	n/a	Y	N
July to September	Y	N	Y on leash	Y	Y	N
July to September	Y	N	Y on leash	Y	Y	N
July to September	Y	N	Y on leash	Y	Y	N

Trip	Difficulty	Duration	Distance	Elevation Gain	High Point
20 Augerpoint Traverse ★	◆◆	2–5 days	31.5 km (19.6 mi) one way	1013 m (3323 ft)	2093 m (6867 ft)
21 Ripple Rock	●	2.5–3.5 hours	8 km (5 miles) round trip	95 m (312 ft)	95 m (312 ft)
22 Flower Ridge	◆	2–3 days	16 km (9.9 mi) round trip	1150 m (3773 ft)	1400 m (4593 ft)
23 Bedwell and Cream Lakes ★	■/◆	2–3 days	8–22 km (5–13.7 mi) round trip	410–830 m (1345–2723 ft)	1380 m (4528 ft)
24 Upper Myra Falls	●	2–2.5 hours	8 km (5 mi) round trip	150 m (492 ft)	500 m (1640 ft)
25 Arnica Lake and Phillips Ridge	◆	2–3 days	15 km (9.3 mi) round trip	810 m (2657 ft)	1200 m (3937 ft)
26 Elk River and Landslide Lake ★	■	2–3 days	12–18 km (7.5–11.2 km) round trip	180–365 m (591–1198 ft)	685 m (2247 ft)
27 Crest Mountain	◆	2 days	10 km (6.2 mi) round trip	1130 m (3707 ft)	1450 m (4757 ft)
28 Upana Caves	●	1 hour	0.7 km (0.4 mi) round trip	30 m (98 ft)	580 m (1903 ft)
29 Nootka Trail ★	◆	3–5 days	36–41.5 km (22.4–25.8 mi) one way	50 m (164 ft)	50 m (164 ft)
30 Tatchu Peninsula	◆	2–4 days	28 km (17.4 mi) round trip	50 m (164 ft)	50 m (164 ft)
31 North Coast Trail	◆◆	5–6 days	43.1 km (26.8 mi) one way	245 m (804 ft)	245 m (804 ft)
32 Cape Scott ★	■	2–3 days	6–41.4 km (3.7–25.7 mi) round trip	100 m (328 ft)	100 m (328 ft)
33 San Josef Bay	●	2 days	6–8 km (3.7–5 mi) round trip	45 m (148 ft)	45 m (148 ft)
34 Raft Cove	●	2 days	6 km (3.7 mi) round trip	65 m (213 ft)	65 m (213 ft)
35 Grant Bay	●	2 days	1 km (0.6 mi) round trip	40 m (131 ft)	40 m (131 ft)

Best Months	Fees	Reservations	Dogs Allowed	Food Storage	Toilet(s)	Water Taxi/ Floatplane Required
Mid-July to September	Y in Core Area only	N	Y on leash but not recommended	Y in Core Area only	Y in Core Area only	N
Year-round	N	N	Y on leash	n/a	Y	N
July to September	N	N	Y on leash	N	N	N
July to September	Y	N	Y on leash	Y but none at Cream Lake	Y but none at Cream Lake	N
Year-round	N	N	Y on leash	n/a	Y	N
July to September	N	N	Y on leash	Y	Y	N
June to October	Y	N	Y on leash	Y	Y	N
July to September	N	N	Y on leash	N	N	N
April to November	N	N	Y on leash	n/a	N	N
May to September	Y	N	Y but not recommended	N	Y at some campsites	Y
May to September	N	N	Y but not recommended	Y at Rugged Point only	Y at Rugged Point only	Y
June to September	Y	N	N	Y	Y	Y
May to September	Y	N	N	Y	Y	N
Year-round	Y	N	Y on leash	Y	Y	N
Year-round	Y	N	Y on leash	Y	Y	N
Year-round	N	N	Y	N	Y	N

Walking along the coastal shelf at low tide on the West Coast Trail (Trip 6)

SOUTHWEST COAST TRIPS

THE SOUTHWEST COAST of Vancouver Island allows you to experience a wide range of scenery. As you travel west through the region, the vegetation transitions from dry grassy bluffs with arbutus and Garry oak trees to wet coastal rainforest with towering Douglas-fir, western redcedar, and Sitka spruce trees. The trips in this section focus on rugged coastal terrain and majestic temperate rainforests.

Getting Around: Saturna Island is easily reached via a scenic BC Ferries ride from Victoria. Highway 14, also known as West Coast Road, stretches west along the coast from Victoria to Port Renfrew and leads to several trailheads via 2WD-accessible gravel spur roads. Past Port Renfrew the coast is roadless, so you will need to head inland from Lake Cowichan along lengthy and bumpy, but 2WD-accessible, logging roads. Port Alberni, reached via Highway 4, is the jumping-off point to the long 2WD-accessible logging road to Bamfield. Shuttle buses provide service to some trailheads, but for others you will need to drive yourself.

Indigenous Context: Many Indigenous groups have traditional territory along Vancouver Island's southwest coast, thanks to the bounty of food it contains. The Quw'utsun (Cowichan), Stz'uminus (Chemainus), sc'əwaθenaʔɬ təməxʷ (Tsawwassen), Semiahmoo, Á,LE̱NENEȻ LTE (W̱SÁNEĆ) (Saanich), Halalt, Ts'uubaa-asatx (Lake Cowichan), Lyackson, and Penelakut Nations have traditional territory on the Southern Gulf Islands, including Saturna Island.

Á,LE̱NENEȻ LTE (W̱SÁNEĆ) (Saanich) territory continues west into the Juan de Fuca Strait, overlapping with Sc'ianew (Beecher Bay), Lekwungen/Songhees, and T'sou-ke Nation territory near Sooke. (The name "Sooke" is a transliteration of T'sou-ke.) These nations are all ethnically and linguistically related, speaking Hul'q'umi'num' (Coast Salish) languages.

Pacheedaht territory includes the Juan de Fuca Trail, the Kludahk Trail, T'l'oqwxwat (Avatar Grove), Port Renfrew, and the eastern part of the West Coast Trail (WCT). Farther west, the Carmanah Valley Trail and the Nitinaht Narrows trailhead for the WCT are both in Ditidaht Nation territory. The western WCT trailhead at Pachena Bay and the Keeha Bay trail are Huu-ay-aht territory. The Huu-ay-aht are a sub-group of the Nuu-chah-nulth people, while the Ditidaht are culturally affiliated with the Nuu-chah-nulth, but not formally part of that group.

Supplies: The Victoria area has lots of grocery stores, gas stations, and outdoor stores. Outside of Victoria, supplies can be limited. Sooke has several grocery stores and gas stations. Port Renfrew, Bamfield, and Saturna Island are very small communities. They have tiny general stores and gas stations with limited hours.

Hiking through old-growth forest on the Juan de Fuca Marine Trail (Trip 3)

Accommodations: Hotels and vacation rentals are widely available in Victoria and Sooke. Port Renfrew, Bamfield, and Saturna Island have a small pool of hotels and vacation rentals. Book well in advance. French Beach Provincial Park and the China Beach campground in Juan de Fuca Provincial Park, both on Highway 14 west of Sooke, have a mix of first-come, first-served and reservable campsites. In Port Renfrew, the Pacheedaht Campground has reservable sites. Pachena Bay Campground in Bamfield, run by the Huu-ay-aht Nation, has reservable sites.

1

NARVAEZ BAY

BACKPACKING TRIP

Difficulty: ●
Duration: 2 days
Distance: 2 km (1.2 mi) round trip

Elevation Gain: 50 m (164 ft)
High Point: 80 m (262 ft)
Best Months: Year-round

Fees and Reservations: Online camping reservations are required from May to September and cost $11.50/site/night. All sites are first-come, first-served from October to April. Camping fees are $10.50/person/night.

Regulations: No fires. Dogs allowed on leash only. No drones.

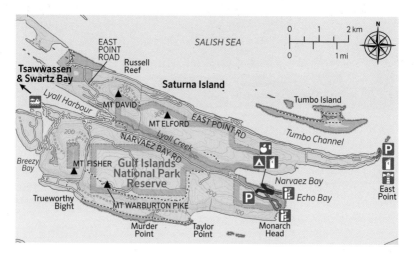

THE EASY HIKE to Narvaez Bay in Gulf Islands National Park Reserve makes a perfect backpacking destination for beginners, families, or those seeking a snow-free backpacking trip in the colder months. The campground is in a grassy clearing next to a beautiful bay surrounded by Douglas-fir, Garry oak, and arbutus trees on the southeastern end of Saturna Island. The beach and nearby trails invite exploration. Discover beautiful viewpoints of tiny coves, towering cliffs, and neighbouring islands. Or search for barnacles, anemones, and starfish clinging to rocks at low tide. The trailhead is a moderate bike ride or hike from the ferry terminal, making a car-free trip possible.

The view from Monarch Head

GETTING THERE

Travel to Saturna Island includes a scenic trip with BC Ferries from Swartz Bay. Check ferry times carefully, because sailings to Saturna are not as frequent as to some of the other Southern Gulf Islands. From the Lyall Harbour ferry terminal on Saturna, head straight up the hill on East Point Road for 1.6 km (1 mi). At the fork by the Saturna General Store, continue straight onto Narvaez Bay Road. Stay on Narvaez Bay Road until it ends 6.4 km (4 mi) later at a parking area. Smooth pavement gives way to lots of potholes and eventually to gravel. However, the road is fine for 2WD vehicles.

If you want to avoid taking a car onto the ferry, the trailhead is a hilly 30- to 45-minute bike ride from the ferry terminal. There is a bike rack at the trailhead. If you have wide tires, you may also choose to bike the trail down to the campground, where there is another bike rack. Alternatively, you could walk the 8 km (5 mi) route from the ferry terminal to the trailhead in about 2 hours. After the first section up to the general store, the road is a quiet walk through the forest, with almost no traffic.

TRAIL

TRIP PLANNER

0 km (0 mi)	Trailhead and parking area
0.3 km (0.2 mi)	Monarch Head Trail junction
0.6 km (0.4 mi)	Echo Bay Trail junction
1 km (0.6 mi)	Narvaez Bay campground

Saturna Island has a chronic water shortage and there is no water source at Narvaez Bay. Plan to bring your drinking water on the ferry with you. You may be able to buy bottled water at the general store.

The trail descends from the northeast corner of the **parking area** on an old road. The path was severely storm-damaged in November 2021 but has been repaired. Watch for bumps and loose gravel if you are biking. About 0.3 km (0.2 mi) along, the **Monarch Head Trail** branches off to the right. Continue following the main trail downhill as it curves left into a grassy clearing. The trail to **Echo Bay** heads off to the right at 0.6 km (0.4 mi).

Your route on the old road goes left past an old apple orchard, planted in the 1920s when this area was part of the Georgeson family farm. In the late summer and fall, visitors are welcome to pick ripe apples from the orchard. Be sure to abide by posted rules designed to protect the trees from damage and avoid overharvesting.

Continue along the old road as it descends gently towards the ocean at Narvaez Bay. Pass the designated overflow camping area and arrive at the **Narvaez Bay campground** 1 km (0.6 mi) from the trailhead. The bay is named for José María Narváez, a Spanish naval officer who was the first European to see the Strait of Georgia. Saturna Island takes its name from his ship, the *Santa Saturnina*. In SENĆOŦEN, the language of the W̱SÁNEĆ (Saanich) Nation, Saturna is called Teketeksen, which means "long nose." The south side of Narvaez Bay is called SNEUES, meaning "in the bay."

CAMPING

The small campground at Narvaez Bay sits at the head of a beautiful small cove. Douglas-fir, Garry oak, and arbutus trees provide a canopy here and on the nearby peninsula.

NATURE NOTE

THE HISTORY OF CAPTIVE ORCAS BEGAN ON SATURNA ISLAND

The confluence of ocean currents at East Point make it a favourite feeding location for orcas, also called killer whales. In 1964 a group from the Vancouver Aquarium harpooned a male orca at East Point, hoping to display his stuffed carcass at the museum. When the whale survived, they displayed him in a pen in Vancouver's harbour until he died four months later. Other aquariums wanted their own orcas, and many whales were captured in the Salish Sea in the 1960s and '70s. Today the whales are protected and the practice of keeping captive orcas has fallen out of favour.

The grassy campground at Narvaez Bay

Campsites: Seven campsites in the main camping area. An overflow area in a grassy field will fit 6 or 7 tents. Sites 1–3 are very close together.
Toilet: On the east side of the campground
Water: None. Bring drinking water with you on the ferry.
Food Storage: Food storage lockers
Other Amenities: Picnic tables, bike rack

EXTENDING YOUR TRIP

Monarch Head: Follow old roads through grassy clearings and regenerating forest to a spectacular viewpoint on high cliffs atop Monarch Head. It is named after the HMS *Monarch*, a British naval ship that patrolled the area in the 1860s. The figure-8-shaped loop is 2.4 km (1.5 mi) long.
East Point: A highlight of Saturna Island is East Point, one of the best places to see orcas (killer whales) from land. The hike along the point is only a 1 km (0.6 mi) round trip, but you'll want to linger a while to watch the wildlife or just marvel at the views from the sculpted sandstone rocks. East Point is 15 km (9.3 mi) from the ferry terminal or 20 km (12.4 mi) from the Narvaez Bay trailhead, so it is best reached by car or bike.

FURTHER RESOURCES

Gulf Islands National Park Reserve: info and reservations *pc.gc.ca/en/pn-np/bc/gulf*
BC Ferries: Saturna Island ferry schedules *bcferries.com*
NTS Map: 092B14

2

EAST SOOKE COAST TRAIL

DAY HIKE

Difficulty: ◆

Duration: 5.5 to 8 hours

Distance: 12.3 km (7.6 mi) one way

Elevation Gain: 65 m (213 ft)

High Point: 65 m (213 ft)

Best Months: Year-round

Fees and Reservations: None

Regulations: No alcohol, smoking, vaping, or cannabis. No camping. No fires. Dogs permitted.

Caution: The stats for this hike make it sound deceptively short and easy. This rough coastal trail has lots of technical ups and downs. Expect slow travel times.

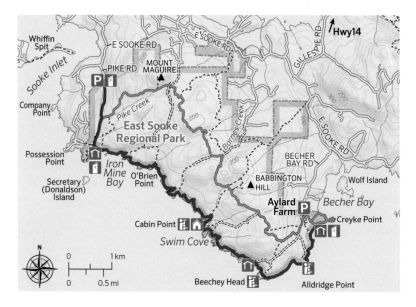

GET A TASTE OF the rugged southwest coast of Vancouver Island with a day hike on the Coast Trail in East Sooke Regional Park. This scenic path hugs the rocky shoreline as it climbs bluffs and plummets into secluded coves. Around every corner you will be treated to incredible views. Gaze along the undulating coastline or across the Juan de Fuca Strait to the mountains of the Olympic Peninsula in Washington State. Watch for seals and shorebirds in the waves below as you walk through groves of arbutus trees and thickets of salal.

GETTING THERE

The East Sooke Coast Trail has two main trailheads: in the east at Aylard Farm and in the west at Pike Road. Several other trailheads lead to the interior of the park, and then eventually to the Coast Trail. The hike described here is a one-way traverse from Pike Road to Aylard Farm, which would necessitate parking a vehicle at each trailhead. Alternatively, you can have a taxi from Sooke transport you between trailheads. An out-and-back trip from either trailhead is also worthwhile.

AYLARD FARM TRAILHEAD

Take Highway 14 west from Langford. Turn right onto Gillespie Road and follow under the new highway underpass, where you turn right again to stay on Gillespie. Stay on Gillespie for 5.6 km (3.5 mi), then turn left onto East Sooke Road. Turn right 2 km (1.2 mi) later onto Becher Bay Road and stay on it until it ends at the Aylard Farm parking lot 1.8 km (1.1 mi) later.

PIKE ROAD TRAILHEAD

Use the directions above to reach the intersection of Gillespie Road and East Sooke Road, but turn right instead and follow East Sooke Road for 7.9 km (4.9 mi). Turn left onto Pike Road. The road ends at the parking lot 0.3 km (0.2 mi) later.

TRAIL

TRIP PLANNER

0 km (0 mi)	Pike Road trailhead
1.5 km (0.9 mi)	Iron Mine Bay
6.8 km (4.2 mi)	Cabin Point
7.2 km (4.5 mi)	Swim Cove
9.5 km (5.9 mi)	Beechey Head and Interior Trail junction
10.9 km (6.8 mi)	Alldridge Point and petroglyph
11 km (6.8 mi)	Squeaky Point and old gravel road junction
12.3 km (7.6 mi)	Aylard Farm trailhead

The trail heads south from the **Pike Road trailhead** on a former logging road that is now a wide gravel trail. Follow the path through a forest of Douglas-fir and western hemlock, dotted with huge old-growth stumps from long-ago logging. As you approach the ocean, you can spot Sitka spruce trees amongst the sword ferns. Ignore junctions with side trails to Anderson Cove, Pike Point, and Silver Spray Drive. About 1.5 km (0.9 mi) from the trailhead, pass an accessible toilet and arrive at **Iron Mine Bay**. A short trail leads down to the shoreline. The pebble beach here is a worthwhile detour at low tide.

Iron Mine Bay

Turn left onto the Coast Trail and pass a covered picnic shelter. The route becomes challenging, with lots of ups and downs but some easy scrambling across rock bluffs. In places, the trail can be a bit indistinct. When in doubt, look for rectangular yellow markers on the rocks and trees, often where the trail changes direction.

Shortly after turning onto the Coast Trail, reach the top of a grassy bluff and your first views of the Juan de Fuca Strait and the mountains of the Olympic Peninsula. Continue along the Coast Trail as it dips and climbs across grassy bluffs, over rocks, through thickets of salal, and past groves of stately arbutus trees.

Junctions at 1.7 km (1.1 mi), 2.4 km (1.5 mi), and 3.6 km (2.2 mi) all lead to the inland trail network. Stay on the Coast Trail, which sometimes heads inland to bypass precipitous gullies. On the open bluffs, look for stonecrop clinging to the rock faces. Its tiny leaves turn from sage green to reddish in the full sun. In summer they produce sprays of pointed yellow flowers. In the spring look for wildflowers, including shooting stars and fawn lilies.

Ignore the **Parkheights Trail** at 5.2 km (3.2 mi). As you hike this challenging section, look ahead down to the coast to spot the old fisherman's cabin at Cabin Point. Follow the Coast Trail over a bluff deep into the back of a cove to a **junction** at 6.6 km (4.1 mi). Stay on the Coast Trail through thick salal along the top of a cliff to **Cabin Point** at 6.8 km (4.2 mi). A bench invites you to rest and soak up the views. Be sure to visit the historic cabin. In the early 20th century, shacks like this one dotted the coast. They were staffed

The historic fishing shack at Cabin Point

by fishermen who used traps tethered to the seafloor to capture fish by the thousands.

Follow the trail away from Cabin Point to another **intersection** at 6.9 km (4.3 mi). Go right to stay on the Coast Trail. (Left leads to the Interior Trail.) The trail curls around the top of a bluff and then descends to sea level at picturesque **Swim Cove** at 7.2 km (4.5 mi). If the weather is warm, this is a good place for a swim. Leave the cove on a set of stairs. Ignore another path branching to the **Interior Trail** at 7.3 km (4.5 mi). The next section of trail climbs onto an open bluff that allows for great views.

A covered picnic shelter at 9.1 km (5.7 mi) provides an opportunity to rest. Continue along the Coast Trail to **Beechey Head** at 9.5 km (5.9 mi). It is named after Rear Admiral Frederick William Beechey, a British navigator and cartographer. A spur trail heads out to a viewpoint, which is a popular place to spot hawks during their fall migration. **Junctions** here and at 9.6 km (6 mi) both lead to the same old road you passed at the picnic shelter.

The last section of the Coast Trail continues ducking and diving along the coast to **Alldridge Point** at 10.9 km (6.8 mi). The point is named for Lieutenant George Manly Alldridge, another British surveyor. Watch for a beautiful, fading Indigenous petroglyph of a sea lion, estimated to be up to 3000 years old.

Squeaky Point, at 11 km (6.8 mi), has an expansive view east across Becher Bay and south to Port Angeles on the Olympic Peninsula. Stay on the Coast Trail, since it winds along the shoreline and is mercifully a bit less

One of the many bluff-top viewpoints

technical. Arrive at a beach, covered picnic shelter, and major **junction** at 12 km (7.5 mi). Head up the stairs to the left to join a wheelchair-accessible trail. It leads through the grassy meadows to the **Aylard Farm trailhead** and parking lot at 12.3 km (7.6 mi).

EXTENDING YOUR TRIP

Creyke Point: Add one more viewpoint by hiking to Creyke Point. From the junction at the beach at Aylard Farm, continue straight (northeast) onto the Creyke Point Trail. It will add 1.2 km (0.7 mi) to your hike.

Loop via Interior Trail: Fit hikers can make an epic loop that takes in both the ocean and forest sections of the park. Take the Coast Trail to the Aylard Farm trailhead, then loop back to Pike Road via the Interior Trail and Mount McGuire Trail. It's a very challenging 22.5 km (14 mi) loop, with innumerable small hills, so allow 10 to 12 hours.

FURTHER RESOURCES

East Sooke Regional Park: info and maps *crd.bc.ca/parks-recreation-culture/parks-trails/find-park-trail/east-sooke*
Sooke Orange Taxi: transportation between trailheads (250) 642-1222
NTS Map: 092B05

3

JUAN DE FUCA MARINE TRAIL

BACKPACKING TRIP

Difficulty: ◆
Duration: 3 to 5 days
Distance: 47 km (29.2 mi) one way

Elevation Gain: 195 m (640 ft)
High Point: 195 m (640 ft)
Best Months: May to October

Fees and Reservations: Camping fees are $10/person/night, payable online. All campsites are first-come, first-served.

Regulations: No drones. No smoking, vaping, or cannabis. Dogs permitted on leash, but the terrain is too challenging for many dogs. Fires allowed below the high-tide line only.

Caution: Parts of this trail are very rough. Use caution on boardwalks, stairs, and bridges.

THE JUAN DE FUCA MARINE TRAIL (JDF) traverses pebble beaches, sandstone shelves, sucking mud pits, and lots of beautiful rainforests as it rambles along the rugged southwest coast of Vancouver Island. The challenging route takes you and up down steep climbs interspersed with sections of old-growth forests and picturesque beach walks. With easy access to Victoria, the trail is a popular introduction to the wonders of coastal hiking. Several access points along Highway 14 allow you to hike the entire trail or sections of it.

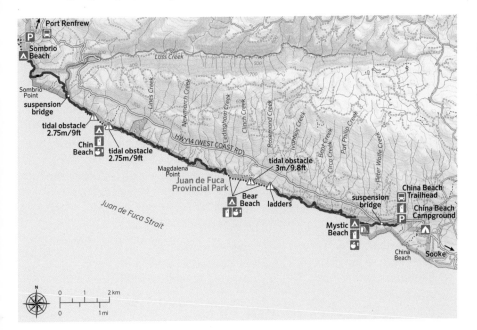

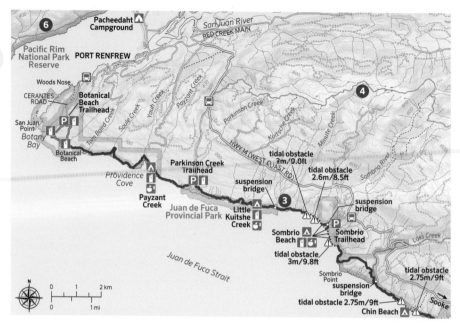

GETTING THERE

The JDF has two main trailheads: Botanical Beach near Port Renfrew in the west and China Beach near Jordan River in the east. Most hikers complete a one-way hike between these two trailheads. Less commonly, you can start the trail partway along at Sombrio Beach or Parkinson Creek.

WEST COAST TRAIL EXPRESS BUS

While you can drive yourself to all trailheads, most hikers use the West Coast Trail Express bus for some portion of their journey. The bus leaves from Victoria, dropping hikers off along Highway 14. From there, you can walk the access roads to the trailheads. You can also use the West Coast Trail Express to travel from one trailhead to another at the beginning or end of your trip. Prices vary based on the distance travelled. Reservations are highly recommended.

CHINA BEACH/JORDAN RIVER TRAILHEAD

The eastern trailhead is located at China Beach near the village of Jordan River. From Victoria, take Highway 1 west. Take exit 14 to merge onto Highway 14 and zero your odometer. Follow Highway 14 for 63 km (39.1 mi), then turn left into the China Beach day-use area parking lot at Juan de Fuca Provincial Park. It is 1.2 km (0.7 mi) after the China Beach campground. The trailhead is 0.2 km (0.1 mi) down the access road.

BOTANICAL BEACH/PORT RENFREW TRAILHEAD

The western trailhead is located at Botanical Beach, near the town of Port Renfrew. From Victoria, take Highway 14 to its end, near the Port Renfrew

Pub. This is the Port Renfrew stop for the West Coast Trail bus. Turn left onto Cerantes Road and follow it to the trailhead and parking lot 3.2 km (2 mi) away.

TRAIL

TRIP PLANNER

0 km (0 mi)	China Beach trailhead
1 km (0.6 mi)	Pete Wolf Creek suspension bridge
2 km (1.2 mi)	Mystic Beach and campground
9.6 km (6 mi)	Bear Beach Centre campground (Clinch Creek)
21 km (13 mi)	Chin Beach campground
23.8 km (14.8 mi)	Loss Creek suspension bridge
29 km (18 mi)	Sombrio Beach West campground and trailhead
32 km (19.9 mi)	Minute Creek suspension bridge
33 km (20.5 mi)	Little Kuitshe Creek campground
37 km (23 mi)	Parkinson Creek trailhead
40 km (24.9 mi)	Payzant Creek campground
45 km (28 mi)	Botanical Beach
47 km (29.2 mi)	Botanical Beach trailhead

The JDF is typically hiked as a one-way traverse between the western trailhead at Botanical Beach (near Port Renfrew) and the eastern trailhead at China Beach (near Jordan River). You can also start the trail in the middle at Sombrio Beach or in the western third at Parkinson Creek. There is no clear advantage to going in one direction over the other. This description starts in the east since BC Parks' official kilometre markers begin there.

The trailhead and the 0 km marker are at the upper parking lot at the **China Beach day-use area.** Your hike begins by undulating through the forest until you cross the **Pete Wolf Creek suspension bridge** about 1 km (0.6 mi) from the trailhead. The trail trends downhill, emerging on the sands of **Mystic Beach** at the 2 km (1.2 mi) mark after descending a set of stairs. Turn left down the beach for a short detour to the spectacular waterfall that rushes over the cliffs.

The main route goes right along the beach, passing campsites and a side trail to the bear cache and toilets. At the west end of the beach, follow the trail up onto a bluff. The trail rambles through the forest and salal with several creek crossings and some brief glimpses of the ocean. Your route runs close to the park boundary here, and clear-cuts are sometimes visible just uphill.

Near the 8 km (5 mi) marker, the trail begins to descend steeply towards the coast on a rough and muddy trail. This section has washed out several

The west end of Bear Beach

times, despite valiant efforts to build ladders and stairs. At the time of writing, a new ladder section had been installed. At the bottom of the slope, begin your journey along 2-kilometre-long (1.2 mi) **Bear Beach**. This stretch of sand and slippery rocks has three separate camping areas.

Pass the first camping area at Rosemund Creek and reach the **Bear Beach tidal obstacle** at 8.7 km (5.4 mi). You can pass below the cliffs at tides lower than 3 m (9.8 ft). Ford Clinch Creek (named for a wrecked American schooner) next to Bear Beach Centre camping area at 9.6 km (6 mi). Continue to the camping area at the end of Bear Beach at Ledingham Creek, 10.5 km (6.5 mi) from the trailhead. At low tide, admire the Rock-on-a-Pillar formation just offshore. Centuries of wind and waves have sculpted the sandstone into this extraordinary top-heavy shape.

Follow the trail steeply uphill. The next section features some huge old-growth western redcedar, Sitka spruce, and western hemlock trees. However, you may have trouble appreciating their beauty as you climb relentlessly up and down numerous hills with many creek crossings. Most have sturdy bridges, but an unnamed creek at the 16.5 km (10.3 mi) mark can pose a bit of a challenge as you navigate a slippery clay stream bank with the help of a muddy fixed rope.

At 20.5 km (12.7 mi) the path leaves the forest and heads down the bluff past a few tent pads and the site of the former Chin Beach emergency shelter (dismantled in 2022). At the bottom of the hill, the trail intersects with **Chin Beach**.

A **tidal obstacle** here is impassable at tides over 2.75 m (9 ft). Continue along Chin Beach to find the creekside campground near the 21 km (13 mi) marker.

At the west side of Chin Beach, a cluster of buoys hanging in the trees marks the beginning of the trail at 21.3 km (13.2 mi). It starts with a tricky rock scramble that is susceptible to waves at high tides. At tides below 1 m (3.2 ft), you can continue along the coast until the 22.1 km (13.7 mi) mark, but most hikers take the forest route.

From here, you are heading into one of the most challenging sections of the JDF. Cross the vertiginous **Loss Creek suspension bridge** at 23.8 km (14.8 mi), which hangs nearly 70 m (230 ft) above the canyon. The sea stacks at the creek's mouth make a great photo op. After the bridge, the trail switchbacks steeply, gaining nearly 150 m (492 ft). The trail joins an old road for about 1 km (0.6 mi), then plummets towards the ocean along a ridgetop trail studded with giant old-growth cedar and Douglas-fir.

Reach Sombrio Point at 26.5 km (16.5 mi), then continue along the tough and technical trail as it scrambles across the tops of rocky cliffs, sometimes with a wire railing for protection. Pause to admire a small waterfall tumbling over the cliff. Follow the trail as it crosses a bridge above the falls and then plunges to the sand of **Sombrio Beach**.

Make a worthwhile detour here by wading through a small creek upstream into a canyon. The vertical moss-covered walls and waterfall at the back of the gorge are like something out of a fairy tale. Please be respectful and do not add to the graffiti that mars the rock.

Back on the main beach, trek west along the sand, passing the campsites at Sombrio Beach Far East (27 km/16.8 mi) and Sombrio Beach East (27.6 km/ 17.1 mi). The tidal obstacle at 28 km (17.4 mi) is passable at tides below 3 m (9.8 ft). Arrive at Sombrio West Camp and the **Sombrio trailhead** at 29 km (18 mi). This area was the site of a Pacheedaht village known as Qwa:qlis.

INDIGENOUS KNOWLEDGE

PEOPLE OF THE SEA FOAM

In a Pacheedaht story, an 8-foot-tall (2.4 m) mound appeared near a village on the San Juan River. The villagers wanted to know what it was, so they asked an old slave to taste it. She declared that it was *pacheed*, or sea foam. The villagers decided to call themselves Pacheedaht, which means "people of the sea foam." Pacheedaht traditional territory stretches along the entire present-day Juan de Fuca Trail, from the east at Sheringham Point near Sooke to Bonilla Point on the West Coast Trail. A pavilion at Sombrio Beach includes lots of information about Pacheedaht culture and history on several beautiful interpretive panels.

Expect to encounter plenty of day-trippers and surfers here, which can be a bit of a culture shock after several days of backpacking.

To continue along the JDF, follow the wide gravel trail towards the parking lot, then go left at a junction to cross the **Sombrio River suspension bridge**. Spanish naval officers gave the river its name, which means "shady river," in 1790. On the far side, follow a newly re-routed trail past **Sombrio Far West Camp**, then back onto the beach. Use caution navigating the slippery rocks to the tidal obstacle at 29.6 km (18.4 mi), which is passable at tides below 2.6 m (8.5 ft). The next tidal obstacle at 30.2 km (18.8 mi) is passable at tides below 3 m (9.8 ft) but does have a short and rough bypass route via an inland trail if you arrive at high tide.

The next section of the JDF leaves the beach and stays in the forest all the way to Little Kuitshe Creek. It is characterized by dark second-growth forest, tunnels of salal, and lots of mud. At 32 km (19.9 mi), cross the final suspension bridge of the trail over **Minute Creek**. Look upstream to find a small waterfall. Reach **Little Kuitshe Creek** campground at 33 km (20.5 mi).

Travel past Little Kuitshe Creek used to be quite slow, due to the poor condition of the trail. But upgrades in 2023 brought new boardwalks, bridges, and stairs, and with it easier hiking. After a short section of old logging road, arrive at the **Parkinson Creek trailhead** at 37 km (23 mi). Proceed through the parking lot to pick up the trail on the other side as it follows more old logging roads, then heads into the second-growth forest.

At 38 km (23.6 mi) the trail emerges at the shoreline. You can stick to the forest trail, or at low tides walk along the slightly sloped reef shelf for the next 1 km (0.6 mi). Watch carefully for marker buoys in the trees that indicate your return to the inland route, which features decaying bridges and boardwalks. Arrive at **Payzant Creek** campground at 40 km (24.9 mi), just after crossing a creek with a small waterfall. The creek is named after Frederick Allison Payzant, who owned land at the mouth of the creek in the early 1900s. Originally from Halifax, he made an unsuccessful trip to the Yukon during the gold rush, then settled on Vancouver Island to work for the telegraph company.

The trail descends towards the ocean, crossing Yauh Creek on a log bridge at 41 km (25.5 mi). On the far side, look for an overgrown trail heading left. It leads to tiny Providence Cove, which is a great place for a snack break. Back on the main trail, the route heads back across the rocky reef shelf for a few minutes at 41.5 km (25.8 mi). The next section of the trail is close to the ocean with lots of viewpoints. You can walk along the shoreline, but it can be slippery and scrambly, so the trail is likely faster.

The trail heads back inland around 43 km (26.7 mi) and passes through some stands of beautiful old-growth trees with the help of mossy boardwalks. Reach **Botanical Beach** at 45 km (28 mi). Try to time your visit for tides below

1 m (3.3 ft) to explore the world-famous tidepools. The Pacheedaht call this beach ɫi:xwa:p, and it was once home to a village with six big-houses. At 46 km (28.6 mi), the trail leaves the beach and begins a slow climb on an old gravel road. Finish your hike at the **Botanical Beach trailhead** at 47 km (29 mi).

CAMPING

There are six official campgrounds on the Juan de Fuca trail, which gives you many options. Fit parties with coastal hiking experience could complete the trail in 3 days, camping at Bear Beach and Sombrio Beach. Most hikers spend 4 days on the trail, staying at Bear Beach, Chin Beach, and Little Kuitshe Creek. A more relaxed approach is to stay at Bear Beach, Chin Beach, Sombrio Beach, and Payzant Creek, finishing the trail in 5 days. If you just want to complete half the trail, the eastern half, from China Beach to Sombrio Beach, is the most scenic. It can be completed in 3 days, with overnight stops at Bear Beach and Chin Beach.

On summer weekends all of the campgrounds can get busy, and some have limited space, so arrive early to secure a spot.

MYSTIC BEACH CAMPGROUND

This small beach with a gorgeous waterfall is close to the trailhead, making it easy for both beginners and raucous partiers to access.

Campsites: Ten wooden tent pads up 2 side trails, a few campsites in flat areas on gravel, and several sandy spots in the middle of the beach, which can flood at high tides
Toilets: Up a steep side trail in the middle of the beach
Water: Collect from a creek at the west end of the beach
Food Storage: Food locker at the side trail to the toilets

BEAR BEACH CAMPGROUND

Choose from three separate camping areas: Bear Beach East (Rosemund Creek) at 8.6 km (5.3 mi), Bear Beach Centre (Clinch Creek) at 9.6 km (6 mi), and Bear Beach West (Rock on a Pillar) at 10.5 km (6.5 mi). Bear Beach Centre is the nicest, with sandy sites near the creek.

Campsites: Each area has a mix of forest campsites, new tent pads, and beach sites above the high-tide line. Centre has the most sites and West has the fewest.
Toilets: All 3 sites have toilets set back from the beach. Look for campground signs and fishing floats in the trees to find them.
Water: At Bear Beach East, collect from Rosemund Creek. At Centre, collect from Clinch Creek. At West, collect from Ledingham Creek to the west.
Food Storage: Food locker near the toilet at all 3 sites

CHIN BEACH CAMPGROUND

Most itineraries include Chin Beach, so it can get crowded. However, there is an overflow area on the bluff at the east end of the beach near the site of the former emergency shelter.

Campsites: A mix of 5 new wooden tent pads and dirt tent sites behind the beach near the creek, plus a few marginal beach sites above the high-tide line. There are also 5 wooden tent pads on the bluff.
Toilets: Two outhouses on the west side of the creek and a third outhouse at the bluff tent pads
Water: Collect from the creek in the centre of camp
Food Storage: Food locker next to the outhouse at both locations

SOMBRIO BEACH CAMPGROUND

Since it is only 0.4 km (0.2 mi) from the Sombrio parking lot, this campground is popular with surfers and partiers on weekends. For more solitude, plan to camp at the east end. There are four main camping areas at Sombrio Beach: Far East Camp, at the easternmost end of the beach at 27 km (16.8 mi); East Camp, at 27.6 km (17.1 mi); West Camp, closest to the parking lot at 29 km (18 mi); and Far West Camp, on the west side of the Sombrio River at 29.3 km (18.2 mi).

Campsites: Each area has plenty of campsites on the beach above the high-tide line. There are also 5 wooden tent platforms at Sombrio Far West and campsites at the top of the bank at Sombrio West.
Toilets: All areas have signed toilets behind the beach.
Water: At East and Far East, collect water from the creek at Far East. At West and Far West, collect from the river above the suspension bridge to avoid salt water, especially at high tide.
Food Storage: Food lockers near the toilets at each camp

LITTLE KUITSHE CREEK CAMPGROUND

This forested campground is set in dark second-growth at the top of a bluff. You can access a rocky shelf above the ocean via a rough trail.

Campsites: Ten new wooden tent pads
Toilets: On a spur trail uphill from campground
Water: Collect from Little Kuitshe Creek on the main trail west of campground
Food Storage: Food locker at the start of the trail to the outhouse

PAYZANT CREEK CAMPGROUND

Set in a thick old-growth forest, this is the only campground without ocean access.

Mystic Beach

Campsites: Ten new wooden tent pads downhill from the main trail
Toilet: Next to the main trail
Water: Collect from Payzant Creek, on the main trail just east of the campground
Food Storage: Food locker on a signed trail near the outhouse

EXTENDING YOUR TRIP

Botany Bay: This little bay is just west of Botanical Beach and has lots of pocket coves to explore at low tide. This worthwhile loop hike adds 1.6 km (1 mi) to your trip.
Kludahk Trail: With a bit of road walking on either end, you could combine the Kludahk Trail (Trip 4) with the Juan de Fuca Trail to create a challenging week-long loop.

FURTHER RESOURCES

Juan de Fuca Provincial Park: info, map, and trail fees *bcparks.ca/explore/parkpgs/juan_de_fuca*
Happiest Outdoors: additional trail info *happiestoutdoors.ca/juan-de-fuca-trail*
Fisheries and Oceans Canada: Port Renfrew tide table *waterlevels.gc.ca/eng/station?sid=8525*
West Coast Trail Express: shuttle bus info and reservations *trailbus.com*
NTS Maps: 092C09; 09C08

4

KLUDAHK TRAIL

BACKPACKING TRIP

Difficulty: ■

Duration: 2 to 4 days

Distance: 40 km (24.9 mi) one way

Elevation Gain: 350 m (1148 ft)

High Point: 1100 m (3609 ft)

Best Months: June to October

Fees and Reservations: All campsites are first-come, first-served.

Regulations: No fires.

Caution: Camping is very limited on this trail. Arrive early and avoid long weekends. The upland bog ecosystem is very fragile. Stay on the trail to avoid erosion. Water sources on this trail are very silty and can clog filters.

WALK THE LENGTH of the San Juan Ridge in a unique subalpine bog and forest ecosystem. In the Nuu-chah-nulth language, Kludahk means "home of the elk." You may spot these majestic ungulates on your hike, along with black bears, cougars, and countless species of birds. The trail follows the crest of

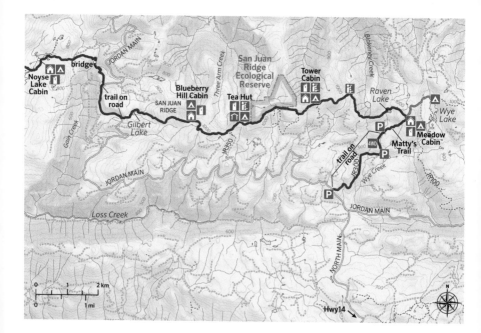

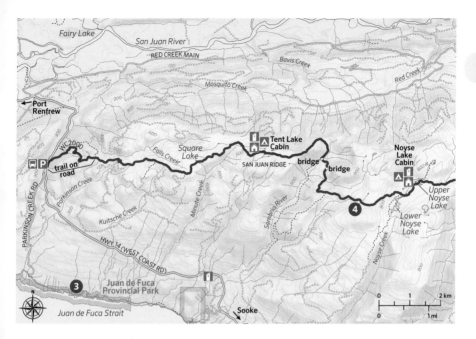

the ridge, meandering past viewpoints, through groves of old-growth trees, and next to countless ponds and lakes. Visit in the spring and early summer to see the wildflowers, including endangered white glacier lilies. In late summer, the bushes drip with blueberries and huckleberries. The Kludahk Outdoors Club has built a series of welcoming cabins along the way, each with an associated camping area.

GETTING THERE

The Kludahk Trail has many access points scattered through the confusing logging road system on the south side of San Juan Ridge. Some access points require 4WD vehicles or are behind locked gates. The two easiest places to reach the trail with a 2WD vehicle are listed below.

The Kludahk Trail is typically completed as a one-way traverse and can be hiked from either direction. That means you will need to arrange a car shuttle or use the West Coast Trail Express bus (details below).

EASTERN/JR300 FOREST SERVICE ROAD TRAILHEAD

From Victoria, take Highway 14 west through Sooke. Zero your odometer at the bridge over the Jordan River. Turn right 2.8 km (1.7 mi) later onto North Main Forest Service Road and zero your odometer again. The turn is directly opposite the entrance to the China Beach campground. Head uphill on North Main, which is a well-graded gravel road suitable for 2WD vehicles. Go left at a fork at 1.7 km (1.1 mi) to stay on North Main. At 9.4 km (5.8 mi) cross a bridge. Immediately after, a road joins from the right. Continue uphill on what is now Jordan Main FSR. At 10.2 km (6.3 mi), an overgrown spur road (JR300 FSR) leaves from the right. This is the trailhead. Park on the wide shoulder of Jordan Main near the trailhead, being careful to get well off the road and out of the way of industrial traffic.

WESTERN/PARKINSON CREEK TRAILHEAD

From Victoria, take Highway 14 west through Sooke. Zero your odometer at the bridge over the Jordan River. Turn left 32.7 km (20.3 mi) later onto Parkinson Creek Road, signed for the Juan de Fuca Trail. Park on the wide shoulder just off the highway. The trailhead is the gravel road immediately to the north across the highway.

WEST COAST TRAIL EXPRESS BUS

The West Coast Trail Express bus service from Victoria is designed for hikers on the Juan de Fuca Marine Trail (Trip 3) and West Coast Trail (Trip 6), but with some planning you can use it for the Kludahk Trail too. The bus stops on Highway 14 at the western trailhead for the Kludahk Trail. It also stops at the entrance to the China Beach day-use area, which is a 1 km (0.6 mi) walk along the highway from the start of North Main FSR. From there it's a 10.2 km (6.3 mi) walk with 660 m (2165 ft) of elevation gain on logging roads to the JR300 trailhead. Prices vary based on the distance travelled. Reservations are required.

TRAIL

TRIP PLANNER

0 km (0 mi)	Eastern trailhead (JR300 FSR)
3.2 km (2 mi)	Start of Matty's Trail
4.4 km (2.7 mi)	Meadow Cabin and campsite
8.4 km (5.2 mi)	Tower Cabin and campsite
11.6 km (7.2 mi)	Tea Hut day-use cabin and campsite
13.9 km (8.6 mi)	Blueberry Hill Cabin and campsite
16.8 km (10.4 mi)	Trail joins Jordan Main FSR
18.5 km (11.5 mi)	Trail leaves logging roads
19.5 km (12.1 mi)	Gain Creek bridge
21.8 km (13.5 mi)	Noyse Lake Cabin and campsite
26.3 km (16.3 mi)	East Sombrio River bridge
27.1 km (16.8 mi)	West Sombrio River bridge
30.5 km (19 mi)	Tent Lake Cabin and campsite
37.5 km (23.3 mi)	Trail joins WC2000 FSR
40 km (24.9 mi)	Western trailhead (Highway 14 at Parkinson Creek Road)

Taking a break at Raven Lake

The Kludahk Trail can be hiked from either direction. The description below starts in the east, which means less overall elevation gain (350 m/1148 ft) than starting in the west (870 m/2854 ft).

From the **eastern trailhead** at 750 m (2461 ft) elevation, walk up JR300 FSR. Alder branches encroach on the roadbed for the first few minutes, but soon you enter a more mature forest and the road surface is clear. Stay right at a fork at 1.9 km (1.2 mi). The road curls east through a more recent clearcut. At 2.5 km (1.6 mi), reach the bottom of a steep hill. If you are okay with branches scratching your car, you can drive a 2WD vehicle to this point and park on the wide right shoulder. You will need a 4WD vehicle with good clearance to make it to the end of the logging road.

Continue up the steep hill on the very loose road. Go right at a fork at 3.2 km (2 mi). If you have a high-clearance 4WD you can drive to this point. Almost immediately after the fork, look for a flagged trail, known as **Matty's Trail**, leaving the road on the left side. Follow the trail gently uphill through wet meadows and patches of forest. You will encounter your first sections of metal tread plate here. The Kludahk Outdoors Club has placed hundreds of pieces of this perforated metal dock ramp across the wet sections, protecting the unique and fragile upland bog ecosystem and providing hikers with a dry place to walk.

Reach a junction at 4.4 km (2.7 mi) and 1000 m (3281 ft) elevation. The Kludahk Trail heads both east and west from here. The route to the east (right) heads to Wye Lake, currently the eastern terminus of the trail. A few decades ago, the trail stretched even farther east, but with more logging and deteriorating access roads, the Kludahk Outdoors Club decided to cease maintenance east of Wye Lake. Your route along the Kludahk Trail heads west (left). You will find the **Meadow Cabin and campsite** just a few steps left of the junction.

Continue west along the Kludahk Trail through a patch of subalpine forest to the shores of **Raven Lake** at 5 km (3.1 mi). On a hot day, this is a wonderful place for a swim. From here, the trail climbs through the forest as you go up and over a high point on the ridge known locally as Deer Mountain. Pass through a spectacular section of old-growth Douglas-fir and hemlock, named John Leesing Grove after a local forester. As you start to descend at about 7.1 km (4.4 mi), look for a short spur trail to the right leading to a great **viewpoint**. Look northeast to a maze of logging roads stretching across the hills that hold the headwaters of the San Juan River.

The trail passes a few small ponds in a marshy saddle before climbing through the forest to the trail's high point at 1100 m (3609 ft), **Tower Cabin and campsite**. The cabin is 8.4 km (5.2 mi) from the start and takes its name from the communication towers just to the west of the cabin. Ignore the towers and take in incredible views to the north of the Blakeney Creek valley and 1117-metre-high (3665 ft) Mount Modeste across the San Juan River.

Follow the trail past the towers and back into the forest. The path heads gently downhill and passes another set of ponds in a wet meadow. A sign at about 10 km (6.2 mi) indicates a side trail to logging roads to the south and the edge of the **San Juan Ridge Ecological Reserve** to the north. Created in 2003, the ecological reserve is not open to the public. It protects an endangered population of white glacier lilies, this being one of only two places on Vancouver Island where this wildflower grows.

The trail stays on the crest of the ridge as it climbs slightly and passes tiny Triangle Lake at about the 11 km (6.8 mi) mark. The path dips slightly into a draw, then climbs to a marvellous vantage point at the **Tea Hut day-use cabin and campsite** at 11.6 km (7.2 mi). Allow a few minutes to go inside and read the extensive interpretive panels explaining the flora, fauna, geology, history, and culture of the area. Sit awhile on one of the stools to enjoy expansive views of Three Arm Creek valley and the hills beyond. You may even be able to spot wildlife in the wetlands below.

From Tea Hut, the trail plummets through the forest, at one point with the help of a fixed rope. Pass two junctions with the **Lily Loop Trail** at 12 km (7.5 mi) and 12.2 km (7.6 mi). In the late spring and early summer, rare glacier lilies bloom here. The Lily Loop also leads farther downhill to meet logging roads branching off from Jordan Main FSR. Follow the Kludahk Trail west as it climbs slightly. Soon the trail breaks out of the forest into pockets of meadow and passes many small ponds on wooden boardwalks.

The view from Tea Hut

Reach the **Blueberry Hill Cabin and campsite** on the shores of a pond at 13.9 km (8.6 mi).

Follow the Kludahk Trail west as it heads into the trees, then swings slightly south to drop steeply off the ridge crest. A few fixed ropes assist your descent. At about 16 km (9.9 mi), the trail breaks out of the forest into open marshland near **Gilbert Lake**. The trail skirts wetlands to the north before descending back to lake level on the west side. Low water in summer and fall may make you wonder why this marsh is called a lake, but in spring, rains fill the basin, inundating the surrounding grass.

Cross the lake outlet on a log bridge, then follow the trail west as it parallels the creek. Emerge on **Jordan Main FSR** at 16.8 km (10.4 mi). Although this road is gated east of here, watch for large industrial trucks on weekdays. Turn right and hike along the road. Ignore a spur at 17.4 km (10.8 mi) and stay on the road as it swings north and climbs a hill. At 18.3 km (11.4 mi), turn left and head downhill on a rough **spur road**. Continue straight at 18.5 km (11.5 mi). Reach the **end of the spur** a few minutes later and follow flagging tape through short switchbacks in a regenerating clear-cut as you lurch downhill. The grade eases a bit as you transition back into the forest.

A large metal bridge at 19.5 km (12.1 mi) helps you across **Gain Creek** at 600 m (1969 ft) elevation. Follow the trail up a steep hillside, using a fixed rope for help in one spot. The ascent becomes more gradual after the rope. Cross a **new logging road** at 20.5 km (12.7 mi), picking up the trail on the far side. The path winds through forest with glimpses of open meadow to the south shore of Upper Noyse Lake. The trail parallels the lake through wet meadows before arriving at the **Noyse Lake Cabin and camp** at 21.8 km (13.5 mi), about 740 m (2428 ft) above sea level.

Leaving Noyse Lake, the trail strikes out south through the meadows, then heads west to cross Noyse Creek. Arrive at a junction with the **Noyse Creek access trail** at 22.6 km (14 mi). This trail heads south to Lower Noyse Lake, and then beyond to a logging road access point. Go straight to continue west along the Kludahk Trail as it heads briefly uphill, then steadily downhill through patches of forest interspersed with open, wet meadows. At about 25.4 km (15.8 mi), the trail enters an old cutblock in a saddle. Shortly after, the route joins an **old, overgrown road** heading due west. Stay on the road for a few minutes, watching for flagging tape that marks your departure from the roadbed.

Follow the trail steeply downhill through cutblocks of varying ages to a large metal bridge over the **East Sombrio River** at 26.3 km (16.3 mi). The next section of trail is very rough as you scramble over huge stumps, gaining and losing elevation in a bushy clear-cut. The trail eventually joins an old road that takes you to a deteriorating road bridge over the **West Sombrio River** at 27.1 km (16.8 mi) and 590 m (1936 ft) elevation. On the west side of the bridge, turn right and follow the old road as it curls around the side of the hill. The road soon ends and the trail climbs steadily along the ridge crest. As you reach the high point around 860 m (2822 ft), you will enter Sombrio Woods, a beautiful grove of old hemlock, Douglas-fir, and cedar trees.

The trail drops down onto a marshy plateau speckled with small ponds and patches of forest. Watch for subalpine fir trees with their huge, dense cones, as well as the Western white pines with their long, soft needles clustered in bundles of five. Arrive at **Tent Lake Cabin and campsite** at 30.5 km (19 mi). Follow the trail along the south shore of the lake, then back into the forest, where it ascends a small rise. The path dips slightly to cross the headwaters of Minute Creek, then trends southwest along the ridge, passing more small ponds and patches of meadow.

Arrive at **Square Lake** at 32 km (19.9 mi). A spur trail down to its shore invites you to take a break. Swimmers beware: the lake is very silty. To continue onwards, follow the trail through the frame of a large abandoned wall tent. The path meanders along the ridge, crossing more wet meadows on boardwalks. **Spur trails** at 33.7 km (20.9 mi) and 34.9 km (21.7 mi) lead south to connect to Minute Creek FSR. At about 36 km (22.4 mi), just after passing Two Duck Lake, the trail parallels the back of a recent clear-cut, easily visible through the trees. The trail through this section is rougher as it winds through a dark forest of yellow- and redcedar.

The trail emerges into a regenerating cutblock, then **joins a road** at 37.5 km (23.3 mi). The rest of the hike is on this logging road, known as WC 2000 FSR. Follow the road as it switchbacks downhill, ignoring any side branches. The road reaches Highway 14, the **western trailhead**, at the 40 km (24.9 mi) mark. At the time of writing, WC 2000 was being regraded. It may be reactivated for logging in the coming years. If this is the case, watch for trucks on the road and check online for closures before your trip.

CAMPING

You must be a member of the Kludahk Outdoors Club (KOC) to sleep in the cabins along the trail. See the KOC website for more info. Anyone else is welcome to camp on wooden platforms next to the cabins, then head inside to warm up or socialize. If you use the cabins, leave them cleaner than you found them, and consider donating to the KOC. Camping is very limited on the trail, so plan to share tent platforms with other groups or be prepared to hike to the next site.

Fast and fit parties willing to hike long hours could finish the trail in 2 days by camping at Noyse Lake. For a 2-night trip, aim for Blueberry Hill and Tent Lake. For a more leisurely 3-night trip, stay at Tea Hut, Noyse Lake, and Tent Lake.

MEADOW CABIN AND CAMPSITE

This campsite is in a clump of trees next to a large meadow is a good place to stay if you got a late start or wish to day hike to Wye Lake.

Campsites: One large wooden tent platform just east of the cabin holds 1 or 2 small backpacking tents. No overflow area.
Toilet: On a trail behind the cabin
Water: Collect from silty ponds to the west along the Kludahk Trail
Food Storage: None. Bring a rope to hang your food in a tree, or use a bear canister or Ursack.
Other Amenities: The cabin has a propane stove, pots, dishes, tables, chairs, a wood stove (winter use only), a water filter, and a small library.

Meadow Cabin

TOWER CABIN AND CAMPSITE

Tower Cabin sits at the trail's high point next to an array of communication towers. A clearing provides amazing views.

Campsites: A flat, dirt clearing near the towers holds 1 tent. A few more marginal flat spots in the forest along the water access trail.
Toilet: Next to the cabin
Water: A signed trail (0.2 km/0.1 mi) descends to the south to access a creek that may run dry later in the year. The cabin also has a rainwater barrel, but please take water from it sparingly.
Food Storage: None. Bring a rope to hang your food in a tree, or use a bear canister or Ursack.
Other Amenities: The cabin has a propane stove, pots, dishes, tables, chairs, a wood stove (winter use only), a water filter, and a small library.

TEA HUT AND CAMPSITE

Built in 2007, Tea Hut is the newest cabin on the Kludahk Trail. It is designed as a day-use shelter with a huge collection of interpretive panels and large windows to let you observe nature in comfort.

Campsites: One large wooden tent platform just east of the cabin holds 1 or 2 small backpacking tents and has an incredible view. No overflow area.
Toilet: Behind the cabin
Water: No water source, so haul in your own water from Triangle Lake. The hut has a rainwater barrel, but please take water from it sparingly.
Food Storage: None. Bring a rope to hang your food in a tree, or use a bear canister or Ursack.
Other Amenities: The cabin has a camp stove, kettle, tables, chairs, binoculars, interpretive panels, and a small library.

BLUEBERRY HILL CABIN AND CAMPSITE

The campsite and cabin at Blueberry Hill sit in an open meadow dotted with tiny ponds and surrounded by blueberry bushes.

Campsites: One large wooden tent platform just west of the cabin holds 1 or 2 small backpacking tents. It is a former helipad and sits about 1 m (3.3 ft) off the ground. No overflow area.
Toilet: Next to the cabin
Water: Collect from the pond next to the cabin
Food Storage: None. Bring a rope to hang your food in a tree, or use a bear canister or Ursack.
Other Amenities: The cabin has a propane stove, pots, dishes, tables, chairs, a wood stove (winter use only), a water filter, a canoe, and a small library.

Noyse Lake is the largest lake on the Kludahk Trail. Two canoes here allow you to explore the shoreline.

Campsites: One large wooden tent platform just east of the cabin holds 1 or 2 small backpacking tents and has a view of the lake. A small dirt clearing next to the cabin can hold one small tent.
Toilet: On a spur trail to the east of the cabin
Water: Follow a stepping-stone path 1 minute west of the cabin to collect from a tiny pond that is not as silty as the lake.
Food Storage: None. Bring a rope to hang your food in a tree, or use a bear canister or Ursack.
Other Amenities: The cabin has a propane stove, pots, dishes, tables, chairs, a wood stove (winter use only), a water filter, canoes, and a small library.

The cabin at Tent Lake is the smallest on the trail and the pond in front is similarly diminutive. But the sunset views of the mountains across the San Juan River valley to the north are breathtaking.

Campsites: One large wooden tent platform behind the cabin holds 1 or 2 small backpacking tents and has a view of the mountains. No overflow area.
Toilet: On a spur trail behind the cabin
Water: Collect from the pond in front of the cabin
Food Storage: None. Bring a rope to hang your food in a tree, or use a bear canister or Ursack.

NATURE NOTE

COUGARS ON VANCOUVER ISLAND

Vancouver Island has the highest concentration of cougars in the world. Also known as mountain lions, cougars are the largest cat in the Americas, weighing 50 to 100 kg (110 to 200 lbs) and measuring about 2.4 m long (7.9 ft). As carnivores, they primarily prey on deer. Cougars are excellent jumpers and climbers who often use stealth and ambush to surprise their prey. The cats avoid humans since they don't see them as food; however, you may see cougar tracks or scat. (For cougar safety tips, see page 23.) Unlike dog or wolf tracks, cougar tracks do not have any claw marks. As well, the space between the pads in canine tracks makes an x-shape, whereas the pads of cougar tracks do not. Cougar scat is usually full of hair and bone fragments, can appear ropey and segmented, and tapers at one end.

Other Amenities: The cabin has a propane stove, pots, dishes, a small table, chairs, a wood stove (winter use only), a water filter, and a small library.

EXTENDING YOUR TRIP

Wye Lake: As the official eastern terminus of the Kludahk Trail, Wye Lake is worth a trip. The sinuous lake is over 1 km (0.6 mi) long and you can explore it via a canoe beached on the shore. The hike is 1.5 km (0.9 mi) one way from Meadow Cabin and loses about 120 m (394 ft) of elevation along the way. If you want to spend the night, the expansive campsite fits 5 or 6 tents and includes a covered fire pit area.

Juan de Fuca Trail: With a bit of road walking on either end, you could combine the Kludahk Trail with the Juan de Fuca Marine Trail (Trip 3) to make an epic loop.

FURTHER RESOURCES

Kludahk Outdoors Club (KOC): info, membership, and donations *kludahk .com*

South Island Natural Resource District road safety information: logging road closures and restrictions *gov.bc.ca/gov/content/industry/natural-resource-use/resource-roads/local-road-safety-information/ south-island-natural-resource-district-road-safety-information*

West Coast Trail Express: shuttle bus info and reservations *trailbus.com*

NTS Map: 092C09; 092B12

Driving Map: *Vancouver Island BC Backroad Mapbook*

Trail Map: Kludahk Trail Maps 1, 2, and 3, available from the KOC

5

T'L'OQWXWAT (AVATAR GROVE)

DAY HIKE

Difficulty: ●
Duration: 1 hour
Distance: 1.25 km (0.8 mi) round trip

Elevation Gain: 110 m (361 ft)
High Point: 180 m (591 ft)
Best Months: Year-round

Fees and Reservations: None

Regulations: No fires. No camping.

Caution: Please stay on the trail to avoid trampling fragile vegetation. Walking on the roots of giant trees reduces their stability and longevity.

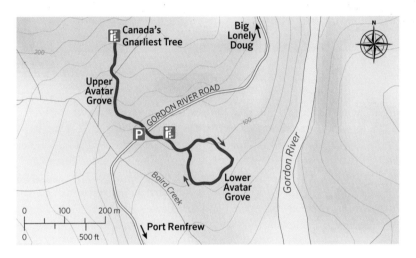

PROTECTED SINCE 2012, the giant western redcedar and Douglas-fir trees of Avatar Grove represent one of the few remaining stands of valley-bottom old-growth forest on southern Vancouver Island. Activists nicknamed the 10-hectare (25 acre) grove for the popular James Cameron film to help publicize the need to save it. In Pacheedaht, the language of the local First Nation, the site is known as T'l'oqwxwat, which means "wide bluff overlooking river." It was a traditional summer salmon fishing camp. Two short trails wind through the forest, to both the Upper and Lower Groves. The highlight is Canada's Gnarliest Tree at the top of the Upper Grove Trail.

The Avatar Grove trailhead

GETTING THERE

From Victoria, drive Highway 14 to Port Renfrew. Turn right onto Deering Road, and zero your odometer. Follow Deering Road across a bridge. Keep right at a Y-junction at 1.5 km (0.9 mi) to stay on Deering and cross another bridge. Turn left at the T-junction at 3 km (1.9 mi) onto Gordon River Road. At 8 km (5 mi), cross the Gordon River on a narrow bridge. The road turns to gravel but is fine for 2WD vehicles. Stay right at an intersection at 9.2 km (5.7 mi). Cross a small bridge over Baird Creek at 9.8 km (6.1 mi). Park shortly after the bridge on the wide shoulder. Trailheads are on either side of the road.

UPPER AVATAR GROVE

TRIP PLANNER

| 0 km (0 mi) | Trailhead |
| 0.3 km (0.2 mi) | Canada's Gnarliest Tree |

The upper trail in Avatar Grove is the more strenuous of the two, gaining nearly 80 m (262 ft) over rough terrain. The trailhead is on the uphill (west) side of the roadside pullout and a large map board shows the locations of key trees along the route. Start your hike by scaling a wooden staircase into the forest. Travel across wooden boardwalks and more stairs as you steadily gain

Canada's Gnarliest Tree

elevation. In some places, the trail is muddy or traverses slick tree roots, so watch your step.

Giant western redcedar trees stand out against the younger forest. The forest floor is covered in moss, ferns, and salal, with new growth springing out of fallen trees. Look for several especially large cedars about 0.2 km (0.1 mi) from the trailhead, where the trail dips to cross a small tributary of Baird Creek. Continue uphill with the help of more stairs to the trail's end at the cedar dubbed **Canada's Gnarliest Tree**. It has a massive 3-metre-wide (10 ft) burl at its base. Take a minute to admire the sinuous twists in its ancient trunk before retracing your steps to the parking area.

LOWER AVATAR GROVE

TRIP PLANNER

0 km (0 mi)	Trailhead
0.05 km (0.03 mi)	Viewing platform
0.1 km (0.06 mi)	Side trail to Douglas-fir
0.15 km (0.09 mi)	Loop junction
0.2 km (0.12 mi)	Gnarly cedar tree
0.4 km (0.25 mi)	Nurse log
0.5 km (0.31 mi)	Loop junction
0.65 km (0.4 mi)	Trailhead

The lower trail in Avatar Grove completes a flattish loop through the forest. However, to get there you will need to descend a steep trail and some stairs, losing about 30 m (98 ft) of elevation.

Start your hike on the downhill (east) side of the road. Almost immediately, arrive at a wooden **viewing platform** with views down into the old-growth forest. Continue downhill along carefully built stairs. A short and rough spur trail to the right leads to the base of a **huge Douglas-fir**.

Back on the main trail, follow the stairs and boardwalks to a junction. Go left to begin the loop. The trail meanders through the damp forest past numerous large trees. Shortly after the junction, reach a **gnarly cedar tree**. While not as large as the one in Upper Avatar Grove, it is still impressive. Continue around the loop, passing more giant trees. Pause to admire a large nurse log near the 0.4 km (0.25 mi) mark. The decaying wood of fallen trees like this one provides nutrients for new trees and bushes to grow.

A few minutes later, arrive back at the junction and retrace your steps up the stairs to the viewing platform and parking area beyond.

EXTENDING YOUR TRIP

Big Lonely Doug: With a 4WD vehicle and a GPS to navigate the backroads, you can visit Big Lonely Doug, a massive Douglas-fir standing alone in a clear-cut. From Avatar Grove, continue along Gordon River Main for 5 km (3.1 mi), then turn right onto Edinburgh Main. The road is rough enough to need a 4WD past here. Cross a bridge over the Gordon River canyon and stay on the road as it veers right and goes uphill. About 5 minutes from the bridge, reach a clear-cut on your right. You can view the tree from the road or make the very short and steep 0.25 km (0.2 mi) hike down a flagged route to close-up views of the massive tree. Please limit your time at the tree base to protect its roots.

FURTHER RESOURCES

Recreation Sites and Trails BC: info and map *sitesandtrailsbc.ca/search/search-result.aspx?site=REC202159&type=Site*
Ancient Forest Alliance Avatar Grove and Port Renfrew Big Trees Map: road and trail map *ancientforestalliance.org/learn-more/port-renfrew-big-trees-map/*
Happiest Outdoors: info *happiestoutdoors.ca/avatar-grove-big-lonely-doug*
Driving Map: *Vancouver Island BC Backroad Mapbook*
NTS Map: 092B05

6

WEST COAST TRAIL ★

BACKPACKING TRIP

Difficulty: ◆
Duration: 6 to 8 days
Distance: 75 km (46.6 mi) one way

Elevation Gain: 213 m (699 ft)
High Point: 213 m (699 ft)
Best Months: May to September

Fees and Reservations: Online trail reservations are required and cost $24.50/person. Trail fees are $130.31/person. National park entry fees are $10.50/person/day. Separate reservations required for Ditidaht Comfort Camping ($90–$120/cabin or luxury tent) and the Nitinaht Narrows Cabins ($150–$200/cabin, $30/camping).

Regulations: No dogs. No drones. Fires allowed below the high-tide line only.

Caution: Parts of this trail are very rough. Use caution on boardwalks, bridges, ladders, and cable cars. Parks Canada officially closes the trail between October and the beginning of May.

THE WEST COAST TRAIL (WCT) in Pacific Rim National Park Reserve is probably the most famous multi-day hiking trail in Canada—and with good reason. Originally a trail and telegraph route built in the early 1900s to assist

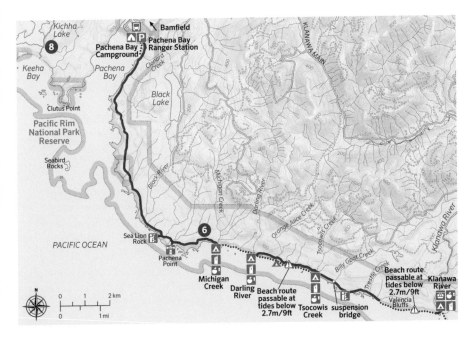

shipwrecked sailors along a wilderness shoreline known as the "Graveyard of the Pacific," it was resurrected in the late 1960s as a challenge for hikers. The rugged trail through temperate rainforest traverses ladders, boardwalks, cable cars, suspension bridges, rushing creeks, smooth sandstone shelves, and plenty of muddy bogs. Each night, hikers camp on a different beautiful sandy beach. The trail can be hiked in either direction, starting near Port Renfrew in the south or Bamfield in the north. Or you can do half of the trail thanks to a newer midway starting point at Nitinaht Narrows.

GETTING THERE

The WCT has two main trailheads: Gordon River near Port Renfrew in the south and Pachena Bay near Bamfield in the north. Most hikers complete a one-way hike between these two trailheads. It is also possible to start the trail at Nitinaht Narrows, near the middle of the trail. From that starting point, you can hike either north or south, completing half of the trail.

WEST COAST TRAIL EXPRESS BUS

While you can drive yourself to all three trailheads, most hikers use the West Coast Trail Express bus service for some portion of their journey. The bus leaves from Victoria and Nanaimo, delivering hikers to all three trailheads. You can also use the West Coast Trail Express to travel from one trailhead to another at the beginning or end of your trip. The route between trailheads is on rough and confusing logging roads and takes about 4 hours, so it's prudent to use the bus service for that leg of your journey. Prices vary based on the distance travelled. Reservations are highly recommended.

GORDON RIVER/PORT RENFREW (SOUTH) TRAILHEAD

From Victoria, take Highway 14 to Port Renfrew. At the entrance to town, turn right on Deering Road and follow it across the bridge. Make the next left onto Pacheedaht Road. The Parks Canada check-in office is at the Pacheedaht campground at the end of the road. You can also pay for overnight parking ($5/day) at the campground office.

PACHENA BAY/BAMFIELD (NORTH) TRAILHEAD

Driving to Bamfield involves travel on rough and sometimes confusing logging roads, but it is 2WD accessible. I recommend bringing a GPS and a copy of the *Vancouver Island BC Backroad Mapbook*. From Port Alberni, take 3rd Avenue south to Ship Creek Road, which becomes Bamfield Road and turns to gravel. Stay on Bamfield Road and follow signs for Bamfield, ignoring all other side roads. About 75 km (46.6 mi) later, look for the Parks Canada sign on your left. Turn down the bumpy access road to arrive at the trailhead and parking lot a few minutes later.

NITINAHT NARROWS (MIDDLE) TRAILHEAD

The route to Nitinaht Narrows at the WCT midpoint involves travel on rough logging roads but is 2WD accessible. Bring a GPS and a copy of the *Vancouver Island BC Backroad Mapbook*. From Duncan, head west on Highway 18 to Lake Cowichan. Zero your odometer, then continue west on Youbou Road as it turns to gravel and becomes North Shore Road, then Cowichan Main Forest Service Road. Follow signs for the Nitinaht Lake Motel and turn left onto Nitinaht Main. At a T-junction 55 km (34 mi) later, go left on Carmanah Main to reach Nitinaht Village a few minutes away. From Nitinaht Village, take a pre-arranged water taxi along Nitinaht Lake to the trailhead at Nitinaht Narrows.

TRAIL

TRIP PLANNER

0 km (0 mi)	Pachena Bay (northern) trailhead
9.5 km (5.9 mi)	Pachena Point Lighthouse
12 km (7.5 mi)	Michigan Creek campground
13.7 km (8.5 mi)	Darling River campground
15 km (9.3 mi)	Orange Juice Creek campground
16.5 km (10.3 mi)	Tsocowis Creek campground
18 km (11.2 mi)	Valencia Bluffs viewpoint
23 km (14.3 mi)	Klanawa River campground
25 km (15.5 mi)	Tsusiat Falls campground
29.7 km (18.5 mi)	Ditidaht Comfort Camping
32.2 km (20 mi)	Nitinaht Narrows (Crab Shack and cabins)
41.5 km (25.8 mi)	Cribs Creek campground
44 km (27.3 mi)	Carmanah Point Lighthouse
46 km (28.6 mi)	Carmanah Creek campground
48 km (29.8 mi)	Bonilla Point campground
53 km (32.9 mi)	Walbran Creek campground
56 km (34.8 mi)	Logan Creek Suspension Bridge
57.7 km (35.9 mi)	Cullite Creek campground via side trail
62.2 km (38.6 mi)	Camper Bay campground
67 km (41.6 mi)	Owen Point
70 km (43.5 mi)	Thrasher Cove campground junction
75 km (46.6 mi)	Gordon River ferry and southern trailhead

The WCT is typically hiked as a one-way traverse between Gordon River (Port Renfrew) in the south and Pachena Bay (Bamfield) in the north. Some hikers also start in the middle at Nitinaht Narrows, then head south or north.

Some people prefer to start with the easier northern portion so they can hit the tough sections in the south with lighter packs. Others choose to start at the southern trailhead to get the hard stuff out of the way first. I have hiked the trail in both directions and do not have a clear preference. This description starts in the north since that's where Parks Canada's official kilometre 0 for the trail is located.

Your trip begins with a mandatory orientation session with a park ranger. It includes important information about tides, wildlife, safety, wilderness ethics, and trail conditions. You'll also learn about the trail's history and Indigenous context. The park ranger will give you your trail permit, a copy of the trail map, and a basic tide table.

On the WCT you will often need to choose between parallel beach and inland routes. Consult your trail map and tide table to see if the beach route is passable. If tides allow, the beach route is usually easier and more pleasant.

You will need to make your first beach versus inland choice at the **Pachena Bay trailhead**. If the tide is below 2.4 m (8 ft), you can take the shoreline route, which travels across flat sand. The inland route uses a few ladders to go up and over a bluff. The two routes converge 0.5 km (0.3 mi) later. The next section is entirely inland on an eroded former jeep road that makes for mostly easy walking. Around 9 km (5.6 mi) from the trailhead, look for the **side trail to Sea Lion Rocks**. It's a short walk to a spectacular clifftop viewpoint where you may be able to spot sea lions on offshore rocks. Binoculars will help you get a better look.

Back on the trail, you'll come to the junction with a side trail to the **Pachena Point Lighthouse**. You can explore the lighthouse grounds, but respect the lighthouse keepers' privacy. Watch for whales from the bluffs and elsewhere along the WCT. About 200 resident grey whales spend the summer along the west coast of Vancouver Island. You can often spy them swimming on their sides to feed on crustaceans and other organisms that live along the ocean floor. Ts'axq'oo-is, a Huu-ay-aht village, was located just east of the point. The name means "village along the west coast with a bay within it."

Continue on the forest trail for another 2.5 km (1.6 mi) until it descends to the ocean at **Michigan Creek campground**. Emerge on the beach and cross Michigan Creek, named for a steamer that wrecked here in 1893. The next 2 km (1.2 mi) of trail is along the beach to **Darling River campground**. Fording the river on the beach is usually a straightforward rock-hop, but use caution at high tide or during heavy runoff. The Huu-ay-aht know the river as ʔI:hwa-nat, meaning "large object in front of beach." The Ditidaht call it iixwaat7aa, which means "big creek." Past here, you can take the sandy beach route for 2.5 km (1.6 mi) at all but the highest tides (less than 2.7 m/9 ft), which makes the forest route a bit overgrown.

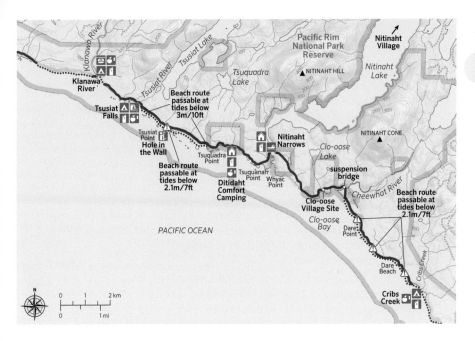

Pass **Orange Juice Creek campground** on the beach route, then arrive at **Tsocowis Creek campground**, 16.5 km (10.3 mi) from the start. In Ditidaht, Tsocowis means "head pointing straight down towards the beach." The forest and beach routes converge here as you head inland on a set of ladders, then cross a suspension bridge.

In the next section, the trail runs across the top of the bluff through thick salal, with several viewpoints. The best one is at **Valencia Bluffs**, where there are two iconic red Parks Canada chairs. This site is named for the steamship *Valencia*, which wrecked here in 1906 (page 88).

Pass a derelict grader and donkey engine beside the trail, then descend ladders back to the beach near the 20 km (14.4 mi) mark. The next section is a mandatory beach hike with no inland option. At lower tides, head down onto the sandstone shelf for the easiest walking. Just be careful of the slippery algae and seaweed.

Reach **Klanawa River campground** on the north bank of the river and get ready to tackle your first cable car. Be careful climbing aboard and loading your pack. Enjoy the downhill ride to the midpoint, then give your arms a workout pulling yourself back up the other side. In Huu-ay-aht, the river is called Tla-na-wa and in Ditidaht, it is known as Tladiiwa, both of which translate to "pieces of blubber on the beach." The next section of trail climbs onto a bluff with help from a few ladders, then traverses a few boardwalks.

Cross the Tsusiat River on a bridge, then drop down to the beach at **Tsusiat Falls campground** on a set of ladders. The word *Tsusiat* (spelled tsusiiyit in Ditidaht and Tsu-si-yat in Huu-ay-aht) means waterfall. The picturesque falls streaming down the sandstone cliffs into a pool on the gravel beach are a highlight for many backpackers. Heading north, consult the tides, then choose between the beach and forest routes for the next 4 km (2.5 mi). The beach route includes some deep sand that can be tiring but gives you the chance to walk through a natural rock arch at Hole in the Wall if the tide is low enough (less than 2.1 m/6.9 ft). The inland trail is slippery, with lots of mud and tree roots, but passes an interesting cave.

Follow hanging buoys to head back into the forest near the 29 km (18 mi) marker. A few minutes later, pass the turnoff to **Ditidaht Comfort Camping**. The trail crosses a few streams, so fill your bottles; this is the last reliable water until Dare Beach, about 10 km (6.2 mi) away.

Follow the trail up and over some bluffs, then inland through the forest to the dock on the north side of **Nitinaht Narrows**. The word *Nitinaht* is an older misspelling of *Ditidaht*, after the Ditidaht Nation. Call across the narrows for the ferry operator to pick you up. After a 2-minute ferry ride, disembark on the south dock. Carl Edgar Jr. and his family from the Ditidaht Nation have been operating a hiker ferry service here since the late 1970s. They now have an excellent restaurant called the **Crab Shack** that serves breakfast, lunch, and dinner, as well as four heated cabins for rent. Be sure to stop for a snack and a chat.

Leaving Nitinaht Narrows, the trail is almost entirely easy walking on an inland boardwalk for 4 km (2.5 mi). In June, watch for signs of digging in the skunk cabbage that lines the boardwalk. The roots are a popular early season food for bears. The trail passes through the semi-abandoned Ditidaht village of Clo-oose, or tluu7uus, which means "camping beach." A small European settlement existed here at the turn of the 20th century. The village has had no permanent residents for several decades, but many members of the Ditidaht Nation spend time fishing and gathering here in the summer months. Respect private property by staying on the trail.

Cross the brackish Cheewhat River on a wide suspension bridge around 36 km (22.4 mi) from the trailhead. In Ditidaht, Cheewhat means "little stream of water comes in." Just past the bridge, choose between a firm-sand beach route and an easy forest route. The two paths come back together just past the 38 km (23.6 mi) marker, where you must take a ladder over an impassable headland.

A few hundred metres later you can descend back to the beach or stick to the forest. The beach starts as sand, but transitions to a rock shelf with some scrambly sections near headlands. Near the 40 km (24.9 mi) mark, choose between coastal and inland routes again. If the tide is below 2.1 m (6.9 ft),

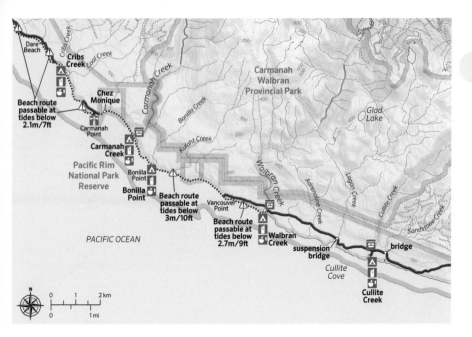

you can take the beach route across rocky shelves. If not, you'll have to take a ladder up into the forest. Both options intersect at **Cribs Creek campground**. The creek takes its name from the sandstone rocks just offshore that act as a natural breakwater.

Heading south, you'll walk along the beach for the first kilometre (0.6 mi). If tides allow (less than 2.1 m/6.9 ft), you can continue along the shoreline to a set of stairs to **Carmanah Point Lighthouse**. Otherwise, take the easy path through the forest, then a side trail to the lighthouse. There are great views from the bluff beside the light station and a huge whale skeleton displayed on the lawn. Respect the privacy of the lighthouse keepers. Past the lighthouse, the trail heads through the forest, then down some ladders to a sandy beach.

Look for an informal beach shack restaurant near the bottom of the ladders at a place the Ditidaht know as qwabaaduwa? ("canoe landing in front of village"). Monique and Peter Knighton operated the Chez Monique restaurant here from the mid-1990s until they passed away in 2017 and 2018. Monique was originally from Quebec and Peter was a member of the Ditidaht Nation. Although their family has tried to resurrect the restaurant, its future is uncertain. If it's open, enjoy a burger and the magnificent view.

Continue along the gorgeous beach as the sand gets deeper, making walking more challenging. Reach **Carmanah Creek campground** and take the cable car or wade across at low water. The route stays on the beach with no inland option south of here. At low tide, be sure to take advantage of the easy walking on the sandstone coastal shelf. Pass **Bonilla Point campground** at

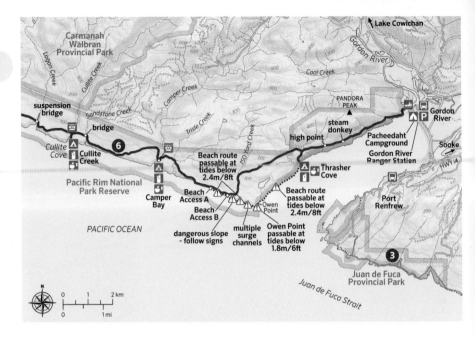

48 km (29.8 mi) and continue along the shelf, then trudge through some deep sand. The point is named after Antonio Bonilla, a senior administrator in Spain's colonization of Mexico and Texas. The Pacheedaht name for Bonilla Point is Botkawat, which means "water around point."

Just before Vancouver Point, near km 51 (31.7 mi), consult your tide table to choose your route. If the tides are right (below 2.7 m/8.9 ft), you can take the beach route and walk on a sandstone shelf all the way to Walbran Creek. It is possible to ford the creek at its mouth at low tide and during periods of low water. At higher tides or if the creek is in flood, you must take the rough and overgrown inland trail to the Walbran cable car. Arrive at **Walbran Creek campground** after crossing the creek.

The next section to Camper Creek is one of the most challenging parts of the WCT. Leaving Walbran Creek, you'll ascend a long set of ladders. Next, traverse a bog on badly deteriorating boardwalks. It is a challenge to keep your feet dry through the many mud holes. Logan Creek at km 56 (34.8 mi) used to have some of the longest and most vertigo-inducing ladders on the trail. But the new **Logan Creek Suspension Bridge**, which opened in 2021, whisks you from one side of the canyon to the other in a few easy minutes.

On the other side of the bridge, slog through another 2 km (1.2 mi) of damaged boardwalks, deep mud, and slippery tree roots. Descend into Cullite Creek on the longest ladder system on the trail: there are 7 ladders on one side of the canyon and 11 on the other. At the bottom, rock-hop across the creek or take the cable car. Follow a short side trail down the creek to **Cullite**

Climbing the ladders out of Thrasher Cove

Creek campground, on the beach. It makes a good lunch stop if you don't plan to camp here. In Pacheedaht, Cullite Creek is called qawšadt.

After the Cullite Creek ladders, the trail travels through a slightly less muddy forest for 1.5 km (0.9 mi) before descending and ascending a few ladders on either side of the Sandstone Creek bridge. Mud holes and tree roots resume in the forest, but the boardwalk in this section is in better shape. Descend ladders and steep trail to **Camper Bay campground**, just past the 62 km (38.5 mi) marker.

Leaving Camper Bay, take the cable car across Camper Creek. You can also ford the creek in low water. Climb up a section of ladders and head back into a stretch of forest trail with a few muddy sections but lots of good boardwalks.

At the 65 km (40.4 mi) marker you'll have a key choice to make. The coastal route travels along the base of a cliff and around **Owen Point**, named in 1846 for a British surveyor. The Pacheedaht name for Owen Point is ʔaxačkt, which means "a hole through under the rock." It's a difficult, rough, and slippery route through jumbled boulders and scrambly surge channels that takes most hikers a few hours to complete. A stunning sea cave provides glorious scenery. Time your hike carefully to ensure you can get through this 5 km (3.1 mi) section without getting trapped against the cliffs by the rising tide. Most of it is passable at tides below 2.4 m (7.9 ft), but you need tides of less than 1.8 m (5.9 ft) to get around Owen Point.

If the Owen Point route sounds too challenging or you don't have the right tides, you'll have to take the rigorous inland route, widely considered one of the hardest sections of the WCT. When the trail was developed for hikers in the late 1960s, this section had recently seen a huge windstorm. As a result, the route zigzags up, over, and around fallen trees with lots of slippery tree roots and mud holes in between. It also includes numerous narrow log crossings, some over 4 m (13.1 ft) off the ground. However, the old-growth trees are spectacular, and if you hike in July and August, you can feast on red huckleberries. Expect very slow travel through this section.

At the 70 km (43.5 mi) marker you'll arrive at a junction. A rough and steep side trail with ladders and switchbacks descends for 1 km (0.6 mi) to **Thrasher Cove campground**, which has a view across Port San Juan to Port Renfrew. While "thrasher" could describe the challenging nature of the trail, the cove takes its name from Abram Thrasher, who received a Crown grant of land near here in the early 1900s. The beach route from Owen Point meets the main trail at the cove. The Pacheedaht call this beach ʔo:yacs', which means "bay facing in the bay," and had a village here.

Continuing straight from the junction will take you along a rough stretch to the WCT's high point, at 213 m (699 ft) above sea level. Only this section of the route was extensively logged, and you will notice that the second-growth forest is much darker and denser than the rest of the trail. Next, pass an old donkey engine left over from logging. The path begins a slow descent to the ocean before arriving at the top of a very tall ladder that is nearly vertical and terrifying for many hikers. Take a deep breath and go slowly.

Use a buoy on a rope next to the ladder to let the ferry operator know you want a pickup, then descend to the beach. Butch Jack from the Pacheedaht Nation will boat you across the river to the **Gordon River trailhead**, 75 km (46.6 mi) from the start. Walk one block up the road to the right to the Parks Canada office to officially check out from the trail.

CAMPING AND CABINS

All WCT campsites are on the beach. Look for fishing floats hanging in the trees to show the way to the toilets and food storage lockers. All toilets are composting toilets, where wood shavings are mixed with the waste to break it down. Follow the instructions posted inside the toilets. With 15 campgrounds, many itineraries are possible. The most common 7-day itinerary includes nights at Michigan Creek, Tsusiat Falls, Cribs Creek, Walbran Creek, Camper Bay, and Thrasher Cove.

MICHIGAN CREEK CAMPGROUND

This campground is popular for first and last nights on the trail and can get crowded. Look for the remains of the *Michigan* shipwreck at low tide.

Campsites: Limited space on the beach above the high-tide line. A few sites in the forest on both sides of the creek.
Toilet: Composting toilet on the north side of the creek
Water: Collect from Michigan Creek
Food Storage: Food hanging pole in the forest north of the creek

DARLING RIVER CAMPGROUND

With lots of soft sand, ample driftwood for campfires, and a small waterfall, Darling River is an ideal place to camp.

Campsites: Lots of flat spots on the sand above the high-tide line
Toilet: In the forest on the south side of the river
Water: Collect from the Darling River
Food Storage: Food locker in the forest south of the river

ORANGE JUICE CREEK CAMPGROUND

This is the only official campground on the WCT with no facilities, so you may have it to yourself. It has a small sea cave above the high-tide line that may be a welcome place to dry off in wet weather.

Campsites: Several in the forest and 2 beach sites above the high-tide line
Toilet: None. Dig a cat hole and use Leave No Trace toilet practices. Make sure you go inland, well away from the campsites and creek.
Water: Collect from Orange Juice Creek. You may have to scramble over the driftwood and follow the creek inland to find enough flow.
Food Storage: None. Bring rope to suspend your food in a tree. Many of the trees have broken branches from failed food hangs, so you may have to walk a few minutes from camp to find a suitable tree.

TSOCOWIS CREEK CAMPGROUND

This campground has a beautiful sandy beach and a shipwreck to explore nearby, but it never gets very busy. The West Coast Trail Guardians cabin here is not open to the public.

Campsites: Spots on the beach north of the cabin, and more to the south near the creek
Toilet: In the forest near the cabin
Water: Collect from Tsocowis Creek
Food Storage: Food locker in the forest near the cabin

KLANAWA RIVER CAMPGROUND

The wide, sandy beach on the north side of the Klanawa River makes a good place to camp. You can also cool off with a swim in the brackish river.

Campsites: On the sand north of the river and in the nearby forest

The Tsusiat Falls campground

Toilet: In the forest behind the beach on the north side of the river
Water: The Klanawa River is tidal and too salty to drink. A small creek a few minutes up the trail on the south side of the river can be accessed via the cable car across the river.
Food Storage: Food locker in the forest on the north side of the beach

TSUSIAT FALLS CAMPGROUND

The most popular campground on the WCT and a common place to take a rest day, Tsusiat Creek pours over a sandstone cliff into a pool on the beach. Taking a "shower" under the falls is a fun way to get some of the mud off.

Campsites: Lots of space on the sand south of the falls, although many sites are very close to each other
Toilet: Against the cliff at the south end of the beach
Water: Collect from Tsusiat Creek. To avoid contamination from swimmers, fill up from the creek before you descend the ladders to the beach. Or wade up to the waterfall and fill up there.
Food Storage: Food lockers and hanging poles at the south end of the beach

DITIDAHT COMFORT CAMPING

If you want to treat yourself, stay at Ditidaht Comfort Camping near Tsquadra Point. Reservations are recommended.

Cabins and Luxury Tents: Wall tents and cabins each sleep 4 on cots
Toilets: In the forest behind the cabins and tents
Water: Collect from the creek that runs through the site
Food Storage: Food lockers outside each tent or store it inside cabins
Other Amenities: Each cabin or tent comes with a table and chairs, and a wood stove. The cabins have covered porches.

NITINAHT NARROWS CABINS

Break up the long hike between Tsusiat Falls and Cribs Creek with a stay at Nitinaht Narrows. The Edgar family runs the Crab Shack restaurant here and also rents out cabins. You can also pitch your tent on their dock. Reservations are recommended.

Cabins and Camping: Four heated cabins with bunks (one sleeps 4–8, the rest 1–5). You can also camp on the floating dock under a tarp.
Toilets: In the forest behind the cabins.
Water: Provided by the Edgar family.
Food Storage: Inside cabins.
Other Amenities: Each cabin has a wood stove or heater and chairs. Some have covered decks and tables.

CRIBS CREEK CAMPGROUND

Due to the spacing of campgrounds, Cribs Creek sees a lot of traffic. A large band of rocks stretches across the mouth of the bay, which makes for dramatic crashing waves as the tide comes in.

Campsites: Lots of space on the sand on both sides of the creek. Be careful: it can be tough to tell if your tent is above the high-tide line.
Toilet: In the forest near the centre of the beach
Water: Collect from Cribs Creek
Food Storage: Food locker and hanging poles in the forest at the centre of the beach

CARMANAH CREEK CAMPGROUND

The Carmanah Creek campground has lots of fine sand and lovely views. It's also less busy than nearby Cribs Creek Camp.

Campsites: Lots of spots on the north side of the creek
Toilet: In the forest on the north side of the creek
Water: Collect from Carmanah Creek. Try to get water at low tide or head far upstream to avoid saltwater contamination.
Food Storage: Food locker in the forest on the north side of the creek

BONILLA POINT CAMPGROUND

This small campground is seldom used, which is a shame since it's one of the prettiest on the trail. It has a beautiful sandy beach, a few campsites in the sand, and a cute little waterfall.

Campsites: A few sites on the beach on the north side of the creek
Toilet: In the forest on the north side of the creek
Water: Collect from the creek
Food Storage: Food locker in the forest north of the creek

WALBRAN CREEK CAMPGROUND

Many hikers say Walbran Creek is their favourite campground on the WCT. Cliffs on the north side of the creek create a deep swimming hole, and the broad gravel beach to the south has lots of campsites.

Campsites: Numerous sites on the beach and in the forest south side of the creek, although some are very close together
Toilet: In the forest on the south side of the creek
Water: Collect from the creek
Food Storage: Food locker in the forest on the south side of the creek

HISTORY
———

THE GRAVEYARD OF THE PACIFIC

During the 1800s, many European fur-trading ships wrecked on the rocky reefs in stormy weather and gave the west coast of Vancouver Island the nickname "the Graveyard of the Pacific." When the SS *Valencia* ran aground near Klanawa River in 1906 and 136 lives were lost, there was a public outcry. The existing rudimentary telegraph line along the northern part of what is now the WCT was upgraded to the Dominion Lifesaving Trail, with aid cabins along it to help shipwreck victims. Today you can see remains of the telegraph wires along the trail between Thrasher Cove and Gordon River. With advances in navigation technology, shipwrecks decreased and the trail fell into disuse. By the 1960s, hikers were exploring the area. The trail was incorporated into Pacific Rim National Park in 1973. Since then, park rangers have added ladders, boardwalks, cable cars, and bridges.

CULLITE CREEK CAMPGROUND

This small campground is in a lovely little cove along a short and rough side trail, which means it sees few visitors.

Campsites: Space for 4 or 5 tents in a clearing above the beach
Toilet: In the forest on the south side of the creek
Water: Collect from the creek
Food Storage: Food locker in the forest south of the creek

CAMPER BAY CAMPGROUND

Camper Bay is often busy. The campsites are arranged along the back of a deep bay, with Camper Creek meandering in front. A West Coast Trail Guardians cabin here is not open to the public.

Campsites: Lots of sites at the back of the beach and around the corner by the creek. The creekside sites can flood during heavy rain.
Toilet: Near the creek at the south end of the campground
Water: Collect from the creek
Food Storage: Food locker near the creek at the south end of camp

THRASHER COVE CAMPGROUND

This small campground is popular for first and last nights on the WCT. It is 1 km (0.6 mi) down a steep side trail in a small cove with a sandy beach and is the best place on the WCT to swim.

Campsites: Lots of sites along the sand and in the forest behind it
Toilet: Near the trail entrance at the south end of the campground
Water: Collect from the small creek in the centre of the beach
Food Storage: Food hanging pole near the outhouse

FURTHER RESOURCES

Pacific Rim National Park Reserve: info, reservations, and map *pc.gc.ca/en/pn-np/bc/pacificrim/activ/SCO-WCT*
Happiest Outdoors: additional trail info *happiestoutdoors.ca/guide-to-the-west-coast-trail*
Fisheries and Oceans Canada: Tofino tide table *tides.gc.ca/eng/station?sid=8615*
West Coast Trail Express: shuttle bus info and reservations *trailbus.com*
Ditidaht Comfort Camping: info and reservations *westcoasttrail.com*
Nitinaht Narrows Cabins: info and reservations (250) 745-3509
NTS Maps: 092C075, 092C076, 092C066, 092C067, 092C057, 092C058
Driving Map: *Vancouver Island BC Backroad Mapbook*

7

CARMANAH VALLEY

BACKPACKING TRIP

Difficulty: ●
Duration: 2 days
Distance: 7 km (4.3 mi) round trip

Elevation Gain: 90 m (295 ft)
High Point: 240 m (787 ft)
Best Months: April to October

Fees and Reservations: Camping fees are $5/person/night, payable online. All camp-sites are first-come, first-served.

Regulations: No drones. No smoking, vaping, or cannabis. No fires. Dogs permitted on leash.

Caution: The trails in the Carmanah valley are unmaintained. Expect broken board-walks, washed-out trails, and fallen trees. Do not camp in the park during periods of high rainfall or snowmelt as the trail and campsites are subject to flash floods.

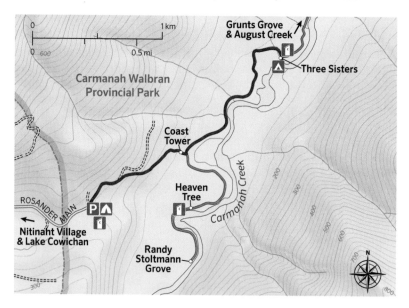

THE CARMANAH VALLEY is a special place. Home to some of the world's largest Sitka spruce trees, Carmanah Walbran Provincial Park protects the Carmanah Creek watershed, which includes huge swaths of B.C.'s remaining old-growth forest. While old-growth logging protests feature prominently in B.C.'s news cycle today, they have their roots here. In the late 1980s, activists built trails to encourage the public to visit, then chained themselves to trees

A gravel bar on Carmanah Creek

and slept in hanging campsites high in the forest canopy to protect the trees from logging. The park was established in 1990, but today it is somewhat forgotten, tucked away in a maze of logging roads. The boardwalks and trails are falling into disrepair, but the beauty of the rainforest endures. Camping amongst these giants is a spiritual experience not to be missed.

GETTING THERE

There's no getting around it: the drive to the Carmanah valley is long and rough. It is usually 2WD accessible, but depending on weather or road conditions, an AWD or 4WD vehicle may be a better choice. For the first part of your journey to Nitinaht Village, refer to the Nitinaht Narrows (Middle) Trailhead driving directions in Trip 6 (page 77). Home of the Ditidaht First Nation, the village has a small store and motel. Continue along Carmanah Main for another 4 km (2.5 mi) to a bridge over the Caycuse River. On the other side, turn right onto Rosander Main, which has some steep and loose sections. Stay on Rosander Main for 29 km (18 mi) to its end at a parking lot in Carmanah Walbran Provincial Park. There are five small drive-up campsites here. Allow 2.5 to 3.5 hours from Lake Cowichan.

TRAIL

TRIP PLANNER

0 km (0 mi)	Trailhead and parking lot
0.3 km (0.2 mi)	Valley Mist Trail begins
1.2 km (0.7 mi)	Coast Tower tree
1.3 km (0.8 mi)	Valley Mist Trail junction
3.5 km (2.2 mi)	Three Sisters camping area

The trail begins at the north end of the parking lot on a gated continuation of Rosander Main. Walk along the old road for 0.3 km (0.2 mi) and look for the signed **Valley Mist Trail** branching downhill to the right. Follow the trail as it descends gradually on a well-constructed gravel trail. After hours of driving through cutblocks to reach the trailhead, it is a sweet relief to find yourself in such a lush old-growth forest, with towering trees overhead and moss, ferns, and huckleberry bushes blanketing the ground.

Reach the first named tree of your hike, the **Coast Tower**, about 1.2 km (0.7 mi) from the start. This massive Sitka spruce tree was once 92 m (302 ft) tall, but a windstorm in 1997 reduced its height by 30 m (98 ft). Sitka spruce trees have shallow roots that are very sensitive, so please stay on the boardwalk around this and other trees in the valley. But use caution on the boardwalks as they are very slippery and falls are almost inevitable.

Continue on the Valley Mist Trail for another minute to a **junction**, 1.3 km (0.8 mi) from the trailhead. Your route to the Three Sisters goes left. (The trail to the right heads to the Heaven Tree and Randy Stoltmann Commemorative Grove.) Continue along the boardwalk as the trail roughly parallels the banks of Carmanah Creek and heads upstream. You'll pass many huge old-growth trees, as well as lots of Sitka spruce, western hemlock, and western redcedar seedlings with lofty aspirations. In the spring, watch for trilliums and fawn lilies blooming in sunny patches.

About 1.7 km (1.1 mi) from the start, the trail heads along the top of the riverbank, which has eroded and **washed out** the trail. Follow a rough re-route across a tributary creek and around some blowdown before rejoining the main trail. Continue following the trail as it meanders through the forest away from the creek. The path passes through several incredible groves of spruce before arriving at the **Three Sisters**, about 3 km (1.9 mi) from the

NATURE NOTE
_____

IDENTIFYING TREES IN B.C.'S COASTAL RAINFOREST

In the Carmanah valley, three types of trees dominate the landscape: western redcedar, Sitka spruce, and western hemlock. To identify these trees, look at their needles. Western redcedar has flat, scale-like needles. Sitka spruce has sharp, pokey needles all the way around a branch. Western hemlock has flat needles on either side of each branch. These trees often grow together. Older fallen trees known as nurse logs decay and provide nutrients for seedlings growing on top of them. As you walk the trail, look for red-tinged western redcedar nurse logs with tiny western hemlock seedlings growing out of them.

Walking through old-growth forest

trailhead. Each of these three Sitka spruce trees is about 79 m (259 ft) tall. Two of the sisters still stand tall, but one fell in a storm over the winter of 2018/19.

Continue along the trail for a few more minutes to a **junction** at 3.3 km (2.1 mi). Turn right to reach the **Three Sisters camping area** on gravel bars at a bend in the creek at 3.5 km (2.2 mi). Continuing straight on the main trail will take you to an outhouse. The trail beyond is no longer maintained, so most hikers make this their destination.

CAMPING

Campsites on the gravel bar provide a beautiful vantage point.

Campsites: Space for 5 or 6 tents in sandy patches. There are also many marginal sites in rockier areas.
Toilet: Follow the main trail upstream for a few minutes
Water: Collect from Carmanah Creek
Food Storage: None. Bring a bear canister, an Ursack, or a rope to hang your food in a tree. Choose wisely to avoid damaging the fragile ecosystem.

The Coast Tower tree

EXTENDING YOUR TRIP

Heaven Tree and Randy Stoltmann Commemorative Grove: Head south from the Valley Mist Trail junction to see some spectacular trees. Reach the 77-m-tall (253 ft) Heaven Tree just 1 km (0.6 mi) from the junction. It is 3.5 m (11.5 ft) across and has a viewing platform at its base. Continue downstream past an outhouse for 0.3 km (0.2 mi) to the Randy Stoltmann Commemorative Grove, named for one of the key activists who pushed to establish Carmanah Walbran Provincial Park and advocated for preserving old-growth trees across B.C. The trees in the grove range from 75 to 89 m (246 to 292 ft) tall. At the time of writing, the trail south of Heaven Tree is unsafe, so it may not be possible to reach the grove.

Grunts Grove and August Creek: The trail is no longer maintained north of the Three Sisters, but intrepid hikers can attempt it across broken board-walks and around fallen trees. Backcountry camping is allowed north of here on gravel bars in the creek at times of low water, but there are no facilities. Reach Grunts Grove, a collection of giant spruce trees, and good camping on a nearby gravel bar, about 2.5 km (1.6 mi) beyond the Three Sisters. August Creek is 6 km (3.7 mi) past the Three Sisters. It is the largest creek that flows into Carmanah Creek, and the trail officially ends here. (It once stretched even farther north, but after a key bridge failed, most of the infrastructure has decomposed back into the forest.) August Creek also has an informal back-country campsite on a gravel bar but no facilities.

FURTHER RESOURCES

Carmanah Walbran Provincial Park: info and trail fees *bcparks.ca/explore/parkpgs/carmanah*
NTS Map: 092C10; 092C15
Driving Map: *Vancouver Island BC Backroad Mapbook*

8

KEEHA BEACH

BACKPACKING TRIP

Difficulty: ■
Duration: 2 days
Distance: 8 km (5.6 mi) round trip

Elevation Gain: 50 m (164 ft)
High Point: 50 m (164 ft)
Best Months: May to September

Fees and Reservations: Online camping reservations are required and cost $11.50/site/night. Camping fees are $10.50/person/night. National park entry fees are also required and cost $10.50/person/day.

Regulations: No dogs. No stereos. No drones. Fires allowed below the high-tide line only.

Caution: Parks Canada officially closes the trail between mid-October and the beginning of May.

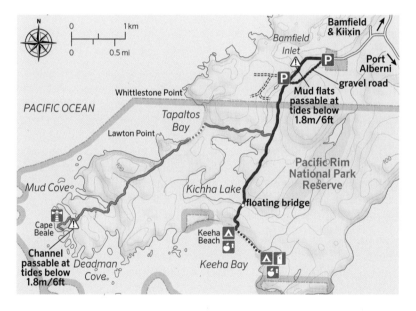

THE TRAIL TO Keeha Beach offers some of the most rugged terrain on Vancouver Island's west coast. The route scrambles over fallen logs, clambers across twisted tree roots, and slogs through boot-sucking mud. But your reward is a spectacular wilderness beach of fine sand. Listen to crashing waves as you relax next to a campfire or explore the trail-less coastline to discover sea caves

The mud flats at Bamfield Inlet

and tide pools. Despite the arduous hike to reach it, devotees of Keeha Beach return year after year to enjoy its wild beauty.

GETTING THERE

DRIVING

The trailhead is near the town of Bamfield. For the first part of your journey to the Parks Canada office near Bamfield, see the driving directions for the Pachena Bay/Bamfield (North) Trailhead in Trip 6 (page 76). Pass the Parks Canada sign and the West Coast Trail office on your left. Continue on Bamfield Road for another 4 km (2.5 mi), then turn left on South Bamfield Road. The main parking area is on your right 1.2 km (0.7 mi) later and has space for about 8 cars. Alternatively, turn left onto the unmarked gravel road just past the parking area. Drive 0.8 km (0.5 mi) down this road and park in a pullout next to the trail crossing. This parking area fits about 5 cars. Parking here will save you 0.5 km (0.3 mi) of hiking.

WEST COAST TRAIL EXPRESS BUS

You can also get to Bamfield via the West Coast Trail Express bus service. The bus leaves from Victoria and Nanaimo and deposits hikers in the town of Bamfield or at the Parks Canada office. You can take a taxi from either of those locations to the trailhead. Or you can walk 2 km (1.2 mi) from Bamfield or 5.5 km (3.4 mi) from the Parks Canada office.

LADY ROSE MARINE SERVICES

If you want to skip the long, bumpy drive to Bamfield, Lady Rose Marine Services offers a passenger and freight service on the MV *Frances Barkley* from Port Alberni to Bamfield a few days a week. From the dock you can walk 2 km (1.2 mi) or take a taxi to the trailhead.

TRIP PLANNER

0 km (0 mi)	Trailhead at the end of South Bamfield Road
0.5 km (0.3 mi)	Trail crosses a gravel road at the alternate parking area
1.6 km (1 mi)	Junction with Cape Beale Trail
3 km (1.9 mi)	Floating bridge at the lake outlet
3.5 km (2.2 mi)	Keeha Beach
4 km (2.5 mi)	Main camping area

From the main parking area, continue down South Bamfield Road for 0.4 km (0.2 mi) to its end. This is the official **trailhead**. The trail is rough from the start with lots of slippery roots and mud. A few minutes past the trailhead, a rough side trail heads right to emerge on mud flats at the back of Bamfield Inlet. At tides below 1.8 m (5.9 ft), you can walk along the wet shoreline for a few minutes and skip the forest trail. The mud-flat route rejoins the main trail after about 0.2 km (0.1 mi), near a creek.

From here, the trail heads into a thick coastal forest. Gnarled salal branches have overgrown the trail in a few places. About 0.5 km (0.3 mi) from the trailhead, the path emerges at a **gravel road**. This is the alternate parking area and trailhead. The trail continues on the other side of the road and heads through the forest. Reach a **junction** marked with a faded wooden sign and some fishing floats at 1.6 km (1 mi) from the trailhead. Your route to Keeha Beach continues straight. The path to the right leads to **Cape Beale**.

INDIGENOUS KNOWLEDGE

KIIX̱IN NATIONAL HISTORIC SITE

While in Bamfield, make time to connect with Huu-ay-aht culture on a tour of Kiix̱in. It is the only known Indigenous village on the southern B.C. coast that still features standing traditional architecture. Kiix̱in is the traditional 19th-century fortified capital village of the Huu-ay-aht and was occupied for over 3000 years. Take a tour with Huu-ay-aht traditional knowledge holders to learn about the history of the Barkley Sound area, as well as its role as an important sacred site today. In 2022, Kiix̱in became a National Historic Site of Canada, managed jointly with the Huu-ay-aht Nation to uphold the three Huu-ay-aht Sacred Principles: ʔiisaak (Greater Respect), Hišuk ma cʼawak (Everything Is One), and ʔuuʔałuk (Taking Care Of).

Past the junction, the trail gets rougher as it transitions into an inland bog near the shores of Kichha Lake. There is mud underfoot almost constantly, some of which seems almost bottomless. Locals hike the trail in rubber boots. Pick your way carefully through this section by balancing on roots, logs, rocks, and the occasional piece of boardwalk. Try to avoid stepping on the fragile vegetation on the edges of the trail, which prevents erosion. While the trail parallels the lake, you will rarely see it. If you aren't too busy staring at your feet, take time to appreciate the unique coastal bog vegetation of stunted trees, nurse logs, skunk cabbage, and salal.

Arrive at the **lake outlet** 3 km (1.9 mi) from the start. A pontoon-style **floating bridge** spans the water. On the other side of the bridge, the trail continues through the forest, which gets lusher as you move uphill and away from the swampy area near the lake. Watch for a huge culturally modified cedar on the right with a hole at its centre. If you look closely, you will see tool marks around the hole where Indigenous people sampled the tree to see if its wood was suitable for canoe building.

A short, stiff climb brings you to the trail's high point on a ridge. From here you will be able to hear and smell the ocean, but it is still a few hundred metres away. The ridge is actually a huge sand dune, likely the product of a tsunami around 1700 CE. Follow the trail as it drops steeply from the ridge. A few fixed ropes in this section help on slippery bits. The trail curves southeast, then back to the southwest as it descends through head-high salal bushes before emerging on the broad sand of **Keeha Bay**, 3.5 km (2.2 mi) from the trailhead.

The beach stretches for nearly 2 km (1.2 mi) in a broad crescent. The northwest side is more sloped and has more pebbles, transitioning to a shallower, fine sand beach as it trends to the southeast. Rough informal trails lead along the coast from both ends of the beach. Follow them to explore pocket coves, sea caves, and tide pools. To reach the **main camping area** at the creek at the southeast end of the beach, turn left and trudge through the sand for 0.5 km (0.3 mi).

CAMPING

You can camp anywhere along the beach, but the best spots are at the southeastern end, near the creek.

Campsites: Numerous sites on the beach above the high-tide line
Toilet: Composting toilet at the southeast end of the beach
Water: Collect from the creek at the southeast end of the beach
Food Storage: Food locker near the outhouse and a second food locker where the trail meets the beach

Waves breaking on Keeha Beach

EXTENDING YOUR TRIP

Cape Beale: The trail to Cape Beale is just as rough and muddy as the one to Keeha Bay. It's a 14 km (8.7 mi) round trip from the trailhead (or 11 km/ 6.8 mi round trip from the Keeha Bay junction), with 85 m (279 ft) of elevation gain. Part of the route follows the shore of Tapaltos Bay before turning inland through forest and bog to reach the cape. You will need to cross the channel at tides lower than 1.8 m (5.9 ft) on the final push to the lighthouse. Built in 1874, the Cape Beale Lighthouse is part of the same telegraph route as the West Coast Trail (Trip 6). Watch for remnants of the line as you hike.

FURTHER RESOURCES

Pacific Rim National Park Reserve: info and reservations *pc.gc.ca/en/pn-np/bc/pacificrim/activ/SCO-WCT*
Fisheries and Oceans Canada: Bamfield tide table *tides.gc.ca/en/stations/ 08545*
West Coast Trail Express: shuttle bus info and reservations *trailbus.com*
Lady Rose Marine Services: passenger ferry info *ladyrosemarine.com/*
NTS Maps: 092C14
Driving Map: *Vancouver Island BC Backroad Mapbook*

Waves breaking against offshore islets on the Wild Pacific Trail (Trip 12)

PORT ALBERNI AND TOFINO TRIPS

THIS REGION OF superlatives is home to Canada's tallest waterfall, largest trees, and biggest waves. The streets of Port Alberni, Tofino, and Ucluelet bustle with locals and tourists. But once you leave the pavement, you can explore remote beaches, stroll along rugged headlands, walk through rainforests, and scale lofty peaks.

Getting Around: The Pacific Rim Highway (Highway 4) cuts west across the Island, passing Port Alberni before reaching its terminus on the ocean in Tofino. Along the way, rough gravel roads snake upwards to trailheads for Mount Arrowsmith and 5040 Peak. A paved road also leads to the dock on Great Central Lake, where you can catch a water taxi or launch a canoe to reach the Della Falls Trail. Once you reach the coast, it's an easy drive through the town of Ucluelet to the trailheads for the Wild Pacific Trail. To reach the Wild Side Trail or the Big Tree Trail, catch a water taxi from the dock in downtown Tofino.

Indigenous Context: The west coast of Vancouver Island is Nuu-chah-nulth traditional territory, comprising 15 related Indigenous groups. The large water bodies of Alberni Inlet, Sproat Lake, and Great Central Lake are the heart of the overlapping territories of the Tseshaht and Hupačasath Nations, which extend to the summit of Mount Arrowsmith as well as the tumbling waters of Della Falls. Many Indigenous territories follow watershed boundaries. 5040 Peak sits at the head of several watersheds and the intersection of Yuułuʔiłʔatḥ, Toquaht, Tla-o-qui-aht, Tseshaht, Hupačasath, and Uchucklesaht territories. Yuułuʔiłʔatḥ (Ucluelet) territory begins on the coast around the town of Ucluelet and extends inland to the mountains around 5040 Peak. The Tofino area, including Meares Island, is the traditional territory of the ƛaʔuukʷiʔatḥ (Tla-o-qui-aht) Nation. Flores Island is the heart of Ahousaht territory. You can visit Indigenous-owned art galleries in Tofino to enjoy and purchase Nuu-chah-nulth art and jewellery.

Supplies: Port Alberni has several grocery stores, gas stations, and outdoor stores. Tofino and Ucluelet each have modest-sized grocery stores and a few gas stations. There is a small outdoor store in Tofino.

Accommodations: Port Alberni, Tofino, and Ucluelet have many hotels, vacation rentals, and private campgrounds. The reservable sites at Green Point Campground in Pacific Rim National Park Reserve are a good option for trips in the Tofino and Ucluelet area. Sproat Lake Provincial Park just west of Port Alberni has a mix of both first-come, first-served and reservable campsites.

9

MOUNT ARROWSMITH (JUDGE'S ROUTE)

DAY HIKE

Difficulty: ◆◆
Duration: 5 to 7 hours
Distance: 6.2 km (3.9 mi) round trip

Elevation Gain: 1060 m (3478 ft)
High Point: 1817 m (5961 ft)
Best Months: July to September

Fees and Reservations: None

Regulations: No fires. Dogs are permitted but not recommended due to scrambly sections.

Caution: The upper reaches of this trail include some sections of scrambling and route-finding.

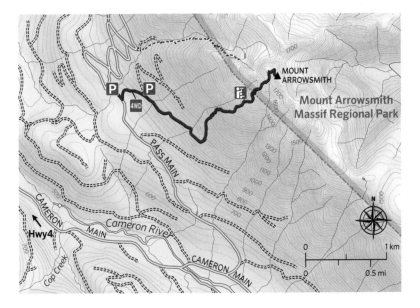

AT 1817 M (5961 FT), the basalt peaks of Mount Arrowsmith stand out as the highest summit south of Strathcona Provincial Park on Vancouver Island. The mountain gets its settler name from Aaron and John Arrowsmith, renowned British cartographers. But the Hupačasath name for the peak, Kuth-Kah-Chulth, meaning "that which has sharp pointed faces," is more apt. Visible from many locations along Vancouver Island's east coast and the Port Alberni area, the summit is a goal for many local hikers. Numerous trails and rock-climbing routes ascend the flanks of the peak, but only one hiking trail takes you to the true summit. The Judge's Route is named after Ralph Hutchinson, a Nanaimo judge who pioneered the route in 1975. The expansive views from the summit are some of the best on southern Vancouver Island. The path is fiercely steep and requires a bit of scrambling, so it's best in good weather and for experienced hikers who aren't afraid of heights.

GETTING THERE

From Highway 19 near Qualicum Beach, turn west on Highway 4 and zero your odometer. Turn left 28 km (17.4 mi) later onto Cameron Main Connector Forest Service Road. The turn is 1.3 km (0.8 mi) past the Port Alberni Summit. Drive through the Mosaic Forest Management gate (check the website for opening dates/hours). The route to the trailhead has some steep and bumpy sections but is fine for 2WD vehicles. Continue on Cameron Main Connector FSR for about 2.7 km (1.7 mi) to a T-junction. Turn left onto Cameron Main FSR and follow it for 7.7 km (4.8 mi). Zero your odometer and turn left (uphill) onto Pass Main FSR. Keep left at a fork at 0.2 km (0.1 mi). Stay on Pass Main, ignoring branch roads. At 2.8 km (1.7 mi), pass a rough gravel road with a gate heading uphill to the right. Park at a pullout on the left a few metres later.

TRAIL

TRIP PLANNER

0 km (0 mi)	Trailhead
1.4 km (0.9 mi)	Old road ends
2.3 km (1.4 mi)	Viewpoint bluff
2.6 km (1.6 mi)	Scrambling begins
3 km (1.9 mi)	Saddle
3.1 km (1.9 mi)	Summit

From the parking area, walk a few metres south along Pass Main, then turn left up the rough gravel road you passed on the drive in. This is the **trailhead**. Follow the old road uphill to a **fork** about 0.3 km (0.2 mi) away. Capable 4WD vehicles with high clearance may be able to make it this far. Turn right at the fork onto a very overgrown road-turned-trail that heads southeast and rises gently.

The **old road ends** 1.4 km (0.9 mi) from the trailhead. Find a dusty trail on the left side of the road that ascends steeply into a forest of subalpine fir and mountain hemlock. The trail is rough, with lots of roots, loose gravel sections,

The view from atop Mount Arrowsmith

and tight switchbacks. The climb is relentless as it heads uphill through the forest. Around 1.7 km (1.1 mi) from the start, at about 1120 m (3675 ft) elevation, the vegetation begins to transition to more open forest and rocky basalt bluffs.

Take a break on a bluff at 2.3 km (1.4 mi) to enjoy the first real **views** to the west. The foreground is a patchwork of cutblocks. In the middle distance, you can see Port Alberni, Alberni Inlet, Sproat Lake, and Great Central Lake. On the horizon to the northwest are the snow-capped peaks of Strathcona Provincial Park, including the distinct summit of Nine Peaks.

Past this point the route gets rougher. At times the path braids and branches. When in doubt, follow flagging tape, cairns, or the most boot-beaten path. At about 2.6 km (1.6 mi) and 1550 m (5085 ft) elevation, the trees thin out even more and a series of rocky **scrambling sections** begins. You may need to use your hands in many places, but there is no real exposure to heights if you stay on the main route.

At about 3 km (1.9 mi), the trail reaches a **saddle** between the main summit of Mount Arrowsmith and a rounded sub-summit to the left. The small grassy meadow hosts pink heather and other wildflowers. Stay on the trail as it works its way towards a notch with a sheer drop to the north. The trail turns right and ascends a cleft to a flattish bench just below the summit. A wooden helicopter platform and a tall conical radio repeater sit on this bench. The true **summit**, with two more radio repeaters, is 70 m (230 ft) higher and is reached by a trail to the southeast.

Snow lingers in the saddle below the summit

From the peak, you will enjoy incredible views of Mount Arrowsmith's many sub-summits, commonly called The Bumps. Jewel Lake sits deep in a rocky bowl just below you with Mount Cokely rising from its far shore. Look north to the Strait of Georgia, with Denman, Hornby, Lasqueti, and Texada Islands breaking its surface. On a clear day, you can also see the peaks of the Sunshine Coast on the mainland. If you are lucky, you might spot the Vancouver Island marmot (page 188) and the Vancouver Island white-tailed ptarmigan (page 167), both endangered species. When you have finished enjoying the view, retrace your steps back to the car. While many hiking apps show trails crisscrossing the Arrowsmith massif, all routes to the summit except for the one you took are mountaineering routes best left to experienced rock climbers.

FURTHER RESOURCES

Mount Arrowsmith Massif Regional Park: info *rdn.bc.ca/mount-arrowsmith-massif-regional-park*

Mosaic Forest Management: road access via Cameron Main Connector FSR *mosaicforests.com/access*

NTS Map: 092F02; 092F07

Driving Map: *Vancouver Island BC Backroad Mapbook*

DELLA FALLS

BACKPACKING TRIP

Difficulty: ■
Duration: 2 to 4 days
Distance: 32 km (19.9 mi) round trip

Elevation Gain: 545 m (1788 ft)
High Point: 625 m (2051 ft)
Best Months: June to October

Fees and Reservations: None

Regulations: No fires. No drones. No smoking, vaping, or cannabis. Dogs permitted on leash.

Caution: The mosquitos can be bad on the lower portion of the trail in June and July.

HIKE UPSTREAM THROUGH the Drinkwater valley to Della Falls in the heart of Strathcona Provincial Park. At 440 m (1444 ft), the towering cascade is one of the tallest waterfalls in Canada. (Other contenders for that honour are mostly on B.C.'s remote Central Coast.) Admire the falls from their base or make a side trip up the steep Love Lake Trail for a breathtaking elevated view of the entire torrent. The route to the falls follows old mining and logging tracks through a beautiful valley, passing five backcountry campsites. To catch the falls in full flow, plan to hike during early summer snowmelt or in the autumn rainy season. In June and early July, visitors will have to time their hike carefully to catch the waterfall at peak runoff and have a snow-free hike to Love Lake.

GETTING THERE

The trailhead is at the west end of Great Central Lake and can only be reached by boat. You can book a ride with Della Falls Water Taxi, or pilot your own boat or canoe. Meet your water taxi or launch a motorized boat at Great Central Lake RV Resort and Marina at the east end of the lake, 35 km (21.7 mi) from the trailhead. Canoeists can shave off about 11 km (6.8 mi) of paddling by launching at Scout Camp Recreation Site.

GREAT CENTRAL LAKE RV RESORT AND MARINA

From Port Alberni, take the Pacific Rim Highway (Highway 4) west. About 7 km (4.3 mi) after crossing the bridge over the Somass River, turn right onto Central Lake Road. Follow it for another 7 km (4.3 mi). Just past a large fish hatchery and the Ash Main logging road coming in from the right, turn right into the RV park and marina. Della Falls Water Taxi leaves from the dock and

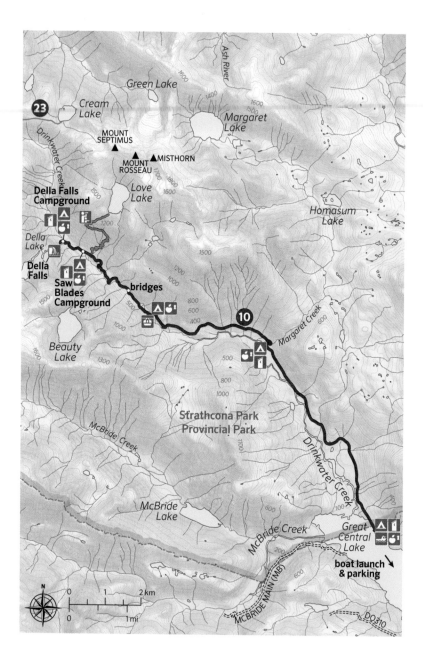

Green Lake

Cream
Lake

Ash River

Margaret
Lake

MOUNT
SEPTIMUS

MOUNT
ROSSEAU

MISTHORN

Love
Lake

Homasum
Lake

Della Falls
Campground

Della
Lake

Della
Falls

Saw
Blades
Campground

bridges

10

Margaret Creek

Beauty
Lake

Strathcona Park
Provincial Park

McBride Creek

Drinkwater Creek

McBride
Lake

McBride Creek

Great
Central
Lake

boat launch
& parking

MCBRIDE MAIN (MB)

DO310

Drinkwater Creek

N

0   1   2 km

0   1 mi

you can pay to launch your boat at the ramp. There is free parking on the wide gravel shoulder of the main road.

SCOUT CAMP RECREATION SITE

This route requires backroad driving on a confusing network of logging roads. The *Vancouver Island Backroads Mapbook* or a GPS with a backroads map layer can help. From Great Central Lake RV Resort and Marina, take Ash Main FSR north, immediately crossing a bridge over the Ash River. Stay on Ash Main for 6.6 km (4.1 mi), then turn left onto Ash 286/Browns Bay Dryland Sort. Stay right at the fork 0.8 km (0.5 mi) later. In another 8.3 km (5.2 mi), turn left and then immediately left again to arrive at Scout Camp Recreation Site. There is a rustic campsite here as well as a launch for small craft.

PADDLING

The paddle to the trailhead is 35 km (21.7 mi) from the marina or 24 km (14.9 mi) from Scout Camp, so paddlers may wish to camp along the way. An informal primitive site at Clark Point on the north shore of the lake, about 21 km (13 mi) from the marina, is the best option. Depending on water levels, the north shore of the lake has a few small beaches suitable for camping between Clark Point and the trailhead. Paddlers may also wish to camp at the trailhead campsite. Great Central Lake can get very windy, especially in the afternoon, so use caution and stay near the shore as you paddle.

TRAIL

TRIP PLANNER

0 km (0 mi)	Boat dock and trailhead campground
6.5 km (4 mi)	Margaret Creek campground
11.5 km (7.1 mi)	Cable car campground
12.5 km (7.7 mi)	Bridges over Drinkwater Creek
15 km (9.3 mi)	Saw Blades campground
16 km (9.9 mi)	Della Falls campground

The trail begins at a small wooden **dock** near the west end of Great Central Lake. The lake was dammed in 1925 for hydroelectric power generation, raising the water levels. As a result, the western end of the lake features huge stands of dead trees rising out of the water. From the dock, ascend a wooden staircase to the **trailhead campground.**

The trail leaves from the north side of the campground. The 100-year-old route is a legacy of mining and logging in the valley (see page 114) and parallels Drinkwater Creek from the lakeshore up to the base of Della Falls. At times the trail runs next to the river, but often the river is downhill and out of sight.

Crossing the bridge over Drinkwater Creek

Hikers with a keen eye for plant identification will enjoy spotting dozens of species along the way. Lower down, the trail is edged in several species of ferns, salmonberry and thimbleberry bushes, and patches of devil's club in the wetter sections. Bunchberry, vanilla leaf, and false lily of the valley carpet the forest floor. In open areas near the creek, the coniferous forest gives way to stands of red alder and bigleaf maple. Higher up you will start to notice blueberry and black huckleberry. In June and early July, watch for wildflowers, including the speckled yellow globes of tiger lily, pointy red columbine, dainty starflower, drooping pink Pacific bleeding heart, and the broad green leaves of hellebore.

Leaving the trailhead campground, the trail is flat and wide as it follows the shoreline of Great Central Lake into the delta of Drinkwater Creek. This section is thick with mosquitos in June and July. As the trail works its way inland, it crosses two **unbridged creeks** at 2.8 (1.7 mi) and 3.9 km (2.4 mi). Later in the year, both are easy rock-hops across, but during snowmelt, they may require a boots-off wade. In a few places, the trail deviates from the old miners' track to bypass boggy sections. Follow flagging tape up onto berms beside the trail, left over from long-ago road building.

Reach the small **campground at Margaret Creek** 6.5 km (4 mi) from the trailhead. The trail makes a hard right here and follows a rough trail uphill alongside Margaret Creek for a few minutes. Arrive at a sturdy wooden bridge spanning the turbulent water of the creek as it cascades through a rocky canyon. On the other side, a rough track plunges steeply downhill to rejoin the old roadbed.

Continue along the old road as it crosses several rocky washes through groves of bigleaf maple. In the early season, you'll have to hop across creeks in a few of these washes. The grade remains mostly steady, with a few short, but sharp, climbs. About 11 km (6.8 mi) from the start, the trail begins to climb as it curves through a broad but short switchback, gaining 80 m (262 ft) in 0.5 km (0.3 mi).

Arrive at the base of the **cable car**, 11.5 km (7.1 mi) into your hike. Drinkwater Creek rolls through a dramatic set of rapids here. Climb the ladder onto the cable car platform, carefully load your pack, and clamber aboard. Be sure to enjoy the view to the rapids below you as you give your legs a rest and use your neglected upper body muscles to pull yourself across.

The next kilometre (0.6 mi) of trail along the west bank of Drinkwater Creek is rough as you clamber over roots and rocks on an undulating route through the forest. Watch for flagging tape as the trail drops to cross two brushy sections across slide paths. Immediately after the final slide path, emerge on the banks of Drinkwater Creek and cross it on two **narrow metal bridges** high above the churning flow. Follow flagging tape up into the forest briefly before descending again to creek level.

Follow the trail as it scrambles alongside the creek for a few hundred metres, weaving over and between giant boulders and traversing a rockslide. A tiny gravel beach flanked by boulders partway along makes a great rest spot. Before long, the trail rejoins the old road as it climbs through a long curve. Cross a bridge near the 14 km (8.7 mi) mark. Shortly after, a straight stretch of trail provides the first view of Della Falls, tumbling over cliffs high above you. A few minutes later, cross another bridge over the rushing waters of Love Creek. Continue down the trail for a few more metres to the **junction** with the Love Lake Trail.

Arrive at **Saw Blades campground** in a grove of hemlock trees, 15 km (9.3 mi) from the trailhead, marked with huge circular blades affixed to trees. There is a small camping area next to the sawblades, but most sites, along with the outhouse and bear cache, are a few metres down the brushy trail to the left.

Continuing past the campsite, the trail rises and then crosses a high bridge over Drinkwater Creek. A few minutes later, the trail emerges from the forest on a slide path of thick brush speckled with boulders. A tall bridge over Della Creek provides a good view of the base of the falls. Arrive at **Della Falls campground** in an island of trees near the 16 km (9.9 mi) mark.

Della Falls seen from the Love Lake Trail

CAMPING

With five campsites along the trail, various itineraries are possible, However, most hikers stay at Saw Blades campground, which makes a good base for hikes to the base of Della Falls and Love Lake.

TRAILHEAD CAMPGROUND

This large campground is set in the forest near the boat dock and makes a good first or last night's camp while waiting for the water taxi or as part of a canoe trip. Many of the campsites are overgrown.

Campsites: Sixteen compact dirt tent pads
Toilets: Two pit toilets at the back of the campground
Water: Collect from Great Central Lake
Food Storage: Food locker on a spur trail beyond the lower outhouse
Other Amenities: Two canoe racks. Some campsites have picnic tables

MARGARET CREEK CAMPGROUND

Camping here is a logical way to break up the long hike to Saw Blades or Della Falls Campground. It is on the former roadbed next to Margaret Creek.

Campsites: Room for 5 or 6 tents along the old road
Toilet: Throne-style pit toilet west of the trail with little privacy
Water: Collect from Margaret Creek
Food Storage: Large plastic barrel with a screw-top lid, near the toilet

CABLE CAR CAMPGROUND

This small campground may be a good option for parties who have taken longer to hike from the trailhead than they planned.

Campsites: Space for 2 or 3 tents at a wider part of the trail
Toilet: None. Dig a cat hole and use Leave No Trace toilet practices. Climb the steep slope north of camp and find a spot amongst the boulders.
Water: Collect from Drinkwater Creek via a steep trail near the cable car
Food Storage: Food locker near the cable car

SAW BLADES CAMPGROUND

This is the largest and most popular campground on the Della Falls Trail. It makes a good base camp for hikes to the foot of the falls or Love Lake. The sites are spread out along the trail between the saw blades and the bridge over Drinkwater Creek.

Campsites: Room for 10–12 tents split between the creekside sites and the clearing near the saw blades. An overflow area just over the Drinkwater Creek bridge fits another 2 or 3 tents.
Toilet: Throne-style pit toilet amongst the boulders on a signed spur trail behind the creekside sites
Water: Collect from Drinkwater Creek
Food Storage: Food storage locker on the outhouse trail

DELLA FALLS CAMPGROUND

Located in a grove of trees near the base of Della Falls, this small campground can be damp with mist from the falls. A short trail behind the food cache leads to a gravel bar and incredible views of the upper Drinkwater valley.

Campsites: Room for 2 or 3 tents. Room for several more tents on the gravel banks of Drinkwater Creek.
Toilet: Throne-style pit toilet on a spur trail just beyond camp
Water: Collect from Drinkwater Creek
Food Storage: Large plastic barrel with a screw-top lid, near the toilet

EXTENDING YOUR TRIP

Della Falls Base: From Della Falls Camp it's a 0.5 km (0.3 mi) round-trip hike to the base of Della Falls. Follow the trail uphill through brush and boulders.

Several cottage-sized rocks at the base are an ideal place to observe the cascade. The spray from the falls will soon soak you, so bring a rain jacket.

Love Lake: Don't miss this 6 km (3.7 mi) return hike for the incredible views of Della Falls. The steep and well-worn miners' track leads from the Drinkwater valley up to Love Lake, gaining 720 m (2362 ft). Many switchbacks make the grade manageable. Be careful at an early creek crossing on a slimy shelf above a waterfall. Enjoy great views of Della Falls, Della Lake, Big Interior Mountain, and Nine Peaks from a bluff at 1180 m (3871 ft) elevation, about 2.5 km (1.6 mi) along. Continue to the trail's end at Love Lake, nestled into the slopes of Mount Septimus, Mount Rosseau, and The Misthorns. Snow lingers into early July at this elevation, so use caution and come equipped with trekking poles, snowshoes, or microspikes early in the season.

FURTHER RESOURCES

Strathcona Provincial Park: info *bcparks.ca/explore/parkpgs/strath*
Happiest Outdoors: additional trail info *happiestoutdoors.ca/della-falls-trail*
Della Falls Water Taxi: info and reservations *dellafallswatertaxi.com*
Recreation Sites and Trails BC: Scout Camp Recreation Site info *sitesand trailsbc.ca/search/search-result.aspx?site=REC5750&type=Site*
NTS Map: 092F06; 092F05

HISTORY
———

MINING IN THE DRINKWATER VALLEY

Joseph Drinkwater was prospecting between Bedwell River and Great Central Lake in the 1890s when he came across the magnificent falls, which he named after his wife, Della. He staked copper claims on Big Interior Mountain and gold at Della Lake, above the falls. More miners followed when the Ptarmigan Mine opened on the mountain in 1906. Between 1900 and 1915, a pack trail was completed up Drinkwater Creek to the base of Della Falls. From there, an aerial tramway led to Della Lake. The tramway carried buckets of gold and ore to the present Saw Blades Camp, where pack horses transported it downstream to Great Central Lake. By 1916, the mine had closed, although a few prospectors remained in the area. Later, loggers widened the trail into a road and extracted timber from the lower valley. As you walk the trail, watch for abandoned machinery and tools from that era.

11

HIŠIMY̓AWIƛ HUT AND 5040 PEAK ⭐

BACKPACKING TRIP

Difficulty: ◆
Duration: 2 to 3 days
Distance: 6 km (3.7 mi) round trip

Elevation Gain: 700 m (2297 ft)
High Point: 1320 m (4331 ft)
Best Months: July to September

Fees and Reservations: Camping is free and all campsites are first-come, first-served. The hut is locked. Reservations are required to get the hut access code. Hut fees are $150/room/night. Make reservations and pay online.

Regulations: No fires. No dogs inside the hut.

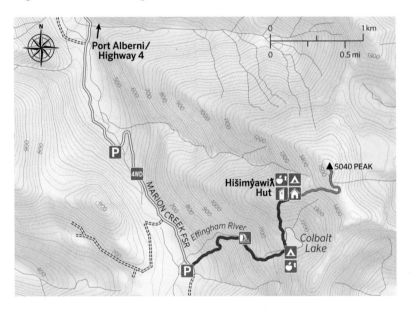

THE APPROACH TO Hišimy̓awiƛ Hut may be relentlessly steep, but the panoramic views from the hut and the summit of nearby 5040 Peak make it well worth the effort. The short trail winds its way up through a regenerating cutblock, and then a gorgeous old-growth forest beside a waterfall, before arriving in the subalpine. Camp lower down on the shores of Cobalt Lake, which is set in a stunning bowl. Or book a stay at the Alpine Club of Canada's palatial Hišimy̓awiƛ Hut. Pronounced hi-SHIM-ya-wit, the hut's name means "gather together" in the Barkley Sound dialect of the Yuułuʔiłʔatḥ (Ucluelet) First Nation.

GETTING THERE

From Port Alberni, follow Highway 4 west. Zero your odometer at the large bridge over the Somass River a few minutes out of town. Turn left 46.5 km (28.9 mi) later onto the Marion Creek Forest Service Road. (The turn is about 5.5 km/3.4 mi after the Sutton Pass Summit.) Follow the Marion Creek FSR for 9.6 km (6 mi) to the trailhead, ignoring all side branches. The road is steep and rough in sections, so an AWD or 4WD vehicle is necessary. Capable 2WD vehicles may be able to make it to the 8 km (5 mi) mark, just before a hairpin bend, where there is a small pullout. Do not attempt to go farther in a 2WD vehicle because the road is very steep and loose and you will spin out, further damaging the road. There are several pullouts for parking just past the trailhead at the 9.6 km (6 mi) mark. Avoid parking on the shoulder, which blocks the road.

TRAIL

TRIP PLANNER

0 km (0 mi)	Trailhead and parking
1.2 km (0.7 mi)	Waterfall
2 km (1.2 mi)	Cobalt Lake
3 km (1.9 mi)	Hišimýawiƛ Hut

The **trailhead** is marked with a large information kiosk. The hike begins in a regenerating cutblock of young Douglas-fir with lots of black huckleberry in the understorey. A few openings in the brush provide good views of Triple Peak to the south and a chance to catch your breath on the brutally steep trail. About 0.5 km (0.3 mi) into the hike, at about 740 m (2428 ft) elevation, the trail **leaves the clear-cut** and enters a beautiful old-growth forest with lots of western redcedar, western hemlock, and Douglas-fir. The trail bed is often rough, with many rocks, roots, and big steps.

The path continues its sharp climb as it swings north towards a creek. These rushing waters are the headwaters of the Effingham River, which flows south to Barkley Sound, near Bamfield and Ucluelet. In a few minutes, the trail turns east and continues to climb. Pause for another breather at a peek-a-boo viewpoint at 830 m (2723 ft) elevation, about 0.8 km (0.5 mi) from the trailhead. The trail scrambles up two rock steps a few minutes apart, about 1 km (0.6 mi) from the trailhead, both with the help of **fixed ropes**.

After the ropes, the grade eases slightly and the vegetation thins out a bit as you enter subalpine terrain. At 1.1 km (0.7 mi), the trail reaches the creek for the first time. This is a good place to fill up with water if you're running

Cobalt Lake and Triple Peak seen from the summit of 5040 Peak

low. The trail sticks close to the creek for a minute to the base of a **waterfall** in a canyon at 1.2 km (0.7 mi). Follow the trail as it makes a hard right turn away from the creek, then switchbacks up a rock slab before continuing uphill parallel to the creek.

Continue along the trail, following markers and cairns through heather meadows, gravel, and intermittent patches of forest. Take care to stay on track through a few indistinct rocky and marshy sections. Arrive on the shores of **Cobalt Lake**, 2 km (1.2 mi) from the trailhead, at 1150 m (3773 ft) elevation. The trail turns left to parallel the shoreline over several small hills and past several campsites to the north end of the lake.

The path leaves the lake and makes a steep ascent to the ridge through an open forest. The footbed can be loose and dusty here. Another **fixed rope** at 1290 m (4232 ft) elevation (2.8 km/1.7 mi from the trailhead) helps you up a final step. Above, the trees dwindle as you gain the gravelly ridge crest. **Hišimy̓awiⱦ Hut** is just ahead, perched on the ridge's shoulder at 1320 m (4331 ft). Enjoy views down to Cobalt Lake and across to Mount Hall, Triple Peak, and The Cats Ears.

CAMPING

COBALT LAKE CAMPING AREA

After the strenuous climb, many hikers are content to camp near the shores of Cobalt Lake, then ascend to the hut and 5040 Peak unburdened.

Campsites: Four or 5 cleared campsites along the west shore of the lake. Please use existing clearings and avoid camping on fragile vegetation.
Toilet: There are plans to build an outhouse at Cobalt Lake. Until then, use the toilet at the hut if possible. Otherwise, dig a cat hole and use Leave No Trace best practices. Aim for the slopes downhill of the northwest side of the lake, and stay well away from the creek.
Water: Collect from the lake
Food Storage: Food locker on the west side of the lake

HIŠIMY̓AWIƛ HUT

The well-appointed interior of Hišimy̓awiƛ Hut allows hikers to stay in the backcountry without roughing it.

Sleeps: Two bunkrooms each sleep 6. Mattresses are provided.
Toilet: Urine-diversion toilet east of the hut. A window in the south wall gives you incredible views of Triple Peak while you do your business.
Water: Melt from snow patches or muddy tarns near the cabin in early summer. Otherwise, haul water up from Cobalt Lake.
Food Storage: On shelves inside the hut
Other Amenities: Tables and chairs, propane cooking stove, dishes and cutlery, wash sink, sleeping mattresses, wood pellet stove for heat, solar lighting

HIŠIMY̓AWIƛ HUT CAMPING

Hikers may camp on the rock slabs and informal gravel clearings near the hut. However, they are not allowed to use the hut without a reservation.
Campsites: Room for half a dozen tents on rock slabs to the east of the hut and gravel areas to the southwest
Toilet: Urine-diversion toilet east of the hut
Water: Melt from snow patches or muddy tarns near the cabin in early summer. Otherwise, haul water up from Cobalt Lake.
Food Storage: Food locker on a rock outcropping east of the hut

EXTENDING YOUR TRIP

5040 Peak: Don't miss the hike to 5040 Peak (named for its estimated elevation above sea level in feet). It's 2 km (1.2 mi) round trip from the hut, with 200 m (656 ft) of elevation gain. The trail starts east of the hut and contours up through meadows and rock bands to a saddle. From there, turn north and follow the ridge to the summit. Watch for cairns, because the trail can be indistinct in places and may require some scrambling. On the ascent enjoy the wildflowers, including red and white heather, Davidson's penstemon, spreading phlox, paintbrush, and arnica. From the 1532 m (5026 ft) peak, look west and southwest over the shoulders of Triple Peak to Barkley Sound, the Broken Group Islands, and the Pacific Ocean near Ucluelet. To the east, you can see the Strait of Georgia, Texada Island, and the Sunshine Coast. The snow-capped peaks of Strathcona Provincial Park dominate the skyline to the north. From the summit you can wander off-trail above the treeline along the adjoining ridges.

FURTHER RESOURCES

Alpine Club of Canada, Vancouver Island section: Hišimỷawiƛ Hut info and reservations *accvi.ca/5040-peak-hut*
NTS Map: 092F03
Driving Map: *Vancouver Island BC Backroad Mapbook*

INDIGENOUS KNOWLEDGE

BEHIND THE NAME *HIŠIMỶAWIƛ*

When the Alpine Club of Canada's Vancouver Island (ACCVI) section built a new hut on the slopes of 5040 Peak in 2018, they wanted to honour the spirit of reconciliation with Indigenous Peoples. Members of the youth Warrior Program in Tofino and Ucluelet, who came from several different Indigenous Nations with traditional territory around the hut, proposed the English name "Gathering Place." Yuułuʔiłʔatḥ Elders suggested "Gather Together" to follow the traditional practice of naming locations for the activity that goes on there. The name was translated into the Barkley Sound dialect of the Yuułuʔiłʔatḥ Nation. Toquaht Elders suggested a small spelling change, and Tla-o-qui-aht Elders formally approved. In the fall of 2019, members of the Warrior Program and ACCVI members hiked to the hut and summitted 5040 Peak. Afterwards, the Warriors sang a Welcome Song and a Victory Song to formally name the hut Hišimỷawiƛ.

12

WILD PACIFIC TRAIL

DAY HIKE

Difficulty: ●

Duration: 1 to 3 hours

Distance: 3 to 10 km (1.9 to 6.2 mi) loop and/or round trip

Elevation Gain: 40 to 80 m (131 to 262 ft)

High Point: 40 to 80 m (131 to 262 ft)

Best Months: Year-round

Fees and Reservations: None

Regulations: Dogs allowed on leash. No drones. No camping.

Caution: Stay on the trail. The many sheer cliffs and the oceanside rocks are frequently scoured by huge waves.

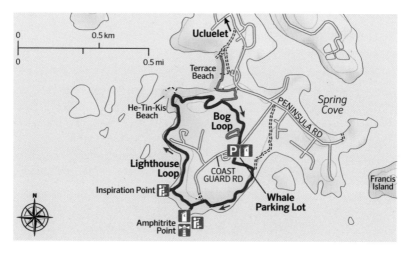

THIS EASY HIKE takes you along the wind-sculpted coastline in Ucluelet. Enjoy old-growth forests, a historic lighthouse, and spectacular views of the rocky bluffs. It's especially gorgeous at the height of the winter storm-watching season. The trail is separated into two parts: the shorter and more popular Lighthouse Loop and a longer section from Brown's Beach to Rocky Bluffs. Both portions have dozens of spur trails leading to cliffside perches with benches that entice you to sit awhile and take in the scenery.

A wind-twisted tree frames a viewpoint on the Lighthouse Loop

GETTING THERE

WHALE PARKING LOT (LIGHTHOUSE LOOP)

From the junction of Highway 4 and Peninsula Road, take Peninsula Road past Ucluelet. Turn right onto Coast Guard Road. About 0.4 km (0.2 mi) later, turn right into a gravel parking lot, following signs for the Wild Pacific Trail.

SEA STAR PARKING LOT (BROWN'S BEACH)

From the junction of Highway 4 and Peninsula Road, follow Peninsula Road for 6.5 km (4 mi). Turn right onto Pacific Crescent, then right again onto Cynamocka Road. Turn left onto Marine Drive. Just after a crosswalk, turn right into a gravel parking lot signed for Brown's Beach.

ANCIENT CEDARS TRAILHEAD

From the junction of Highway 4 and Peninsula Road, follow Peninsula Road for 5.5 km (3.4 mi). Park on the wide gravel shoulder on the right, near the large Wild Pacific Trail sign.

TRAIL

The Wild Pacific Trail is split into two sections. It is possible to link the two sections by walking approximately 3.5 km (2.2 mi) of road through the town of Ucluelet. (See the NTS map in the Further Resources section for details.)

But since most hikers tackle the sections separately, I have chosen to present them that way here.

The Lighthouse Loop section is easier and more popular, with spectacular views of the coast and Amphitrite Point Lighthouse. The northern section, from Brown's Beach to Rocky Bluffs, includes hillier trails, remote windswept coastline, and giant old-growth trees.

LIGHTHOUSE LOOP

TRIP PLANNER

0 km (0 mi)	Whale parking lot trailhead
0.8 km (0.5 mi)	Amphitrite Point Lighthouse
1.7 km (1.1 mi)	Inspiration Point
3 km (1.9 mi)	Whale parking lot trailhead

The main Lighthouse Loop Trail makes a 3 km (1.9 mi) loop around the end of the Ucluth Peninsula. The wide gravel trail is flat with a few small hills, making it easy to complete in about 30 minutes. However, dozens of spur trails lead to picturesque ocean viewpoints, most with benches. Each one somehow seems more fantastic than the last. If you want to visit many of these vistas, allow an hour for this walk.

Begin your hike at the **Whale parking lot** on Coast Guard Road. The trailhead is on the south side of the lot, near a large info sign. Follow the path slightly downhill through the tight rainforest for a few minutes to the coast, where it turns right and runs along the top of a bluff. You'll encounter the first of many viewpoints here.

About 0.8 km (0.5 mi) from the start, emerge from the forest into an open area near the **Amphitrite Point Lighthouse**, built in 1915. Named for a British navy ship that served on the B.C. coast in the 1850s, its squat concrete construction is designed to withstand the gale-force winds and pounding waves that are common here. The lighthouse and rocky viewpoints along the Wild Pacific Trail are great places to watch storms make landfall in the winter months.

Past the lighthouse, the trail winds and twists along the coast through thickets of salal, passing still more gorgeous viewpoints. About 1.7 km (1.1 mi) from the trailhead, follow a short trail signed for **Inspiration Point** to descend several sets of stairs to a clifftop perch.

Back on the main trail, reach a junction at 1.8 km (1.1 mi). The main loop heads uphill to the right. Left leads 0.2 km (0.1 mi) downhill to **He-Tin-Kis Beach**. Continuing along the loop, the trail turns inland and climbs a hill. At 2.5 km (1.6 mi), reach a junction with the trail to **Terrace Beach**. Your route goes right and uphill slightly towards the parking lot. A sign marks the turnoff to the **Bog Woodland Interpretive Loop** at 2.8 (1.7 mi) km. Take the left fork to cross Coast Guard Road and arrive back at the **Whale parking lot.**

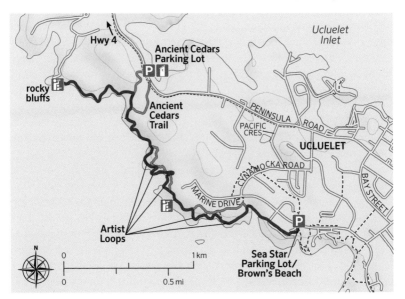

BROWN'S BEACH TO ROCKY BLUFFS

TRIP PLANNER

0 km (0 mi)	Sea Star parking lot at Brown's Beach
0.5 km (0.3 mi)	Start of Artist Loops
1.3 km (0.8 mi)	Observation deck
2.1 km (1.3 mi)	End of Artist Loops
2.6 km (1.6 mi)	Ancient Cedars Trail south junction
2.7 km (1.7 mi)	Ancient Cedars Trail north junction
3.5 km (2.2 mi)	Bluff viewpoint at trail's end

This section of the Wild Pacific Trail can be walked as a point-to-point hike if you can arrange a pickup at the Ancient Cedars trailhead. It also makes a pleasant out-and-back hike from the Sea Star parking lot at Brown's Beach.

From the parking area, follow the Wild Pacific Trail to the right. (You can also detour to check out Brown's Beach by going left, then retrace your steps back to the parking lot.) The first few minutes of the trail run between some houses. About 0.2 km (0.1 mi) from the trailhead, cross **Odyssey Lane** and pick up the trail on the other side. A few minutes later, a spur trail leads out to the first of many beautiful viewpoints.

About 0.5 km (0.3 mi) from the trailhead, reach a junction. Going left will take you on a series of rougher oceanside trails known as the **Artist Loops**. (If you stay right at the junction, you'll remain on the direct route that is flatter but lacks views.) Each loop trail winds along the top of rocky bluffs and offers a slightly different view of the crashing waves, tiny islets, and deep surge channels along the rugged coast. You'll pass countless viewing platforms and benches that are great locations for photography or plein-air painting. Between the 0.5 km (0.3 mi) and 2.1 km (1.3 mi) mark, the Artist Loops leave and rejoin the main trail several times. Choose the left-hand path at each junction to get the best views. Don't miss the spectacular **observation deck** at the 1.3 km (0.8 mi) mark.

After the Artist Loops end, the main trail continues along the top of the bluffs, passing even more viewpoints. At 2.6 km (1.6 mi), the south side of the **Ancient Cedars Trail** branches right. You will meet the other side of the loop at 2.7 km (1.7 mi). Add this 1 km (0.6 mi) loop past several huge old-growth trees to your trip. Or use it to head to the Ancient Cedars parking lot on Highway 4.

Continuing onward, the trail heads inland for a few minutes before tracking the top of the cliffs once more. Watch for seals and sea lions on the rocks below. The path dead-ends at a **rocky bluff viewpoint** at the 3.5 km (2.2 mi) mark. The Wild Pacific Trail Society has plans to extend the path in the future, but for now the trail terminates at private property. Therefore, you'll need to retrace your steps to the Sea Star parking lot at the start or the Ancient Cedars parking lot on Highway 4.

EXTENDING YOUR TRIP

Terrace Beach: This small beach is the site of a Yuułuʔiłʔatḥ Nation canoe landing and shell midden. Interpretive signs explain traditional plant use. It's a 1 km (0.6 mi) round trip from the junction on the Lighthouse Loop Trail.

Bog Woodland Interpretive Loop: At just 0.3 km (0.2 mi), this one-way loop makes an interesting add-on to the Lighthouse Loop. Info signs at regular intervals explain the unique bog plants.

Ancient Cedars Trail: Visit the oldest trees on the Ucluelet Peninsula on this 1 km (0.6 mi) loop that leads from the Wild Pacific Trail down to Highway 4 and back again. Look for giant western redcedar, Sitka spruce, and western hemlock, some of which are over 800 years old.

FURTHER RESOURCES

Wild Pacific Trail Society: info and maps *wildpacifictrail.com*
NTS Map: 092C13

13

BIG TREE TRAIL

DAY HIKE

Difficulty: ●
Duration: 2 hours
Distance: 3.5 km (2.2 mi) loop

Elevation Gain: 10 m (32 ft)
High Point: 10 m (32 ft)
Best Months: Year-round

Fees: Round-trip water taxi costs $30/person and includes trail fees.

Regulations: No dogs. No camping.

Caution: The trail can be very muddy. Stay on boardwalks and avoid walking around the base of the large trees, which can damage their root systems.

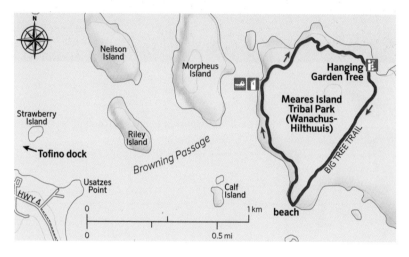

A SHORT WATER TAXI RIDE away from Tofino you can discover what the coastal rainforests of Clayoquot Sound looked like before logging. The Big Tree Trail on Meares Island is an easy loop hike along boardwalks that lead to numerous huge western redcedar, Sitka spruce, and western hemlock trees that are over 800 years old. The highlight is the Hanging Garden Tree, which is estimated to be 2000 years old. Today the trail is protected in the Tla-o-qui-aht Nation's Meares Island Tribal Park, known as Wanachus-Hilthuuis. In the 1980s and '90s it was at the centre of a protest movement known as the War in the Woods, which tried to stop old-growth logging and preserve groves of large trees all across B.C.

Entering the rainforest from the boat dock

GETTING THERE

Take Highway 4 to Tofino. There is pay parking on side streets in Tofino and at the municipal lot at 121 Third Street. Book a water taxi to Meares Island with one of the many operators in town. The trip takes about 10 minutes.

TRAIL

TRIP PLANNER

0 km (0 mi)	Water taxi pickup/drop-off
1.2 km (0.7 mi)	Hanging Garden Tree
2.2 km (1.4 mi)	Beach
3.5 km (2.2 mi)	Water taxi pickup/drop-off

To start the hike, your water taxi operator will drop you off at a small dock. Follow a ramp up into the forest to a junction and a new composting out-house. Turn left to follow the boardwalk towards the largest trees, which are 800 to 1300 years old. (You will complete the loop on the path to the right.) The first section of the trail winds through the forest on boardwalks made of hand-hewn cedar planks. You will pass by several huge old-growth trees, some of which have carved name placards, such as the Cedar of Life.

About 1.2 km (0.7 mi) from the trailhead, reach the largest tree, known as the **Hanging Garden Tree** due to all the ferns and small trees growing out of it. This massive tree is 18 m (59 ft) wide, almost 43 m (141 ft) tall, and approximately 2000 years old.

The boardwalk ends at the Hanging Garden Tree, and a rough and muddy flagged route through the forest begins. Some hikers retrace their route to the water taxi dock from here, but I recommend continuing to make a loop hike. Tla-o-qui-aht Tribal Parks Guardians are coordinating ongoing maintenance on this part of the trail to lengthen the boardwalk and reduce the muddy sections. Follow the wet and mucky trail through the forest for about 1 km (0.6 mi) across a peninsula to the south side of Meares Island. You may need to duck under or climb over several fallen trees.

Rough-hewn boardwalks protect fragile tree roots

Several side trails lead to the marshy tidal flats of Browning Passage. Take a break on the **beach** to watch for shore birds like herons, and look across the channel to the houses of Tofino. Continue your hike along the forest trail as it weaves in and out of salal thickets and passes several large old-growth trees. You are just a few minutes away from the trailhead, so you may want to call your water taxi to arrange a pickup from this section of the trail.

FURTHER RESOURCES
Tla-o-qui-aht Tribal Parks: info *tribalparks.com*
District of Tofino: parking info and prices *tofino.ca/parking*
Jamie's Whaling Station: water taxi *jamies.com*
Meares Island Water Taxi: *mearesislandwatertaxi.ca*
Ocean Outfitters: water taxi *oceanoutfitters.bc.ca*
Tofino Water Taxi: *tofinowatertaxi.com*
NTS Map: 092F04

14

WILD SIDE TRAIL ★

BACKPACKING TRIP

Difficulty: ■
Duration: 2 days
Distance: 22 km (13.7 mi) round trip

Elevation Gain: 5 m (16 ft)
High Point: 5 m (16 ft)
Best Months: May to September

Fees and Reservations: Trail fees are $15/person/day, payable in cash at the trail office at the Ahous Fuel Stop in Ahousaht. Camping is first-come, first-served.

Regulations: Dogs are not recommended. No drones. No smoking, vaping, or cannabis. Fires permitted below the high-tide line only.

Caution: This area has an active wolf population. Wolves are highly territorial and have attacked dogs and harassed hikers. Do not bring dogs or allow dogs from Maaqtusiis to follow you onto the trail. See the wildlife section (page 23) for more tips on backpacking in wolf habitat.

ESCAPE THE BUSTLE of Tofino with a short water taxi ride to the nearly deserted lush rainforest and white-sand beaches of Flores Island. The Wild Side Trail is in the traditional territory of the Ahousaht people and passes through Gibson Marine and Flores Island Provincial Parks. The route also

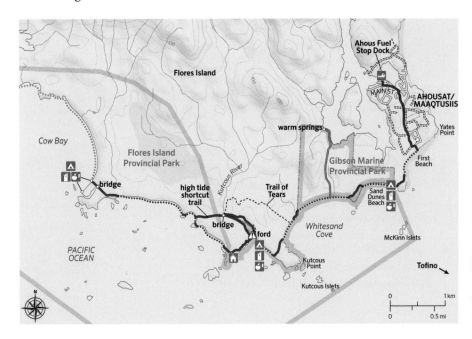

features interpretive signs about Ahousaht history and culture. The highlight is camping on the 2-km-long (1.2 mi) crescent of sandy beach at Cow Bay, where grey whales feed offshore and the sun sets into the Pacific Ocean, lighting up the sky in a spectacular show of pinks and purples.

GETTING THERE

Take Highway 4 to Tofino. There is overnight pay parking at the municipal lot at 121 Third Street. Water taxis leave from the First Street dock. Head down to the dock to ask about departure times, or phone one of the water taxi operators to arrange a charter. Fares are cash only and vary by vessel.

TRAIL

TRIP PLANNER

0 km (0 mi)	Trail check-in at Ahous Fuel Stop dock
1.6 km (1 mi)	First Beach
2.5 km (1.6 mi)	Sand Dunes campground
3.7 km (2.3 mi)	Junction with Warm Springs Trail
5.8 km (3.6 mi)	Kutcous River campground/low-tide river ford
6.8 km (4.2 mi)	Kutcous River bridge/junction with high-tide shortcut trail
7.5 km (4.7 mi)	Junction with the low-tide river ford
8 km (5 mi)	Emergency shelter cabin
9 km (5.6 mi)	Junction with high-tide shortcut trail
11 km (6.8 mi)	Cow Bay campground

This area is the traditional territory of the Ahousaht, one of the 14 members of the Nuu-chah-nulth Tribal Council. In the Nuu-chah-nulth language, Ahousaht means "our backs against the mountains," a reference to the Ahousaht territory sandwiched between the waters of Clayoquot Sound and the tall peaks of Vancouver Island. The Wild Side Trail uses traditional paths that the Ahousaht people have used for thousands of years to hunt, gather, and engage in spiritual practices. Along the trail, watch for interpretive signs explaining key places of cultural importance, such as Wo'aihsi at the Kutcous River bridge, an important battleground in the Ahousaht-Otsosaht war in the early 19th century.

Your hike begins when your water taxi driver drops you off at the **Ahous Fuel Stop dock** on the south side of Ahousaht Harbour. Check in to start the hike and pay your trail fees at the fuel dock office. From here, follow the green and yellow Wild Side Trail signs through the town of Maaqtusiis (also spelled Marktosis) to the trailhead. Watch for signs or ask locals for directions to stay on track through several turns.

Beach hiking as the tide comes in

In general, head up the road from the fuel dock, then turn left on Main Street. Follow it past the sports field and then turn right into the gravel area in front of the school. Walk along the side of the school and pick up a trail through the brush heading south. A few minutes later, emerge on a paved road. Turn right and walk the road south for a few minutes to a roundabout. Head straight through the roundabout into a neighbourhood and keep heading south towards the beach. Follow the Wild Side Trail sign between two houses and across some carved boardwalk to **First Beach**.

Turn right and walk down the beach for a minute. Head into the forest on an inland trail marked with a fishing float. The first forested sections of trail feature whimsical curved boardwalks made of hand-split cedar planks. These boardwalks were built in the late 1990s, when the trail was first opened, so they are weathered and often very mossy. The first section of the inland trail is barely 100 m (328 ft) long, and at low tide you can bypass it by staying on the beach. Pop out onto the sand for a quick minute, then head back into the forest on a longer trail section.

About 2.5 km (1.6 mi) from the trailhead, emerge on **Sand Dunes Beach**, sometimes called Second Beach. The campsite is just ahead, along the beach. Continue along the beach for another 0.5 km (0.3 mi) to another section of inland trail marked with fishing floats. A few minutes later, emerge on yet another beautiful beach at Whitesand Cove.

Partway down the beach, pass the turnoff for the **Warm Springs Trail**. Follow fishing floats into the forest at the end of the beach for a quick inland section. On the next beach, pass the turnoff onto the Trail of Tears and continue to the end of the beach. The Trail of Tears is an important historical route for the Ahousaht Nation, because their people escaped along this route during a conflict with their former neighbours, the Otsosaht. It leads inland to meet up with the main Wild Side Trail at the Kutcous River bridge. However, the Trail of Tears is no longer regularly maintained, so you should stay on the main trail.

At the end of the beach, follow the inland trail for a few minutes through the forest across Kutcous Point, called Katkwuuwis in Nuu-chah-nulth. The name means "cut people's heads off in warfare." The mouth of the river was the site of an important conflict in the Ahousaht-Otsosaht war in the early 1800s. After the Ahousaht gained control of the point from the Otsosaht, they occupied a summer village here, where they hunted for seals and halibut and gathered sedge grasses.

Walk down the beach towards the **Kutcous River camp**. At low tide, you can take a **shortcut** and save 1.5 km (0.9 mi) of hiking by **fording the river** here. At tides below 1.5 m (4.9 ft), cross the river at its mouth. If the tide is 1.5 to 2 m (4.9 to 6.7 ft), you can walk about 100 m (328 ft) upstream, cross there, then scram-

Moss coats the inland boardwalks

ble across the rocks back towards the beach. Regain the trail at a marker on the other side.

At tides above 2 m (6.7 ft), follow the trail just past the campsite into the forest. The path parallels the river and passes a large cedar and then a huge culturally modified cedar tree with a large square hole cut out of it. A few minutes past the tree, arrive at a large metal **bridge over the Kutcous River**, where the overgrown Trail of Tears joins the main trail from the right.

On the other side of the bridge, you can take the rough high-tide shortcut trail to the right if you want to save 1.4 km (0.9 mi). It's a brushy and technical route and is slow going. To stay on the more scenic main trail, head left as it parallels the west bank of the Kutcous River back to the low-tide crossing at its mouth.

The next section of the Wild Side Trail is in the forest, with glimpses down the bank to the rocky shoreline. About 0.5 km (0.3 mi) from the river mouth, you'll pass by an old cabin. It has a sleeping loft and an outhouse nearby, but officially it should only be used as an **emergency shelter**. A few minutes later, hike out of the forest onto the first in a series of small sandy beaches. Follow the trail across a tiny headland into another sandy pocket cove. The **high-tide shortcut trail** meets the main trail in the middle of the beach.

Hike over another tiny headland to a large sandy beach that is about 1 km (0.6 mi) long. At the end of the beach, take the trail into the forest. A few minutes later, cross Cow Creek on a bridge made from a giant Sitka spruce log. Continue for 100 m (328 ft) to the white sand of **Cow Bay**. The crescent of sand stretches to the north for 2 km (1.2 mi). Watch for grey whales and orcas feeding offshore and wolves patrolling the beach in the early morning. The trail used to extend to the top of nearby Mount Flores, but the route has been swallowed back into the forest and is not recommended.

CAMPING

There are 3 designated campgrounds on the trail. You can also camp on any of the beaches if you are prepared to hang your food and use Leave No Trace toilet practices. However, water is scarce, so you will have to haul it from elsewhere along the trail.

INDIGENOUS KNOWLEDGE

CULTURALLY MODIFIED TREES

Watch for culturally modified trees as you hike the Wild Side Trail. The most prominent example is a huge old-growth cedar along the trail on the east side of the Kutcous River. Initially, you will notice the large box cut out of it, where the inner wood was tested to see if it would make a good canoe. If you look closer, you will also see that two planks have been removed from the tree lower down. A core sample taken from the modified portion of the tree dates the modifications to about 150 years ago, likely during the Ahousaht-Otsosaht war. The Ahousaht were careful to remove only the parts of the tree they needed, which is why it lives on today.

The Cow Bay campground

SAND DUNES CAMPGROUND
This campground is close to the town of Maaqtusiis.

Campsites: Two wooden platforms and lots of slanted space in the dunes
Toilet: Outhouse in the trees
Water: Collect from a seasonal stream at the west end of the beach. It is usually dry in the summer, so plan to bring your own water.
Food Storage: Food locker in the trees

KUTCOUS RIVER CAMPGROUND
The sandy beach on the east side of the river is a splendid place to camp.

Campsites: Two wooden tent platforms in the brush behind the beach and lots of space on the beach above the high-tide line
Toilet: Throne-style pit toilet in the trees
Water: Collect from the Kutcous River. It is tidal, so go upriver and collect water at low tide to ensure the water is not brackish.
Food Storage: Food locker in the trees

COW BAY CAMPGROUND
This exquisite sandy beach is the most popular place to camp on the Wild Side Trail. It faces west into the open Pacific Ocean, so it gets incredible sunsets and can be windy.

Campsites: Several tent platforms in the trees at the south side of the beach and lots of space along the beach above the high-tide line

Toilets: Outhouse where the trail meets the beach and a second outhouse at the south end of the beach near the tent platforms

Water: Collect from Cow Creek at the south end of the beach at low tide. At high tide, walk back up the trail to the bridge and collect from there to avoid saltwater contamination.

Food Storage: Food locker on a marked trail near where the main trail meets the beach, and a second food locker near the tent platforms

EXTENDING YOUR TRIP

Warm Springs: From Whitesand Cove, make the 2 km (1.2 mi) round-trip hike on a rough, muddy, and often overgrown route through thick forest and bog to Warm Springs, on the shores of Matilda Inlet. The water at this naturally occurring spring is not that warm (approximately 25°C/77°F) and the small concrete tub is usually full of algae, but a soak is possible.

Cow Bay: Explore the beautiful sand of Cow Bay. The main beach is nearly 2 km (1.2 mi) long, and at low tide you can scramble around or across rocky headlands for a further 2 km (1.2 mi).

FURTHER RESOURCES

Wild Side Trail: trail info *wildsidetrail.com*

Happiest Outdoors: additional trail info *happiestoutdoors.ca/wildside-trail-guide*

Flores Island Provincial Park: info *bcparks.ca/explore/parkpgs/flores_is*

Gibson Marine Provincial Park: info *bcparks.ca/explore/parkpgs/gibson*

Fisheries and Oceans Canada: Tofino tide table *tides.gc.ca/eng/station?sid=8615*

District of Tofino: overnight parking info and prices *tofino.ca/parking*

Ahousaht Nation: water taxi operator listings *ahousaht.ca/water-taxi-info.html*

Wild Side Trail Map: available from the Wild Side Trail office in Ahousaht

NTS Map: 092E08

COURTENAY-COMOX TRIPS

THE MOUNTAINS OF Strathcona Provincial Park rise steeply away from the flat farmland near Courtenay and Comox. Locals have been heading to the high peaks and meadows for over a century, which means a well-developed network of backpacking trails. Closer to sea level, day hikers can enjoy clifftop views on Hornby Island or explore historical sites in the Cumberland Community Forest.

Getting Around: The paved road to the Mount Washington ski area provides the easiest access to the subalpine on Vancouver Island and acts as the gateway to the Forbidden Plateau area of Strathcona Provincial Park. A gravel road leads to the Wood Mountain trailhead, an alternative access point to the plateau. Highway 19 runs north to south through the region, providing access to Cumberland and the Buckley Bay ferry terminal, the departure point for trips to Hornby Island.

Indigenous Context: The east coast of Vancouver Island is the traditional territory of many members of the Coast Salish group of Indigenous Peoples, who are ethnically and linguistically related. The K'ómoks, Homalco, Halalt, Ts'uubaa-asatx (Lake Cowichan), Tla'amin/Sliammon, Lyackson, and Penelakut Nations all have traditional territory on Hornby Island and the coastal parts of eastern Vancouver Island. K'ómoks territory extends inland to the mountains of Strathcona Provincial Park, where it overlaps with the traditional territory of the We Wai Kai and We Wai Kum Nations, both Kwakwaka'wakw groups related closely to other nations on northern Vancouver Island.

The We Wai Kai origin story tells of a great flood. Chief Way Key gathered his tribe in four canoes that were lashed to the top of a tall mountain to ride out the high waters. When the current became too strong, one canoe was set loose. It drifted south to Washington State. Later, another canoe escaped in strong currents. It drifted to B.C.'s north coast. As the flood waters receded, two canoes remained in place. The descendants from those two canoes became the We Wai Kai and the We Wai Kum, related to other coastal Indigenous groups from Washington in the south to Kitimat in the north.

Visit the U'mista Cultural Centre in Alert Bay to learn more about Kwakwaka'wakw history, culture, and art. The Nim Nim Interpretive Centre and the I-Hos Gallery in Courtenay allow you to enjoy K'ómoks art and culture. In Campbell River, the We Wai Kum House of Treasures has Indigenous art and souvenirs. Or visit the Nuyumbalees Cultural Centre on Quadra Island to view We Wai Kai potlatch regalia.

Supplies: The Courtenay-Comox area has many grocery stores, gas stations, and outdoor stores. Cumberland has a small grocery store and two gas stations. The Mount Washington residential community does not have any services. Hornby Island has a small general store and a gas station.

Accommodations: There are lots of hotels and vacation rentals in Courtenay, Comox, and Cumberland. Hornby Island and the Mount Washington ski area also have a limited amount of accommodation. The Cumberland Campground on Comox Lake, managed by a local non-profit, has reservable sites a few minutes from Cumberland. Kin Beach Provincial Park, a few minutes from Comox, and Kitty Coleman Provincial Park, a few minutes north of that, both have first-come, first-served campsites.

A carved trail sign at Kwai Lake (Trip 18). Photo: Reid Holmes

15

HELLIWELL LOOP

DAY HIKE

Difficulty: ●
Duration: 1.5 hours
Distance: 4 km (2.5 mi) loop

Elevation Gain: 50 m (164 ft)
High Point: 50 m (164 ft)
Best Months: Year-round

Fees and Reservations: None

Regulations: No fires. No drones. No smoking, vaping, or cannabis. No camping. Dogs permitted on leash.

Caution: The trail follows clifftops, which are prone to crumbling, so stay well back from the edges.

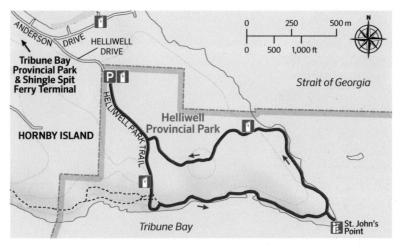

WITH CLIFFTOP MEADOWS, expansive ocean views, and opportunities to spot rare flora and fauna, Helliwell Provincial Park is a premier hiking destination. Located on Hornby Island, one of the northernmost Gulf Islands, the small park includes a unique coastal bluff meadow that provides habitat for endangered butterflies and teems with wildflowers in the spring.

GETTING THERE

Getting to Hornby Island requires two ferries, the first from Vancouver Island to Denman Island, and the second from Denman to Hornby. The ferries cannot be reserved, and multiple-sailing waits are common, so go early on

Looking east to the cliffs lining Tribune Bay

summer weekends. Strong cyclists willing to deal with a few hills can leave their car at Buckley Bay on Vancouver Island and bike across Denman and Hornby Islands to the trailhead. It's a 50 km (31 mi) round trip.

From Highway 19 between Parksville and Courtenay, take exit 101 east to Buckley Bay Road. Continue straight through the traffic light into the Buckley Bay ferry terminal. Catch the ferry to Denman Island. Once on Denman, follow signs across the island to the Hornby Island ferry terminal, 11.5 km (7.1 mi) away, using Denman Road and East Road. Take the ferry to Hornby Island.

When you arrive on Hornby, follow Shingle Spit Road, which curves right and becomes Central Road after 2.9 km (1.8 mi). At a major 4-way intersection 5.9 km (3.7 mi) later, turn left onto St. John's Point Road. At the next intersection, in 0.8 km (0.5 mi), turn right again to stay on St. John's Point Road. Follow this road for 3.2 km (2 mi). It becomes Anderson Road near its end. Turn right at the fork onto Helliwell Drive. The road ends at the parking lot and trailhead 0.45 km (0.3 mi) later.

TRAIL

TRIP PLANNER

0 km (0 mi)	Trailhead and parking lot
0.4 km (0.2 mi)	Totem pole junction
0.7 km (0.4 mi)	Junction
2 km (1.2 mi)	St. John's Point
3.6 km (2.2 mi)	Totem pole junction
4 km (2.5 mi)	Trailhead and parking lot

From the **parking lot**, follow the trail into the forest past an information board and outhouse. The wide path climbs gently to a junction at a wide clearing. Pause to admire the totem pole, erected by the K'ómoks Nation in 2018 as part of a larger project to place poles throughout their traditional territory. The pole was carved by Karver Everson (Gayustistalas) of the K'ómoks and Kwakwa̱ka̱'wakw Nations and depicts a thunderbird and a double-headed sea serpent. A sign here explains the significance of these figures in local Indigenous stories.

When you are ready to continue onward, turn right and follow the wide trail south towards the ocean. Find another **outhouse** just before the path breaks out of the trees. Stay on the path as it heads through the grass to avoid crushing fragile vegetation.

As you approach the ocean, the **trail forks**, following the shoreline to the east and west. The route to the west (right) leads out of the park, while your route heads east (left). Be sure to stay back from the edge of the bluffs as you walk. The cliffs are made of gravel and fist-sized rocks cemented together with finer-grained sand, silt, and clay. This conglomerate, a type of sedimentary rock, crumbles easily.

The trail rambles along the top of the cliffs as it heads towards St. John's Point, at the eastern end of the park. Several benches invite you to rest and enjoy the scenery. To the south, you'll get excellent views of the coastal communities of Vancouver Island, with the jagged peaks of Mount Arrowsmith (Trip 9) looming behind. Look down at the eroding cliffs or admire the hairy manzanita bushes, red-barked arbutus trees, and towering Garry oaks, the only species of oak native to British Columbia.

In 2015, BC Parks began a restoration project designed to expand the cliffside meadows by removing young Douglas-fir, lodgepole pine, and shore pine trees to allow the oaks to flourish. They also planted native grasses, sedges, and flowers. These plants provide important habitat for endangered Taylor's checkerspot butterflies. In the spring, see if you can spy these small orange, black, and white butterflies.

Follow a short spur trail out to the tip of **St. John's Point** and gaze across to tiny Flora Islet, which is also part of Helliwell Provincial Park. Divers flock here to swim with the rare bluntnose sixgill shark. These elusive sharks usually live in water that is too deep for divers, but a small population spends their summers in the rocky reef around Flora Islet.

From the point, follow the trail as it curves northwest and continues to parallel the coast, weaving in and out of small patches of trees, including Pacific yews. Look west across the Strait of Georgia to the hills of Texada Island, with the mountains of the Sunshine Coast behind. Find another **outhouse** shortly after the trail leaves the shoreline and enters a beautiful open forest

Chrome Island in Boyle Point Provincial Park

of Garry oak, bigleaf maple, western redcedar, and Douglas-fir. Continue through the forest for a few more minutes before arriving back at the **totem pole junction**. Turn right and retrace your steps back to the **parking lot**.

EXTENDING YOUR TRIP

Tribune Bay Provincial Park: This exquisite 600-m-long (1969 ft) sandy beach is just a few minutes' drive or bike from Helliwell Provincial Park. Take a walk along the white sand or on the trail that parallels it through a bushy meadow.

Boyle Point Provincial Park: Break up the trip across Denman Island with a quick hike in Boyle Point Provincial Park, near the Gravelly Bay (Denman East) ferry terminal. It's an easy 3 km (1.9 mi) out-and-back trip to magnificent viewpoints over Eagle Rock and the Chrome Island lighthouse. If you're up for a longer hike, explore the less-travelled trails that wind through the forested western part of the park. They lead to hidden beaches and more clifftop viewpoints.

FURTHER RESOURCES

Helliwell Provincial Park: info and map *bcparks.ca/explore/parkpgs/helliwell*
BC Ferries: ferry schedules for Denman and Hornby *bcferries.com*
NTS Map: 092F10

16

CUMBERLAND COMMUNITY FOREST

DAY HIKE

Difficulty: ●

Duration: 1.5 to 2 hours

Distance: 5 km (3.1 mi) loop

Elevation Gain: 75 m (246 ft)

High Point: 225 m (738 ft)

Best Months: Year-round

Fees and Reservations: None

Regulations: No fires. No camping. Dogs permitted.

Caution: This area is primarily for mountain biking, but most trails on this route are shared multi-use trails with low bike traffic. Watch for bikes at all times.

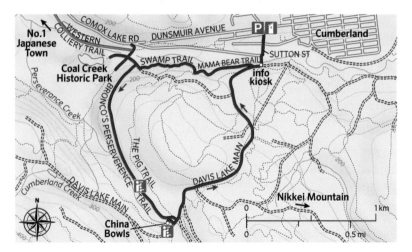

CUMBERLAND LOCALS HAVE worked to protect the forest next to their town while also developing a huge network of trails. This loop hike takes you to some highlights of the Cumberland Community Forest. Marvel at the sculpted sandstone formations at China Bowls in the Perseverance Creek canyon. Learn from interpretive panels at the site about the town's former Chinatown in Coal Creek Historic Park. And sample some of the community-built multi-use trails through the beautiful mossy forest that protects habitat for dozens of species, including the northern red-legged frog and coastal cutthroat trout, both considered species at risk. The forest is home to lots of interesting plant life too, including many mushroom species, which are celebrated each fall at Fungus Fest.

GETTING THERE

From Highway 19 near Courtenay, take exit 117 east onto Cumberland Road. Follow the road into the town of Cumberland, where it becomes 4th Street. Turn right onto Dunsmuir Avenue, then turn left onto Sutton Road and immediately left again, into a large gravel parking lot. There is a washroom building here.

TRAIL

TRIP PLANNER

0 km (0 mi)	Trailhead and parking lot
0.2 km (0.1 mi)	Community Forest information kiosk
1.4 km (0.9 mi)	Coal Creek Historic Park
1.7 km (1.1 mi)	Junction with Bronco's Perseverance Trail
3.2 km (2 mi)	China Bowls/Cumberland Potholes
4.8 km (3 mi)	Community Forest info kiosk
5 km (3.1 mi)	Trailhead and parking lot

From the **parking lot**, turn left and walk downhill on Sutton Street for two blocks on the multiuse path. At the bottom of the hill, follow the gravel road to a yellow gate and the entrance to the Cumberland Community Forest. Arrive at a T-junction with an **information kiosk** and map. Turn right and follow the road for a few metres, then take the signed **Mama Bear Trail** branching to the right. This is one of the Community Forest's nature trails, designed to be enjoyed on foot, so you are unlikely to see many bikes here.

Bronco's Perseverance Trail

The trail undulates through a regenerating forest, with plenty of moss, sword ferns, and huckleberry bushes. About 0.8 km (0.5 mi) from the start, turn right onto the signed **Swamp Trail**, another nature trail. The trail drops slightly to parallel a marshy area. A wide clearing a few minutes later may be slightly confusing—follow

China Bowls, at low water

the trail to the right, continuing to parallel the swamp. A few more minutes after that, stay right again, ignoring an old road going uphill in a straight line. Continue on the Swamp Trail as it continues next to the marsh. At a prominent dip, go straight and uphill out of the dip, ignoring a less-trodden trail to the left.

About 1.3 km (0.8 mi) from the parking lot, emerge on an **old gravel road**. Turn right and follow it across a **boardwalk** to a clearing with a picnic pavilion at 1.4 km (0.9 mi). You have arrived at **Coal Creek Historic Park**, the former site of Cumberland's Chinatown during the town's coal-mining heyday, from the 1880s to the 1960s. Take a few minutes to explore the park. A map at a nearby interpretive kiosk shows the routes to 17 sites of interest in the park, each with its own information plaque. Don't miss Jumbo's cabin, the last remaining building.

When you have finished learning about Cumberland's Chinatown, retrace your steps back across the boardwalk, and turn right onto the **Bronco's Perseverance Trail**. This is a lightly used mountain bike trail, so keep an eye out for descending riders. Follow the trail as it climbs gently through the mossy and mature second-growth forest. In a few minutes, keep right at the fork.

After the trail begins to flatten a little, watch for a **viewpoint** on the right, near the 2.6 km (1.6 mi) mark. Peer down into the depths of the Perseverance Creek canyon far below you, but be careful to keep back from the dangerous drop.

Continue along Bronco's Perseverance for a few more minutes. The trail merges with another mountain bike trail called The Pig and then joins a gravel road. Turn right and follow the road for a few minutes to the edge of Perseverance Creek, under a road bridge. This site is commonly called **China Bowls**, Cumberland Potholes, or Perseverance Potholes. Centuries of running water have sculpted the sandstone rock into intricate bowls, curves, and chutes. At times of low water, you can wander down the creek bed for a few minutes to admire the formations. Do not descend the dangerous cliffs, and be careful near the edges, which are slippery.

After you've enjoyed the potholes, head back along the **gravel road** and follow it as it snakes its way downhill. Ignore the many mountain bike trails and secondary roads and stay on the main gravel road, called Davis Lake Main. Eventually, the road will bring you back to the T-junction and **information kiosk** at the entrance to the Cumberland Community Forest. Turn left to walk back around the yellow gate, then up the multi-use path to the **parking lot**, completing the loop.

EXTENDING YOUR TRIP

Cumberland Community Forest: If you don't mind sharing trails with bikes, the Cumberland Community Forest provides nearly endless loop-hike possibilities. Admire the view from the top of Nikkei Mountain or grab a photo op at the giant wooden chair on the Rapture Trail. Use the map posted at the kiosk or on the Trailforks app to find your way.

No. 1 Japanese Town: For more local history, take the Wellington Colliery Trail west from the Chinatown interpretive site to the location of Cumberland's Japantown, which was active between 1891 and 1942. A short trail with nine interpretive stops tells the story of the area. This out-and-back detour will add 2 km (1.2 mi) and 40 minutes to your hike.

FURTHER RESOURCES

Cumberland Community Forest Society: info and maps *cumberlandforest.com*
United Rides of Cumberland: info and maps *unitedridersofcumberland.com*
NTS Map: 092F11

17

FORBIDDEN PLATEAU TRAVERSE

BACKPACKING TRIP | Trail map on pp. 162–63

Difficulty: ■
Duration: 2 to 3 days
Distance: 24 km (14.9 mi) one way

Elevation Gain: 150 m (492 ft)
High Point: 1240 m (4068 ft)
Best Months: July to September

Fees and Reservations: Camping fees are $10/person/night payable online or in cash at the trailhead for campsites in the Forbidden Plateau Core Area. The campsite at McKenzie Lake is free. All campsites are first-come, first-served.

Regulations: No fires. No drones. No smoking, vaping, or cannabis. Dogs permitted on leash.

THE PARADISE MEADOWS and Mount Becher trails are both deservedly popular destinations for day hikers. Leave the crowds behind on a one-way hike that connects these two scenic areas, travelling across Forbidden Plateau through the gorgeous subalpine of Strathcona Provincial Park. The term "plateau" is a bit of a misnomer, because the area is actually composed of an interesting combination of sloping ridges, low peaks, and picturesque lakes. The designated campsite at McKenzie Lake makes a great place to break up your journey. You can also enjoy swimming and exploring at nearby Douglas Lake.

GETTING THERE
The Forbidden Plateau Traverse can be hiked one way or as an out-and-back from either trailhead to the campsite at McKenzie Lake. If you're completing the traverse, you'll need to arrange to have someone pick you up at the end, or park a vehicle at each trailhead.

While the traverse can be completed from either direction, hiking from west to east has less overall elevation gain. It also means you will descend the dusty and shadeless abandoned ski runs at the eastern trailhead instead of having to ascend them with full packs. That's the direction described below. However, the terrain between the two trailheads is rolling, with lots of small hills, so you will have plenty of short climbs and descents no matter which direction you choose.

PARADISE MEADOWS TRAILHEAD
From Highway 19 just north of Courtenay, go west on Strathcona Parkway (also known as Mount Washington Road) for 17 km (10.6 mi). Turn left onto Nordic Drive, following signs for Raven Lodge and Strathcona Provincial Park. Follow this road for 2.5 km (1.6 mi) until it ends at a large gravel parking

One of many picturesque tarns along the traverse. Photo: Reid Holmes

lot. The trailhead is on the left, next to the small Strathcona Wilderness Centre, which provides visitor information.

FORBIDDEN PLATEAU/WOOD MOUNTAIN TRAILHEAD

From Highway 19 just north of Courtenay, go east on Piercy Road for 1.5 km (0.9 mi). Turn right onto Forbidden Plateau Road and follow it over the highway and up the mountain for 15 km (9.3 mi), ignoring smaller second roads. The pavement peters out about 9.5 km (5.9 mi) along. The remaining distance to the summit is on a 2WD-accessible gravel road with lots of dust and some washboard sections. The road ends at a large gravel parking area. The old ski area here was known both as Forbidden Plateau and Wood Mountain, so you will see signs referencing the two names along the trail.

TRAIL

TRIP PLANNER

0 km (0 mi)	Paradise Meadows trailhead
2.8 km (1.7 mi)	Battleship Lake
3.7 km (2.3 mi)	Lake Helen Mackenzie junction (east)
7.3 km (4.5 mi)	Forbidden Plateau Trail/Kwai Lake junction
14 km (8.7 mi)	McKenzie Lake junction
20.6 km (12.8 mi)	Mount Becher junction
22.2 km (13.8 mi)	Top of old ski runs
24 km (14.9 mi)	Forbidden Plateau trailhead

From the **trailhead at Paradise Meadows,** you will enter an interconnected network of wide gravel and boardwalk loop trails, which present several different options for the first section of your hike. Read the signs at each junction carefully to stay on track. In general, follow signs that give the shortest distance to Battleship Lake. This area is a popular destination for day hikers and backpackers staying at one of the popular campgrounds in the Forbidden Plateau Core Area. (See Trips 18 and 19.)

For the most direct route, turn right at the **first junction** and follow it past several small ponds to a **second junction.** Go left here, following a boardwalk alongside a pond. At the third **junction,** turn right onto the **Crooked Creek Trail,** then turn right again at the next **junction** to continue towards Battleship Lake.

Follow the trail up a small hill. At the top, several spur trails lead to viewpoints on the shores of **Battleship Lake.** The path parallels the lake to another junction at 3.7 km (2.3 mi). Turning right here will take you downhill to the **Lake Helen Mackenzie campground.** Continue straight on the trail as it passes the end of Battleship Lake and then heads up a short, steep hill to Lady Lake. Next, follow the trail downhill to the group campsite at **Croteau Lake,** at the 6.1 km (3.8 mi) mark.

Past here, the trail switchbacks downhill through the forest into a grassy meadow. Soon after, reach a key **junction with the Forbidden Plateau Trail** at 7.3 km (4.5 mi). You will follow this trail for the rest of your hike. As you

HISTORY

DEBUNKING THE LEGEND OF FORBIDDEN PLATEAU

A popular story says that Forbidden Plateau got its name from a K'ómoks legend. In that legend, goes the story, the K'ómoks sent their women and children up to the plateau while they fought off raiding parties from other coastal Indigenous groups. On one occasion the women and children vanished, and the K'ómoks believed they had been eaten by evil spirits. It became taboo to visit the plateau, hence the name. The K'ómoks have no record of this legend in their oral history. In reality, they travelled across the plateau to trap and hunt or to trade. Historians record that Clinton S. Wood, a local businessman and mountaineer, wrote an article about Forbidden Plateau for a Comox newspaper in 1925. To garner more publicity for the area, he added a bit of mystery to the description. The editor of the paper later embellished Wood's story, and after *The Province* newspaper picked it up, the (false) story continued to spread for decades.

turn left at this junction, you will leave the crowds of the core area behind. You are unlikely to encounter many other hikers until you reach the slopes of Mount Becher, near the end of the traverse. (If you want to spend your first night on the trail at **Kwai Lake**, continue straight for 0.5 km/0.3 mi to the campground, then backtrack to this junction in the morning.)

From the junction, the Forbidden Plateau Trail descends slightly through grassy meadows and past small ponds. At the 8.2 km (5.1 mi) mark, a carved wooden sign marks a trail to **Mariwood Lake**, leaving to the right. Carry on through more sections of meadows interspersed with forest. The trail bed is narrower than it was in the core area, but it remains distinct and easy to follow. In places, weathered plank bridges carry you over muddy areas. You can thank the Comox District Mountaineering Club for these, as well as other improvements, along the way. Volunteers from the club are responsible for trail maintenance here.

Arrive at a **junction** marked with many carved wooden signs at the 9 km (5.6 mi) mark. Turn left and cross a small creek, following signs for the Wood Mountain ski area. The creek you just crossed is the outlet for **Panther Lake**. John Brown, a 1920s prospector, gave the lake its name after he was treed by a family of cougars here. (Cougars are sometimes referred to as panthers.) If you want to go for a dip or fish for rainbow trout, take the faint trail to the right before the creek. Your trail parallels the eastern shoreline for a minute before heading into a denser forest out of sight of the lake. The route gains elevation as it contours the side of the hill above the lake, then follows a draw up to a saddle, with a **junction** at 10 km (6.2 mi). If you want a quick side trip, go left to **Johnston Lake**. It is periodically stocked with rainbow trout.

The main trail curls south and climbs onto a rocky bluff before turning east again. Follow the trail as it undulates across a plateau with an open forest and lots of clearings. At 11.5 km (7.1 mi) a **large clearing with a pond** to the north makes a great place to take a break.

Continuing onward, the trail dips through the forest, then turns north across a rock outcropping. From here, the trail begins to descend beside a **steep-sided canyon** with interesting volcanic rocks. After a few minutes, the path swings away from the canyon and descends more gently, passing more ponds interspersed with thickets of trees. After the final pond, the trail swings north and plunges downhill in a thicker forest of amabilis fir and mountain hemlock. In late summer and fall, watch for many types of mushrooms here, especially in the days immediately following a rainstorm. You may spot several huge bolete varieties, some of which can be over 25 cm (9.8 in) across! Keep in mind that you are in a provincial park, where mushroom picking is prohibited.

As the trail descends through the forest, it crosses two rocky creeks. Both are unbridged but should be easy to cross and nearly dry in the summer. At the 14 km (8.7 mi) mark, reach a **junction** marked with flagging and several signs. If you plan to camp at **McKenzie Lake**, 0.5 km (0.3 mi) away, turn left just past the sign and follow the overgrown trail through salmonberry bushes and brush to a meadow with shoulder-high grass. The route through the meadow may seem hard to locate, but look carefully for a depression in the grass that hides a firm footbed below. As you walk through the meadow the long grass obscures your feet, so step carefully. The trail stays on the left edge of the meadow and is marked with flagging on tall bushes in a few places. Then it leaves the grassy area and heads into the forest. The campsite at the south end of McKenzie Lake is just a few minutes away. The lake is named after John McKenzie, the mayor of Courtenay in the late 1920s.

Back on the main trail, the traverse route continues straight from the McKenzie Lake junction. It heads southeast through a brushy forest over several fallen logs and then begins to sidehill around the back of McKenzie Meadows, which you can see to your left through the trees. At 14.8 km (9.2 mi), arrive at another signed **junction**. The path to the left is an older route that cuts through the middle of **McKenzie Meadows**, back towards McKenzie Lake. However, it travels through boggy and ecologically fragile terrain, so the meadows bypass route you took is a more responsible choice.

From the junction, the trail makes a rising traverse to the southeast through a beautiful old-growth subalpine forest. Follow a marked side trail at the 15.8 km (9.8 mi) mark uphill for a few minutes to a splendid **viewpoint** atop a bluff. From here you can look down to your campsite at McKenzie Lake, with Douglas Lake beside it to the west. In the northwest, you can see the ski hill at Mount Washington. Look due west to the summit of Mount Albert Edward, Castlecrag Mountain, and the snow-capped summits of the Comox Range.

A few minutes later, the main trail passes a few grassy ponds, then begins working its way southwest through a forest with lots of blueberry bushes in the understorey. The trail was originally built for horses, so the grade is fairly gentle. At 17.7 km (11 mi), arrive at a signed **junction**. A trail to **Slingshot Meadows** and the logging roads beyond descends to your right. The path to the left leads to **Drabble Lakes**, a pleasant 10-minute detour. Continue straight on the main trail as it hugs the steep north side of Mount Becher. In a few places, you can spot rocky cliffs uphill to your right through the trees.

Just after a small meadow, arrive at a prominent **junction** with the trail to the top of **Mount Becher**, at 20.6 km (12.8 mi). The route to the summit is a popular day hike for locals and a worthwhile addition to the traverse. (See Extending Your Trip for details.) Pronounced "Beecher," the mountain is

Hiking through the tall grass near McKenzie Lake. Photo: Reid Holmes

named after Rear Admiral Alexander Bridport Becher, who was a surveying officer in the British navy in the 1800s.

From the junction, continue straight towards the old Forbidden Plateau ski area. Within a few minutes, the trail widens into an old cat track as it descends gently, passing a few ponds and brushy areas. At 22.2 km (13.8 mi), emerge at the **top of the old ski runs**. Turn left and follow the old ski access roads downhill for almost 2 km (1.2 mi) to the parking lot and **trailhead**. The old ski runs present a few options for the descent, but the most direct route follows the widest road, which generally heads east. Thanks to clean-up efforts between 2017 and 2019, the crumbling infrastructure of the former ski area has been removed, but it will take a few decades for the vegetation to recover.

CAMPING

The first leg of this trip (west of Johnston Lake) is in the Forbidden Plateau Core Area of Strathcona Provincial Park. In that zone, you must camp at designated campgrounds and pay camping fees. On the rest of the trail, you may camp anywhere for free. However, the most ethical option is to stay at the designated campground at McKenzie Lake.

The traverse is commonly completed as an overnight trip, camping at McKenzie Lake. But parties on a 2-night trip could plan to stay in the

Forbidden Plateau Core Area on the first night. Alternatively, you can do an out-and-back trip from either trailhead to McKenzie Lake. The western side is more aesthetically pleasing, but the eastern half has the bonus of an optional summit of Mount Becher.

FORBIDDEN PLATEAU CORE AREA CAMPGROUNDS

There are two campgrounds in the core area that are good options for a first night's camp: Lake Helen Mackenzie and Kwai Lake. Find more details in Trip 18. You must pay camping fees at these sites.

Campsites: Fifteen at Kwai, and 10 at Helen Mackenzie
Toilets: Each campsite has a urine-diversion toilet
Water: Collect from the lake at each site
Food Storage: Each site has food lockers

MCKENZIE LAKE CAMPGROUND

Not to be confused with Lake Helen Mackenzie in the core area, this campground sits on the south shore of a sinuous subalpine lake. There is good swimming and an interesting historical cabin just a few minutes' walk away, at neighbouring Douglas Lake.

The old cabin at Douglas Lake

Campsites: Room for 3 or 4 tents in dirt clearings. There is also 1 site at nearby Douglas Lake that will fit 1 or 2 tents.

Toilets: Two plastic throne-style pit toilets—one on a spur trail behind the campsite and the other next to the Douglas Lake cabin

Water: Collect from McKenzie or Douglas Lakes

Food Storage: None. The trees do not have long enough branches to make a proper bear hang, so bring a bear canister or Ursack.

Other Amenities: The tiny Douglas Lake cabin has a small counter and 1 rudimentary wooden bunk.

EXTENDING YOUR TRIP

Mount Becher: From the top, there are great views of the Comox area and the Strait of Georgia to the east, and the peaks of the Comox Range to the southwest. The trail climbs steeply above the treeline with a few rope-assisted scrambles to the peak. From the junction with the Forbidden Plateau Trail, it is a 3.5 km (2.2 mi) round trip to the summit, with about 300 m (984 ft) of elevation gain.

Helen Mackenzie, Kwai, and Circlet Lakes: Add an extra night or two to your trip by combining this trip with Trip 18 or 19. Be sure to allow time to complete the worthwhile day hikes to Mount Albert Edward and Cruickshank Canyon.

Augerpoint Traverse: Plan an epic 4- to 7-day, 55.5 km (34.5 mi) trip through Strathcona Provincial Park by beginning at the old Forbidden Plateau ski area, hiking through the Forbidden Plateau Core Area to Circlet Lake (Trip 19), then completing the Augerpoint Traverse (Trip 20) to Buttle Lake.

FURTHER RESOURCES

Strathcona Provincial Park: info and fees *bcparks.ca/explore/parkpgs/strath*

Trail Map: Forbidden Plateau Trails Map, Strathcona Wilderness Institute

NTS Map: 092F11

18

HELEN MACKENZIE AND KWAI LAKES LOOP

BACKPACKING TRIP | Trail map on p. 162

Difficulty: ●
Duration: 2 to 3 days
Distance: 8.3 to 15.4 km (5.2 to 9.6 mi) loop

Elevation Gain: 190 m (623 ft)
High Point: 1270 m (4167 ft)
Best Months: July to September

Fees and Reservations: Camping fees are $10/person/night payable online or in cash at the trailhead. All campsites are first-come, first-served.

Regulations: No fires. No drones. No smoking, vaping, or cannabis. Dogs permitted on leash. No swimming in Kwai Lake.

Caution: Campgrounds in this area can be very busy on weekends. Arrive early to ensure you get a spot.

THIS EASY LOOP through subalpine lakes in the popular core area of Strathcona Provincial Park is an ideal introduction to the Forbidden Plateau. The paved road to the Paradise Meadows trailhead at the Mount Washington ski area makes for the easiest access to Vancouver Island's mountains. Gentle terrain and non-technical trails are perfect for beginners, families, and those who prefer a laid-back multi-day outing. And choices abound: choose from a long or short loop hike, each with its own lakeside campground. You can also add a day hike to your trip or connect with Trips 17, 19, and 20 for a longer backpacking trip. Many of the small lakes in the area are stocked with rainbow trout, which make a delicious addition to any backcountry dinner.

GETTING THERE
Refer to the Paradise Meadows driving directions in Trip 17 (page 146).

TRAIL

TRIP PLANNER

0 km (0 mi)	Paradise Meadows trailhead
2.8 km (1.7 mi)	Battleship Lake
3.7 km (2.3 mi)	Lake Helen Mackenzie junction (east)
7.8 km (4.8 mi)	Kwai Lake campground

Easy hiking on the boardwalk through Paradise Meadows

12.1 km (7.5 mi)	Lake Helen Mackenzie junction (west)
15.4 km (9.6 mi)	Paradise Meadows trailhead

The Forbidden Plateau area has a fantastic network of trails. This trip uses beginner-friendly paths in the core area to make two linked clockwise loops. The shorter loop is 8.3 km (5.2 mi) and includes camping at Lake Helen Mackenzie. Stay overnight at Kwai Lake on the longer 15.4 km (9.6 mi) loop. You can also venture farther into the area on the Forbidden Plateau Traverse (Trip 17), the ascent of Mount Albert Edward from Circlet Lake (Trip 19), or the Augerpoint Traverse (Trip 20).

Start your hike at the **trailhead** next to the Strathcona Wilderness Institute (SWI) Visitor Information Centre. Staffed by volunteers, this is a great place to get the latest weather report, trail conditions, and information on animal sightings or flowers in bloom.

The first section of the path through the ponds of Paradise Meadows is a mix of wide gravel trail and boardwalk. Thanks to the efforts of BC Parks, the Rotary Club of Campbell River, and the SWI, this portion of the trail system is wheelchair accessible. On the boardwalk sections, small metal ramps on each stair allow the TrailRider, a single-tire off-road wheelchair, to ascend and descend smoothly. Contact the SWI to arrange to use the TrailRider.

In June and July, watch for wildflowers, especially blue lupines, white and pink heather, red paintbrush, and pink and yellow monkeyflower. Within a few minutes, arrive at the first of many junctions. Read signs at trail junctions carefully to stay on track. Turn right here for the most direct route. (Left is the Centennial Loop Trail along Paradise Creek.) Continue along the wide trail past several small ponds to the **Paradise Ponds junction**. Turn left, following signs for Battleship Lake. The trail to the right is your return route.

Just ahead, reach a **junction with the Crooked Creek loop** trail. Stay right at this junction and the next one to continue towards Battleship Lake. The path climbs a hill forested in yellow-cedar, amabilis fir, and mountain hemlock before emerging in an open marshy area. It's just a few minutes from here to **Battleship Lake**. Follow spur trails to several viewpoints at the north end of the lake. This is a fabulous spot for an extended break, and there's an outhouse along the main trail. Several long, low islands dot the waters, their boat-like shape giving the lake its name. From here you'll leave the wheelchair-accessible trail and head onto more rugged backcountry trails.

The trail roughly parallels the western shore of Battleship Lake, which you can glimpse through the trees. About 3.7 km (2.3 mi) from the trailhead, arrive at the **junction with the Lake Helen Mackenzie Trail**. If you want to camp at Kwai Lake and complete the longer loop, stay on the main trail. To camp at Lake Helen Mackenzie and hike the shorter loop, turn right. The campground is just 0.3 km (0.2 mi) away, on a spur trail. To complete the shorter loop, continue along the Lake Helen Mackenzie trail from the campground for a further 1.1 km (0.7 mi), then turn right to head back to the trailhead via the Paradise Ponds junction. The lake is named after Helen Maud Hutton

NATURE NOTE

IDENTIFYING PLANTS IN PARADISE MEADOWS

With many species abundant in the area, Paradise Meadows and the trails of Forbidden Plateau are perfect places to practise plant identification. Beginners may recognize common wildflowers like red heather, lupine, and fireweed. But as your skills sharpen, you may be able to spot green false hellebore, leatherleaf saxifrage, partridgefoot, mountain arnica, globeflower, and countless others. Plant ID apps like iNaturalist or field guides like *Plants of Coastal British Columbia* by Jim Pojar and Andy MacKinnon can be very helpful.

Mackenzie. She and her uncle, Lieutenant Governor Robert Randolph Bruce, were present at the formal opening of trails into the Forbidden Meadows area in 1929.

If you are continuing to Kwai Lake, follow the trail south as it heads past the end of Battleship Lake, then past tiny Kooso Lake on your right. The path climbs a short but steep hill before arriving at Lady Lake, set in a thick forest. Descend gradually through the trees to **Croteau Lake** at the 6.1 km (3.8 mi) mark. A large campground with a yurt is available only to large groups that have made a reservation. The present-day campground is the latest in a series of group camps at the lake. It is named after Eugene Croteau, who operated the Croteau Guest Camp here in the 1930s. To take a break at Croteau Lake, follow the trail across the bridge at the lake outlet, then take a spur trail to your right to explore the lakeshore.

Past the lake, the trail descends into a narrow grassy meadow. On the other side, arrive at the **junction with the Forbidden Plateau Trail**, which leads to McKenzie Meadows and beyond to the trailhead at the old Wood Mountain ski area (Trip 17).

Continue straight as the trail descends through the forest to **Kwai Lake campground**, 7.8 km (4.8 mi) from the trailhead. Pass spur trails to campsites as you stay on the trail around the lake. The word *kwai* is believed to be an anglicized version of the Quw'utsun (Cowichan) word for wood. The lake may be named to honour Clinton S. Wood and his family, who pioneered modern hiking trails through Forbidden Plateau. On the south side of Kwai Lake, arrive at a **junction**. Heading left takes you to Mariwood Lake and **Cruickshank Canyon**, both worthwhile side trips. It's also one option for heading to **Circlet Lake** and Mount Albert Edward (Trip 19).

Stay on the main trail as it climbs a forested ridge to another **junction**. Going left would take you to **Hairtrigger Lake and Circlet Lake** (Trip 19), but your route heads right through subalpine meadows dotted with tiny ponds. Pass by the **ranger station** around 1.5 km (0.9 mi) from Kwai Lake. On calm days, the small tarn in front of the cabin has stunning reflections.

Past the ranger station, the trail continues across more mixed forests and meadows before heading into a dense forest as it descends steeply towards the southwest corner of Lake Helen Mackenzie. The trail is a little rougher in this section, so watch your step on the rocks, mud, and tree roots. You'll catch glimpses of the water as the route contours along the hillside on the west side of the lake. However, the path doesn't descend to lake level until you reach a junction and an outhouse at the north end.

Continue straight to head back towards the trailhead. (Turning right here takes you on the connector trail to the east side of the loop and **Lake Helen**

Mackenzie campground.) The path descends quickly in the trees beside the lake's outlet stream before emerging in a marshy area with boardwalks and several small ponds. Follow the trail back into the trees as it hugs the side of a ridge. Reach the **Paradise Ponds junction** again 6.6 km (4.1 mi) from Kwai Lake Camp. It's an easy walk on familiar terrain back to the **trailhead** from here: just keep left at both junctions.

CAMPING

There are two campgrounds on this route, both of which can be incorporated into a loop hike. Lake Helen Mackenzie is a good option if you're short on time and stamina. Kwai Lake is a little farther and makes a good base camp for day hikes along the plateau.

LAKE HELEN MACKENZIE CAMPGROUND

Set at the northeast corner of the lake, this campground is off the main trail and can be quieter than others in the area. It also has good swimming.

Campsites: Ten sites on wooden platforms on a loop trail
Toilet: Urine-diversion outhouse at the top of the campground
Water: Collect from the lake
Food Storage: Food locker near the outhouse

KWAI LAKE CAMPGROUND

Tiny Kwai Lake is a gorgeous place, especially when the air is still enough for mirror-like reflections.

Campsites: Space for about 15 tents on a mix of wooden platforms and dirt tent pads on the east side of the lake. A small informal overflow area on the north side of the lake will hold a few more tents.
Toilet: Urine-diversion toilet on the east side of the lake
Water: Collect from the lake
Food Storage: Food locker near the outhouse

EXTENDING YOUR TRIP

Mariwood Lake: Kwai Lake is the water source for the campground, so you can't swim in it, but you can take a dip in nearby Mariwood Lake. It's an easy 1.5 km (0.9 mi) round-trip hike to the lake.

Cruickshank Canyon Lookout: This viewpoint makes a great side trip from Kwai Lake. It is a 4.5 km (2.8 mi) round trip with 60 m (197 ft) of elevation gain, the trail winding past several picturesque lakes before ending on a sheer cliff high above the Cruickshank River. Clear-cuts in the valley bottom (outside the park) somewhat mar the view, but the vistas of rocky Castlecrag Mountain and Moat Lake make up for it.

Lake Helen Mackenzie seen from the campground

McKenzie Lake and the Forbidden Plateau Traverse: Combine this outing with Trip 17, either by day hiking to McKenzie Lake and back (16 km/10 mi round trip from Kwai Lake) or camping there, then thru-hiking all the way to the old Forbidden Plateau ski area to make a one-way traverse.

Circlet Lake and Mount Albert Edward: Circlet Lake is 3.8 km (2.4 mi) one way from Kwai Lake, making it a good day trip destination. Or combine this outing with Trip 19 to spend a few more nights in the area and summit Mount Albert Edward.

FURTHER RESOURCES

Strathcona Provincial Park: info and fees *bcparks.ca/explore/parkpgs/strath*
Trail Map: Forbidden Plateau Trails Map, Strathcona Wilderness Institute
NTS Map: 092F11

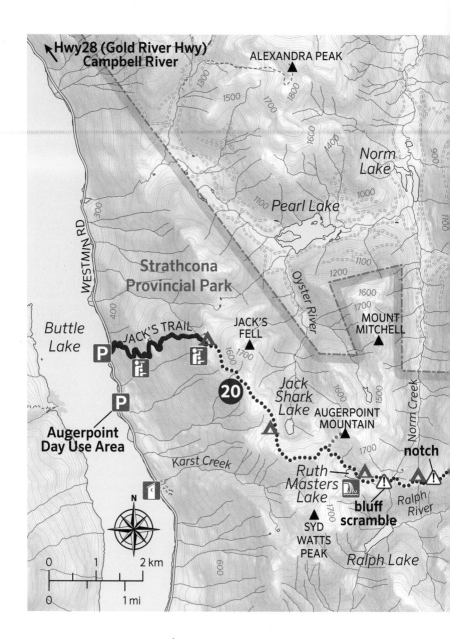

Hwy28 (Gold River Hwy)
Campbell River

ALEXANDRA PEAK

Norm Lake

Pearl Lake

Strathcona Provincial Park

WESTMIN RD

Buttle Lake

JACK'S TRAIL

JACK'S FELL

Oyster River

MOUNT MITCHELL

Augerpoint Day Use Area

Jack Shark Lake

AUGERPOINT MOUNTAIN

Norm Creek

notch

Karst Creek

Ruth Masters Lake

bluff scramble

Ralph River

N

SYD WATTS PEAK

Ralph Lake

0   1   2 km

0   1 mi

17 FORBIDDEN PLATEAU TRAVERSE I p. 146

18 HELEN MACKENZIE AND KWAI LAKES LOOP I p. 154

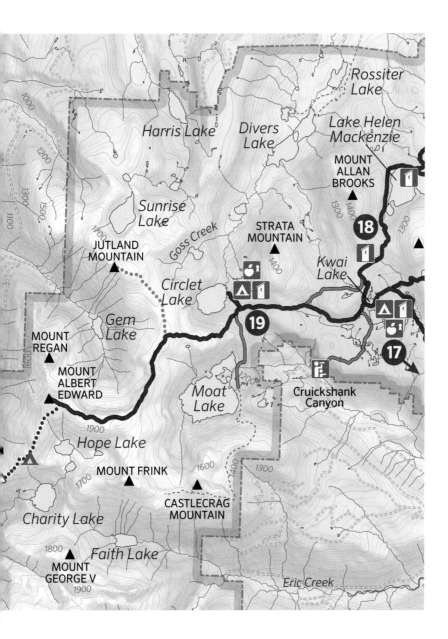

19 CIRCLET LAKE AND MOUNT ALBERT EDWARD | p. 164

20 AUGERPOINT TRAVERSE | p. 168

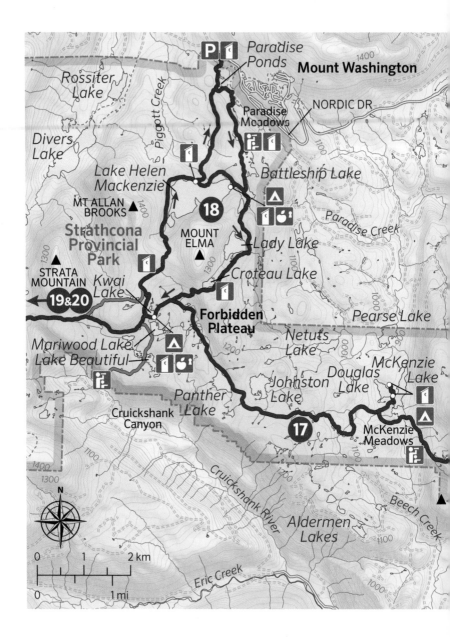

17 FORBIDDEN PLATEAU TRAVERSE | p. 146

18 HELEN MACKENZIE AND KWAI LAKES LOOP | p. 154

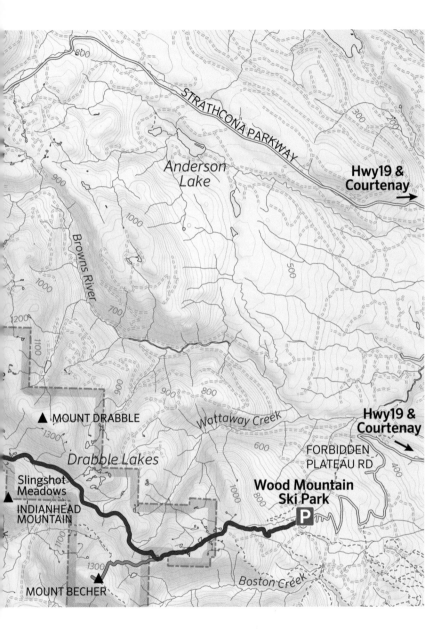

19 CIRCLET LAKE AND MOUNT ALBERT EDWARD | p. 164

20 AUGERPOINT TRAVERSE | p. 168

CIRCLET LAKE AND MOUNT ALBERT EDWARD ⭐

BACKPACKING TRIP | Trail map on p. 161–62

Difficulty: ■
Duration: 2 to 3 days
Distance: 22.6 km (14 mi) round trip

Elevation Gain: 195 m (640 ft)
High Point: 1230 m (4035 ft)
Best Months: July to September

Fees and Reservations: Camping fees are $10/person/night payable online or in cash at the trailhead. All campsites are first-come, first-served.

Regulations: No fires. No drones. No smoking, vaping, or cannabis. Dogs permitted on leash.

Caution: Circlet Lake campground can be very busy on weekends. Arrive early to ensure you get a spot.

HIKE DEEP INTO the core of the Forbidden Plateau area in Strathcona Provincial Park to camp on the shores of Circlet Lake. From there, tackle the arduous (but worthwhile) trek to the summit of Mount Albert Edward. The trip takes you past numerous tarns and lakes as you meander through subalpine meadows. Set up camp at picturesque Circlet Lake, a great spot for a swim. With a daypack full of snacks and water, set off into the alpine to follow cairns across rock outcroppings and then along the treeless and snowy ridge to the peak, the sixth-highest mountain on Vancouver Island.

GETTING THERE

Refer to the Paradise Meadows driving directions in Trip 17 (page 146).

TRAIL

TRIP PLANNER

0 km (0 mi)	Paradise Meadows trailhead
0.3 km (0.2 mi)	Centennial Loop Trail junction
1 km (0.6 mi)	Paradise Ponds junction
1.2 km (0.7 mi)	Crooked Creek Loop junction (north)
1.6 km (1 mi)	Crooked Creek Loop junction (south)
2.8 km (1.7 mi)	Battleship Lake
3.7 km (2.3 mi)	Lake Helen Mackenzie junction (east)
6.1 km (3.8 mi)	Croteau Lake

Looking south to Castlecrag Mountain from the meadows near Circlet Lake

7.3 km (4.5 mi)	Forbidden Plateau Trail junction
7.8 km (4.8 mi)	Kwai Lake campground
8.1 km (5 mi)	Kwai Lake junction
8.3 km (5.2 mi)	Cruickshank Canyon junction
9.7 km (6 mi)	Hairtrigger Lake junction
11 km (6.8 mi)	Circlet Lake camp junction
11.3 km (7 mi)	Circlet Lake campground

There are two possible routes through the network of trails at Paradise Meadows to reach Circlet Lake. The eastern route via Kwai Lake is 1.5 km (0.9 mi) longer but has smoother trails, gentler hills, and arguably more pleasant scenery. That is the recommended route described here. If you wish, you can take the western route back to the trailhead via Hairtrigger Lake, the ranger station, and Lake Helen Mackenzie, as described in Trip 18.

The beginning of this trip up to Kwai Lake is described in Trip 18 (page 154). From the **trailhead**, follow signs for **Battleship Lake**, then Kwai Lake. From the **Kwai Lake campground**, follow the trail southwest around the lake to a **junction**. Turn left and head downhill, following signs for Circlet Lake. Arrive at another **junction** at 8.3 km (5.2 mi). Stay right to continue towards Circlet Lake. (Left goes to the Cruickshank Canyon viewpoint.)

The summit ridge of Mount Albert Edward

The trail curls to the west, meandering past small ponds through Whiskey Meadows. At 9.7 km (6 mi), reach a **junction**. Your route to Circlet Lake continues to the left. The trail to the right is the optional return route via Hairtrigger Lake. The trail climbs a small rise through patches of intermittent forest, then descends slightly to a final **junction** at 11 km (6.8 mi).

Turn right to follow a wet trail next to a small pond to the **Circlet Lake campground**. In the 1920s, prospector John Brown named it Circle Lake, a reference to its shape. In 1939, Circlet Lake was adopted as its official name, perhaps because the lake sits within a cirque. The lake is sporadically stocked with rainbow trout, so you might choose to pack in a fishing rod. The main trail continues onward to Mount Albert Edward, a worthwhile day hike objective.

CAMPING

Picturesque Circlet Lake is nestled up against steep rock walls below Jutland Mountain. The campground sprawls along the eastern shore and is a rewarding destination on its own. The lakeside day-use area makes a great swimming spot. But most hikers use it as a base camp for the challenging day hike to the summit of Mount Albert Edward.

Campsites: Sixty campsites spread out between the upper pond and the eastern shore of the lake, connected by a spiderweb of trails
Toilets: Two outhouses, one near the pond and another near the north end of the campground
Water: Collect from Circlet Lake or the pond
Food Storage: Food lockers near the outhouses
Other Amenities: Dishwashing sinks with greywater drains, near the outhouses

EXTENDING YOUR TRIP

Mount Albert Edward: At 2093 m (6867 ft), Mount Albert Edward is the sixth-highest mountain on Vancouver Island. The summit is a 12 km (7.5 mi) round-trip hike, with 880 m (2887 ft) of elevation gain from the Circlet Lake campground junction. The initial climb is steep and rough as you gain the ridge crest, then head south up a series of rocky steps. The final push swings around to the west. The route can be hard to follow in places, even with frequent cairns to mark the way, so do not attempt this hike in poor weather. For a full description, see the beginning of Trip 20 (page 168).

Moat Lake: The shoreline of Moat Lake is incredibly picturesque, with a rock island rising out of the lake and the crenellated summits of Castlecrag Mountain and Mount Frink looming behind. The lake is 1.5 km (0.9 mi) from the Circlet Lake campground junction. Follow the trail towards Mount Albert Edward for 0.15 km (0.1 mi), then turn left on a less-trodden trail marked with a wooden sign for Moat Lake. A faint route continues past the lakeshore towards Castlecrag, but it involves a lot of route-finding and some easy scrambling so is best left for mountaineers and experienced hikers.

Augerpoint Traverse: This hike to Circlet Lake makes up the first leg of the Augerpoint Traverse (Trip 20), a 31.5 km (19.6 mi) point-to-point hike through less-travelled terrain in the craggy heart of Strathcona Park, finishing on the shores of Buttle Lake.

FURTHER RESOURCES

Strathcona Provincial Park: info and fees *bcparks.ca/explore/parkpgs/strath*
Trail Map: Forbidden Plateau Trails Map, Strathcona Wilderness Institute
NTS Map: 092F11

NATURE NOTE

VANCOUVER ISLAND WHITE-TAILED PTARMIGAN

As you climb across the rocky slopes of Mount Albert Edward, see if you can spot a Vancouver Island white-tailed ptarmigan. These chubby birds are about 30 cm (12 in) tall. In the summer, they have grey-brown plumage that provides clever camouflage against the rocks and distinctive white feathers on their tails and feet, and the edges of their wings. In the winter, the ptarmigan transition to all-white feathers so they don't stand out against the snow. These unique birds live only on high-elevation mountains on Vancouver Island. Due to low population density and declining habitat, they are a species of special concern in B.C. If you see one of these rare birds, give it plenty of space to avoid interfering with its natural behaviour.

20

AUGERPOINT TRAVERSE ★

BACKPACKING TRIP | Trail maps on pp. 160–62

Difficulty: ♦♦
Duration: 2 to 5 days
Distance: 31.5 km (19.6 mi) one way

Elevation Gain: 1013 m (3323 ft)
High Point: 2093 m (6867 ft)
Best Months: Mid-July to September

Fees and Reservations: Camping fees are $10/person/night payable online or in cash at the trailhead for campsites in the core area. All other campsites are free. All campsites are first-come, first-served.

Regulations: No fires. No drones. No smoking, vaping, or cannabis. Dogs permitted on leash but not recommended due to scrambly sections.

Caution: This is a very rugged route, with scrambling sections and exposure to heights. The section between Mount Albert Edward and the top of Jack's Trail is a sporadically marked route, not a trail. This trip is recommended only for fit and experienced hikers with experience in off-trail navigation. Do not attempt this trip in snowy conditions unless you have mountaineering skills and avalanche training.

CHALLENGE YOURSELF WITH this partially off-trail traverse through the alpine heart of Strathcona Provincial Park. The route begins at Paradise Meadows, then travels above the treeline to the summit of Mount Albert Edward, the sixth-highest mountain on Vancouver Island. From there, use infrequent flagging and cairns, along with your map and compass skills, to chart a path downhill to spectacular Ruth Masters Lake. Continue navigating off-trail along the flanks of Augerpoint Mountain and Jack's Fell and past tiny alpine tarns, before plunging downhill on Jack's Trail to finish on the shores of Buttle Lake.

GETTING THERE

The Augerpoint Traverse is usually hiked as a one-way point-to-point hike. You will need to arrange to have someone pick you up at the end, or park a second vehicle at the other trailhead. You can also arrange to have a shuttle service take you to and from the trailheads.

Hiking from east to west is more popular because it involves less overall elevation gain (1013 m/3323 ft of net elevation gain and 1818 m/5965 ft of net descent). That's the direction described below. If you start in the west, you can reverse those statistics.

PARADISE MEADOWS TRAILHEAD

Refer to the Paradise Meadows driving directions in Trip 17 (page 146).

Descending the south ridge of Mount Albert Edward

BUTTLE LAKE TRAILHEAD

From Campbell River, take Highway 28 west for 47 km (29.2 mi) into Strathcona Provincial Park. At the T-junction, continue straight onto Westmin Road and zero your odometer. Continue for another 19.5 km (12.1 mi) to a gravel pullout on the right side marked with flagging tape and a large blue arrow on the road. The Augerpoint day-use area is 1 km (0.6 mi) farther up the road and has additional parking.

TRAIL

TRIP PLANNER

0 km (0 mi)	Paradise Meadows trailhead
11 km (6.8 mi)	Circlet Lake campground junction
13 km (8.1 mi)	Jutland–Mount Albert Edward junction
17 km (10.6 mi)	Mount Albert Edward summit
18 km (11.2 mi)	Upper Albert Edward ridge informal camping area
19.7 km (12.2 mi)	Lower Albert Edward ridge informal camping area
21.5 km (13.4 mi)	Ruth Masters Lake informal camping area
24.5 km (15.2 mi)	Saddle informal camping area
27 km (16.8 mi)	Top of Jack's Trail informal camping area
31.5 km (19.6 mi)	Buttle Lake trailhead

The interconnected trail network beginning at the **Paradise Meadows trailhead** provides several different options for the first leg of this trip. The smoother trails, gentler hills, and superior scenery make it easy to recommend a route on the eastern side of the circuit via **Battleship Lake** and **Kwai Lake** to Circlet Lake, despite it being slightly longer than other possibilities. The first 11 km (6.8 mi) of this trip to the Circlet Lake campground junction are described in Trips 18 and 19.

From the **Circlet Lake campground junction**, continue on the main trail towards Mount Albert Edward as it climbs through an open forest and meadow. A few minutes later, at 11.2 km (7 mi), ignore a faint trail branching left to **Moat Lake**. Stay on the main trail as it ascends steeply over a rough footbed through thinning trees. The grade eases as you reach an undulating **plateau** sprinkled with ponds at 1500 m (4921 ft) elevation, about 12 km (7.5 mi) from the trailhead. This is a good place to catch your breath and enjoy views to the southeast of Moat Lake and Castlecrag Mountain.

Several unmarked trails cross the plateau, so take care to stick to the most obvious one. It curls around to the east to start a rocky climb to a ridge crest. As you emerge above the treeline, metal posts with reflective markers show the route. The route beyond here to the summit of Mount Albert Edward can be confusing in poor visibility. This area has been the subject of many search-and-rescue incidents. Watch carefully for cairns, footbeds, and metal markers as you hike. A GPS or map and compass are essential for navigation beyond this point, no matter the weather.

HISTORY

WHO WAS RUTH MASTERS?

Ruth Masters led an adventurous and passionate life. She joined the Comox District Mountaineering Club in the 1930s and remained a member until she died in 2017 at age 97. Masters first climbed Comox Glacier at age 18 and led hiking trips into the mountains of Vancouver Island for decades. She proposed formal names for over 50 features in Strathcona Park and the Beaufort Range, many honouring locals who died in World War II. Her iconic carved trail signs are found throughout the park. As a wilderness activist, she campaigned against trophy hunting and mining in Strathcona Provincial Park in the 1980s (page 205) and championed local issues in the Comox Valley. She signed her protest letters to politicians with "S.S.D.," meaning "Senior Shit Disturber." In 2004 she donated 7.3 ha (18 acres) of her property along the Puntledge River in Courtenay to create the Masters Greenway and Wildlife Corridor.

Reach the ridge crest at 13 km (8.1 mi) and arrive at a large stone cairn with carved wooden signs pointing left (south) towards Mount Albert Edward and right (north) to **Jutland Mountain**. Turn left and follow the ridge as it climbs gradually through rocky terrain interspersed with tenacious patches of heather. About 14 km (8.7 mi) along, the path dips slightly as it rounds the back of a rocky cleft. The sheer sides of Mount Albert Edward and Jutland Mountain drop precipitously to tiny Gem Lake below.

Continue gradually upward along the cairned route. In places, you'll scramble upwards over natural rock steps, but for the most part the path winds through gravel and dirt. About 15 km (9.3 mi) from the start, the path begins to swing due west as you approach the final summit ridge. This portion of the ridge is very gentle, a welcome reprieve from the tough ascent earlier. Snow patches may linger late into summer, perhaps creating a fleeting melt-water tarn that will allow you to refill your bottles. If walking through snow, take care to remain in the centre of the ridge, because dangerous cornices can form on the north side.

After a final push up a steep and rocky slope marked with orange spray-painted rocks, reach the **summit of Mount Albert Edward**, 17 km (10.6 mi) from the Paradise Meadows trailhead. Drink in the lofty views of the Salish Sea and the Comox Valley to the east and south and the mountains of Strathcona Provincial Park to the west. The mountain is named after Albert Edward, the Prince of Wales who went on to become King Edward VII.

Past here, you will be following the occasional flag, cairn, or beaten boot track as you navigate the central off-trail portion of the Augerpoint Traverse. You can drop directly off the summit and head south down the ridge. An alternative is to backtrack a few minutes down the main trail to 2000 m (6562 ft) elevation, then follow that contour around the side of the peak to the apex of the southwest ridge. The route takes a steep and direct line down the ridge through talus slopes and rock outcroppings. Watch for cairns to help you find the gentlest route through some rock steps and micro-terrain.

Don't forget to look up from careful footwork on the descent to enjoy the views. Ralph Lake and the headwaters of the Ralph River are straight ahead of you, dropping down into Buttle Lake in the distance. To the east, you can see Hope and Charity Lakes below Mount Frink. Look west to Ruth Masters Lake in a hanging valley, with Augerpoint Mountain above it to the north, both farther along on your route. A few shelves on the ridge hold small seasonal ponds and flat areas that can work as **campsites**. The first option is at 1800 m (5906 ft), about 18 km (11.2 mi) from the trailhead.

Continue working your way down the ridge, following cairns to choose the best path. About 19.5 km (12.1 mi) from the trailhead, at 1475 m (4839 ft) elevation, pay close attention to cairns and flags to trend left (south) onto a narrow and bushy shelf that leads you around a sheer cliff. Once you are off the ledge, contour back right (west) to follow the faint boot path down a rocky step into a steep-sided **notch**. The final descent into the notch is sheer and slightly exposed, but not very high. Less-confident hikers may wish to remove their packs and pass them down, then spot each other through the drop.

At the bottom of the notch, scramble up a dirt slope into the brush and then onto a rocky bluff at 19.7 km (12.2 mi) and 1440 m (4724 ft) elevation. Some flat ground and small ponds make this another good **camping option**. Continue heading east and downhill into a steep-sided **col** at 1300 m (4364 ft) elevation and 20.1 km (12.5 mi) from the trailhead. Cross the wet meadows north of the pond. It can be tough to locate the trail here, where it disappears into the open forest. A few flags show the way as the trail heads south uphill, paralleling the pond before curving back west.

The route winds upward through a series of open rock bluffs, gullies, and ledges. With a bit of careful route-finding (and perhaps a GPS), it is fairly straightforward to find the pieces of faint boot path that link up short sections of scrambling over rock outcroppings. For the most part, the route is non-technical, but one 8-m-high (26 ft) bluff at 1330 m (4364 ft) can be tricky when wet. This bluff and other parts of this section are much easier to ascend than descend. Less-confident parties completing the traverse in the other direction may appreciate the comfort of a rope.

Reach the top of the climb next to a small pond. Follow a boot path southwest down into a meadow that curves around to reveal a beautiful stream and a small waterfall. The flat ground and clumps of trees at the edge of the meadow provide well-sheltered campsites, but even better options are just ahead at Ruth Masters Lake. A spur trail leads to the bottom of the 15 m (49 ft) waterfall, which is a good place to cool off on hot days. The main path winds through a thicket of trees before emerging on rocks above the waterfall.

Continue alongside the creek, running in a small canyon here, to the cascades that mark the outlet of **Ruth Masters Lake** at 21.5 km (13.4 mi). The lake occupies a cirque, surrounded by cliffs and imposing mountains. Find several great campsites in clearings on the shore of the lake near the outlet. The lake is named after Ruth Masters, a local mountaineer and wilderness activist (page 170).

A path leads across rock bluffs along the east shore of the lake, then through a talus field. After the talus, keep left along the south shore of a small pond with a massive boulder in the middle. Reach the gravel flats at the north end of the lake and look for cairns marking a route uphill to the col between Augerpoint Mountain and an unnamed 1760 m (5774 ft) peak to its left.

Taking an icy dip in Ruth Masters Lake

Sporadic cairns and flagging mark the route up the steep slope. Thick brush and gravel slopes complicate the ascent in a few places, and the route is often indistinct. Choose the gentlest line and keep the col in sight to stay on track.

Reach the **shoulder of Augerpoint Mountain**, 22.6 km (14 mi) from the trailhead. The route turns left and continues to climb up loose scree and over a false summit. Contour around the left side of the ridge on a narrow path to the top of the unnamed 1760 m (5774 ft) peak. The views back towards Ruth Masters Lake from the ascent are incredible. Thankfully, the descent to the west is gentle as you ramble along a nearly flat ridgetop for about 0.5 km (0.3 mi). In an emergency, a few clearings tucked into the trees would make for good, though waterless, campsites.

At the end of the ridge, ascend a small rocky bluff, then descend into a notch above a chute that is snow-filled for most of the year. To avoid the dangerous snow, follow cairns and footbed upslope to the west, then along a treed ledge that runs north for a few minutes. The ledge soon widens to a broad, rocky ridge with patches of gravel. Pick your way down the ridge, following intermittent cairns and aiming for a saddle with a sprinkling of small ponds. Be sure to look right (east) as you descend to spot Jack Shark Lake in

Ruth Masters Lake seen from the shoulder of Augerpoint Mountain

the deep bowl below you, with Augerpoint Mountain and your route across the ridge to the southeast.

Reach the ponds and a few cleared **campsites** at about 24.5 km (15.2 mi) along. To continue, follow faint footbeds and cairns through the trees to the northwest as you climb low-angled slopes to the top of an unnamed 1586 m (5203 ft) peak. As you descend from the peak, look for the first white rectangular markers on trees. You have finished the off-trail portion of the traverse and can follow a good trail to Buttle Lake.

Follow cairns, footbed, and intermittent markers as you descend to the northwest in an open forest. The trail curls around the west flank of Jack's Fell, and in a few places you'll get good views down to Buttle Lake. Jack's Fell and Jack Shark Lake take their name from Jack Shark, a member of the Comox District Mountaineering Club who pioneered many routes and trails in Strathcona Provincial Park, including the Augerpoint Traverse. Cross a creek above a tight rocky canyon, then descend through grassy meadows to a great **camping area** next to a small pond at 27 km (16.8 mi).

Past the pond, Jack's Trail (also named for Jack Shark) begins and plunges very steeply downhill. The trail is often very loose, with pea-sized gravel that challenges you to stay upright at each footstep. There are also several short ledges with sheer drop-offs. Take your time through these sections. The steepest part of the trail is at the 1280 m (4199 ft) elevation; however, the entire descent to Buttle Lake, losing more than 1100 m (3609 ft) in just over 4 km (2.5 mi), is knee-crushing. For the most part, the trail zigzags through tight switchbacks, but the grade does ease slightly on longer switchbacks in the middle section. A **pond** at 860 m (2822 ft) elevation (about 29 km/18 mi from the trailhead) makes a good place to take a break or perhaps sample the abundant blueberries. Two clearings here make it a good emergency campsite too.

Leaving the pond, the trail descends a long switchback to the south, then begins zigzagging again, although not as tightly as higher up the slope. A **viewpoint** at about 30 km (18.6 mi) and 665 m (2182 ft) elevation provides a good vantage point over Buttle Lake and another excuse to take a break. Notice how the vegetation has changed as you descended. Near the top, the rocks were interspersed with stonecrop and phlox and the understorey was dominated by black huckleberries. As the forest closes in and Douglas-fir begins to proliferate lower down, look for red huckleberry bushes and deciduous trees like alder and bigleaf maple. As you approach the end, you will be able to hear cars whizzing by on Westmin Road. The trail spits you out unceremoniously on the shoulder, marking the end of the challenging Augerpoint Traverse.

CAMPING

The first leg of the traverse is in the Forbidden Plateau Core Area of Strathcona Provincial Park, where you must camp in designated campgrounds and pay fees. Once you pass over the summit of Mount Albert Edward, you may camp anywhere for free, but there are no designated campsites or facilities. However, several sites are frequently used.

Fast and experienced parties planning 1 night on the trail should stay at Ruth Masters Lake. For 2 nights, camp at Circlet Lake and Ruth Masters Lake. Most parties will want a 3-night trip, staying at Circlet, Ruth Masters, and Saddle camp or at the top of Jack's Trail. On a more relaxed 4-night trip, stay at Circlet, the shoulder of Albert Edward, Ruth Masters, and Saddle informal camp or Top of Jack's Trail informal camp.

FORBIDDEN PLATEAU CORE AREA CAMPGROUNDS

There are three campgrounds in the core area: Lake Helen Mackenzie, Kwai Lake, and Circlet Lake. Find more details on these campgrounds in Trips 18 and 19. You must pay camping fees at these locations.

Campsites: Sixty sites at Circlet, 15 at Kwai, and 10 at Helen Mackenzie
Toilets: Each campground has 1 or more toilets
Water: Collect from the lake at each campground
Food Storage: Each campground has 1 or more food lockers

SHOULDER OF MOUNT ALBERT EDWARD INFORMAL CAMPING AREAS

The long southwest ridge of Mount Albert Edward has several small plateaus with tiny ponds. They can be quite windy but have several flattish areas for a few tents. The best options are at 1800 m (5906 ft) elevation (18 km/11.2 mi from the trailhead) and 1440 m (4724 ft) elevation (19.6 km/12.2 mi along).

Campsites: There are no clearings at either area. Pitch your tent on flat patches of bare rock or gravel. Avoid camping on the fragile meadows.
Toilet: None. Dig a cat hole and use Leave No Trace best practices. Head downslope of the ponds towards the northeast or southwest sides of the ridge, but watch for cliffs.
Water: Collect from the stagnant and silty ponds. Bring a good filter.
Food Storage: None. The trees are too small to make a bear hang, so bring a bear canister or Ursack.

RUTH MASTERS LAKE INFORMAL CAMPING AREA

Don't miss spending a night at Ruth Masters Lake, a truly special place tucked into a spectacular hanging valley. Swim in the lake, shower under the waterfall, and explore the tarns above the east end of the lake.

Campsites: Three cleared gravel campsites at the lake outlet, plus a few more marginal spots. Room for lots of tents in the more sheltered grassy meadow a few minutes to the east.
Toilet: None. Dig a cat hole and use Leave No Trace best practices. It is impossible to get out of the watershed for the lake, so head well upslope (at least 70 adult paces) and bury your waste well.
Water: Collect from the lake outlet stream
Food Storage: None. The trees are too small to make a proper bear hang, so bring a bear canister or Ursack.

SADDLE INFORMAL CAMPING AREA

A good place for your final night on the traverse. The hollows of the ponds keep you a bit sheltered from the wind, and there are great views of Jack Shark Lake, Augerpoint Mountain, Pearl Peak, and your route from Ruth Masters Lake.

Campsites: Two or 3 cleared gravel sites, plus a few more marginal spots. Avoid camping in the fragile heather meadows.
Toilet: None. Dig a cat hole and use Leave No Trace best practices. Head down the east side of the ridge to avoid contaminating the ponds.
Water: Collect from the ponds
Food Storage: None. The trees are too small to make a proper bear hang, so bring a bear canister or Ursack.

TOP OF JACK'S TRAIL INFORMAL CAMPING AREA

This site next to a small pond is a great first or last night's camp. Wander through the trees to the east to reach a rocky bluff and unparalleled views of Buttle Lake, Flower Ridge (Trip 22) in the southwest, and the snowy tops of Nine Peaks and Big Interior Mountain, near Bedwell Lakes (Trip 23) and Della Falls (Trip 10), in the distance.

Campsites: Three cleared dirt sites, plus more marginal gravel sites
Toilet: None. Dig a cat hole and use Leave No Trace best practices. Head down the east side of the ridge to avoid contaminating the pond.
Water: Collect from the pond
Food Storage: The trees are too small to make a proper bear hang, so bring a bear canister or Ursack

EXTENDING YOUR TRIP

Jutland Mountain: Hikers with extra energy could add the summit of Jutland Mountain to their trip. It's a 4 km (2.5 mi) round trip from the Jutland–Mount Albert Edward junction. You will gain 190 m (623 ft) on the way to the 1821 m (5974 ft) peak. The route to the top is sometimes marked by cairns, but it mostly follows the ridge crest. From the summit, there are magnificent views of the imposing north faces of Mount Regan and Mount Albert Edward, as well as of Gem Lake below.

Augerpoint Mountain: If you have clear weather and time to spare, scramble up to the 1839 m (6033 ft) summit of the route's namesake. There is no trail, but experienced scramblers can route-find to the top across rock bluffs and scree following a few cairns and a bit of boot path. The summit is about a 1 km (0.6 mi) round trip, with 200 m (656 ft) of elevation gain from the col above Ruth Masters Lake.

Forbidden Plateau Traverse: Add an extra day or two to your adventure by beginning at the old Forbidden Plateau ski hill near Courtenay. You'll hike across Forbidden Plateau to meet up with trails from Paradise Meadows near Kwai Lake. (See Trip 17.)

FURTHER RESOURCES

Strathcona Provincial Park: info and fees *bcparks.ca/explore/parkpgs/strath*
Ambassador Transportation: shuttle info and reservations *ambassador transportation.net*
Trail Maps: Forbidden Plateau Trails Map and Buttle Lake/Elk River Area Trails Map, Strathcona Wilderness Institute
NTS Maps: 092F11, 092F12

The waterfall below Ruth Masters Lake makes a great photo op

CAMPBELL RIVER TRIPS

THE TRIPS IN this region take you on a journey up the Campbell River to its headwaters in the myriad creeks draining into Buttle Lake. Twenty-three-kilometre-long (14.3 mi) Buttle Lake dominates the centre of Strathcona Provincial Park. Steep trails leave the lakeshore and switchback into the mountains above, sometimes gaining over 1000 m (3281 ft) of elevation. But the sweaty climbs are well worth it when you gain the ridgetops to walk through subalpine meadows, summit rocky peaks, swim in icy tarns, and gaze at the sea of snow-capped peaks of the highest mountains on Vancouver Island. Or meander through the valley bottoms and beside the ocean, gaining elevation more gradually as you hike past huge old-growth trees.

Getting Around: The Gold River Highway (Highway 28) and Westmin Road snake along the shores of Buttle Lake and adjacent Upper Campbell Lake, providing access to trailheads.

Indigenous Context: The K'ómoks and Homalco Nations, both Coast Salish tribes, have traditional territory along the coast, including Campbell River and nearby Ripple Rock. The mountains of Strathcona Provincial Park and Buttle Lake are also the traditional territory of the K'ómoks, along with the We Wai Kai and We Wai Kum Nations, both Kwakwaka'wakw peoples. On the west side of Strathcona, We Wai Kai and We Wai Kum territory overlaps with the territory of the Mowachaht/Muchalaht, a west coast Nuu-chah-nulth tribe.

The U'mista Cultural Centre in Alert Bay is worth a visit to learn from exhibits on Kwakwaka'wakw art, history, and culture. Head to Courtenay to enjoy K'ómoks art and culture at the Nim Nim Interpretive Centre and the I-Hos Gallery. In Campbell River, visit the We Wai Kum House of Treasures to view and purchase Indigenous art and souvenirs. Or visit the Nuyumbalees Cultural Centre on Quadra Island to view We Wai Kai potlatch regalia.

Supplies: Campbell River has several grocery stores, gas stations, and outdoor stores. Stock up here, as no supplies are available once you head west on Highway 28 into Strathcona Provincial Park. If you are hiking Crest Mountain or the Elk River Trail, the village of Gold River is a 15-minute drive west. At the time of writing, it had a gas station and a small deli, and a grocery store was planned.

Accommodations: You will find lots of accommodation options in Campbell River. Gold River has a handful of hotels. Strathcona Park Lodge, near the entrance to the park, is the only hotel along Highway 28. If you want to camp near Campbell River, Quinsam Campground at Elk Falls Provincial Park, just outside of town, has a mix of reservable and first-come, first-served

Tents at Bedwell Lake (Trip 23)

campsites. There are several campgrounds along Highway 28 and Westmin Road: Upper Campbell Reservoir Campground, managed by BC Hydro, has first-come, first-served sites. You can also reserve a site at Ralph River Campground and Buttle Lake Campground, both in Strathcona Provincial Park. The Gold River Municipal Campground has first-come, first-served sites a few minutes west of town.

21

RIPPLE ROCK

DAY HIKE

Difficulty: ●   **Elevation Gain**: 95 m (312 feet)
Duration: 2.5 to 3.5 hours   **High Point**: 95 m (312 feet)
Distance: 8 km (5 miles) round trip   **Best Months**: Year-round

Fees and Reservations: None

Regulations: No fires. No camping. Dogs permitted on leash.

Caution: Ticks are prevalent in the spring and summer months.

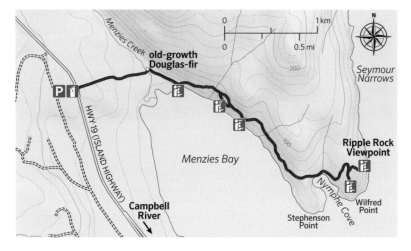

HIKE TO A VIEWPOINT over Ripple Rock in the turbulent waters of Seymour Narrows. It is the site of one of the world's largest planned non-nuclear explosions to remove part of an underwater island that caused many shipping accidents. The path winds through a verdant mossy forest, with detours to several scenic bluff viewpoints. Take breaks on the beach at Menzies Bay and Nymphe Cove. The final climb to the Ripple Rock viewpoint is steep enough to need stairs, but the views of the rapids and nearby islands are worth it.

GETTING THERE

From Campbell River, head north on Highway 19 (Island Highway). Zero your odometer as you go across the bridge over the Campbell River. About

The ocean swirls around Ripple Rock in Seymour Narrows

16 km (9.9 mi) later, turn right into a gravel parking lot signed for the Ripple Rock Trail. There is a portable toilet in the parking lot.

TRAIL

TRIP PLANNER

0 km (0 mi)	Trailhead
1.3 km (0.8 mi)	Menzies Bay
2 km (1.2 mi)	First bluff viewpoint
2.6 km (1.6 mi)	Second bluff viewpoint
3.6 km (2.2 mi)	Nymphe Cove
4 km (2.5 mi)	Ripple Rock viewpoint

Find the **trailhead** at the northeast corner of the parking lot. The first section of the trail follows a gravel power-line access road as it heads downhill, losing nearly 80 m (262 ft) of elevation. At the bottom, cross **Menzies Creek** on a sturdy bridge, then look for a huge old-growth Douglas-fir next to the trail. Boardwalks carry you through a wet section.

Arrive at the edge of shallow and muddy **Menzies Bay**, about 1.3 km (0.8 mi) from the trailhead. This is a good place to have a snack and watch the tiny tugboats zipping around in the log-booming grounds across the bay. The creek and bay are named after Archibald Menzies, a Scottish physician and botanist who visited the B.C. coast on fur-trading and exploratory voyages in the 1780s and '90s. The arbutus (*Arbutus menziesii*) and Douglas-fir (*Pseudotsuga menziesii*) trees bear Menzies' name because he was the first European to document them.

From the edge of the bay, the trail becomes rougher as it climbs into the forest. Moss drips from every tree branch, and sword ferns carpet the ground. In the spring, look for pink and white fawn lilies blooming in open patches of forest. In the fall, watch for mushrooms bursting through the duff.

Arrive at a side trail branching right to the **first bluff viewpoint**, about 2 km (1.2 mi) along. Look down at the log booms in Menzies Bay and across to the mountains in Vancouver Island's interior. You can see 2195 m (7201 ft) Golden Hinde and 2194 m (7198 ft) Elkhorn Mountain to the southwest and 2163 m (7096 ft) Victoria Peak to the west. These are the three tallest mountains on Vancouver Island. Continue along the main trail to **another open bluff** with similar views at 2.6 km (1.6 mi). Past here, the trail climbs and dips as it curves along the headland.

Descend to the shores of tiny **Nymphe Cove**, 3.6 km (2.2 mi) from the trailhead. Take a break on the gravel beach above the high-tide line, or take your shoes off and wander along the sand-and-mud shoreline. Unfortunately, the cove is a bit too shallow for swimming. It gets its name from the HMS *Nymphe*, a British warship based in Esquimalt in the 1890s.

The trail now climbs steeply, gaining 95 m (312 ft) in less than 0.5 km (0.3 mi). Follow the trail as it curls around the side of the cove, then heads uphill. A side trail to the right leads out onto another rocky bluff, with a view that is mostly obscured by trees. Continue on the trail as it climbs a wooden staircase to the top of a bluff. Follow the markers as the trail rambles across the rock outcropping, past power-line towers to a **viewpoint** high on a cliff, 4 km (2.5 mi) from the start.

The waters of Seymour Narrows churn below you. If you're lucky, you'll spot huge cruise ships or Alaska Marine Highway ferries navigating the passage. The submerged site of Ripple Rock is directly across from you, in the middle of the channel. At low tide, Ripple Rock's former summit was just below sea level. In 1958 the top was blasted off Ripple Rock, completing a 2-year federal government project that used over 1 km (0.6 mi) of fuse and 1,250,000 kg (2,750,000 lbs) of explosives. An interpretive panel at the trailhead tells the full story.

FURTHER RESOURCES

Recreation Sites and Trails BC: trail map and brochure *sitesandtrailsbc.ca/search/search-result.aspx?site=RECO472&type=Trail*
NTS Map: 092K03

FLOWER RIDGE

BACKPACKING TRIP

Difficulty: ◆
Duration: 2 to 3 days
Distance: 16 km (9.9 mi) round trip

Elevation Gain: 1150 m (3773 ft)
High Point: 1400 m (4593 ft)
Best Months: July to September

Fees and Reservations: None

Regulations: No fires. No drones. No smoking, vaping, or cannabis. Dogs permitted on leash only.

Caution: The mosquitos can be bad in July.

THE HIKE TO Flower Ridge provides a long ramble along the top of a subalpine ridge, a rarity on Vancouver Island. Getting there involves a steep grunt through the forest, gaining a whopping 1150 m (3773 ft), but in early August, the grassy meadows are awash in colourful blooms. Camp at informal sites next to picturesque tarns, then day hike farther along the rocky spine of the ridge. You will enjoy striking views of Buttle Lake as well as Strathcona Provincial Park's many summits, including imposing Big Interior Mountain and snowy Mount Septimus.

GETTING THERE

From Campbell River, take Highway 28 west for 47 km (29.2 mi) into Strathcona Provincial Park. At the T-junction, continue straight onto Westmin Road and zero your odometer. Stay on Westmin, passing the Ralph River Campground. Just before the bridge over Henshaw Creek at 29.5 km (18.3 mi), look for the signed Flower Ridge Trail on the left next to a gravel parking area. A trail at the north end of the parking lot leads to a pit toilet.

TRAIL

TRIP PLANNER

0 km (0 mi)	Trailhead
2.5 km (1.6 mi)	Buttle Lake viewpoint
3.5 km (2.2 mi)	Bluff viewpoint
5 km (3.1 mi)	Rock outcropping viewpoints
6 km (3.7 mi)	Muddy ponds
7 km (4.3 mi)	Ridge highpoint viewpoint
8 km (5 mi)	Informal camping near two tarns

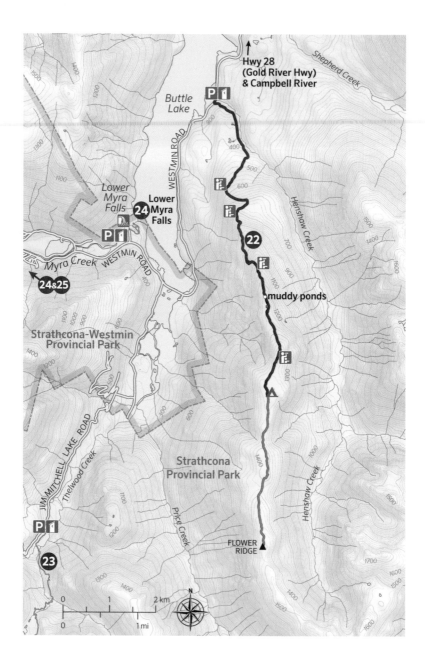

Hwy 28
(Gold River Hwy)
& Campbell River

Buttle
Lake

Shepherd Creek

WESTMIN ROAD

Lower
Myra
Falls

24 Lower
Myra
Falls

Myra Creek   WESTMIN ROAD

24&25

Henshaw Creek

22

muddy ponds

**Strathcona-Westmin
Provincial Park**

JIM MITCHELL LAKE ROAD

Thelwood Creek

**Strathcona
Provincial Park**

Price Creek

Henshaw Creek

23

0   1   2 km

0   1 mi

N

FLOWER
RIDGE

Hiking through meadows along the wide ridge

The trailhead is on the far side of Henshaw Creek, so use the pedestrian walkway on the east side of the road bridge to cross and pick up the trail. There is no reliable water on the ascent, so be sure to fill up your water bottles at the creek. The first portion of the trail gains elevation quickly, sometimes with the help of stairs. About 0.7 km (0.4 mi) from the trailhead, the route reaches a forested bench above Henshaw Creek, and the grade eases for a few minutes. In a few places, you can peer downhill to the creek below. There is also an obscured view of a **waterfall**. In the early season, watch for coralroot and tiger lilies on the lower slopes.

Before long, the trail begins to climb again as the footbed swings away from the creek valley and onto the shoulder of Flower Ridge. Near the 2.5 km (1.6 mi) mark, you can glimpse **Buttle Lake** below you, just before the path begins to climb southwest. You've reached an elevation of 580 m (1903 ft), having already gained 230 m.

Continue slogging up the steep slope through the forest. In some areas, thimbleberry and Oregon grape crowd the trail. In others, the understorey opens up to expose carpets of moss. Around 3 km (1.9 mi) from the start, at an elevation of 725 m (2379 ft), a **seasonal creek** may provide drinking water, but it dries up later in the summer. At 3.5 km (2.2 mi) and 800 m (2625 ft) elevation, a spur trail to the right leads to an open **bluff with a great view** of Phillips Ridge (Trip 25) across Buttle Lake. You will also be able to see the scarred landscape around the Myra Falls mine (see page 205).

Continuing uphill, the grade eases slightly as you pass through a brushy area that can be a bit overgrown. The trail gains the ridge crest around 5 km (3.1 mi) from the trailhead, at 1150 m (3773 ft) elevation. The forest slowly begins to thin, giving way to subalpine vegetation, punctuated by **rock outcroppings**. Several of these provide sensational vistas as you look behind you to the north down the length of Buttle Lake.

Emerge above the treeline near the 6 km (3.7 mi) mark, at an elevation of 1250 m (4102 ft). Two small and **muddy ponds** are nestled amongst the rocks here. They may run dry later in the season, but if you're out of water, they will do in an emergency. Follow the trail as it ascends a rocky ridge speckled with wind-battered trees. A bluffy **high point** of 1400 m (4593 ft) at 7 km (4.3 mi) provides even more views, this time to the east across the Henshaw Creek valley to Shepherd Peak and south along the bumpy backbone of Flower Ridge.

The ridgetop broadens as you continue to hike, and grassy slopes stretch away to both sides. Hollows between hills hide carpets of wildflowers, which take root in the wetter soils. Look for bright red paintbrush, indigo lupines, pink and white heather, and yellow asters. Tenacious plants like spreading phlox grow in the smallest patches of soil in the rocks.

NATURE NOTE

VANCOUVER ISLAND MARMOTS

If you are lucky, you may encounter a Vancouver Island marmot along the high-elevation trails in Strathcona Provincial Park. These large (and adorable) members of the squirrel family are genetically distinct from their mainland counterparts. Like other marmots, they live in burrows in mountain meadows and eat grasses and wildflowers. On Vancouver Island, the marmots' alpine habitat is surrounded by low-elevation forest that juvenile marmots must traverse when searching for a new home away from their parental colony. Increased clear-cutting has fragmented this habitat, and fewer than 30 Vancouver Island marmots were left in the wild in 2004. Since then, the Vancouver Island Marmot Recovery Foundation has bred marmots in captivity, reintroduced them into the wild, and supported existing marmot colonies. Today about 250 marmots are spread amongst the mountains of Strathcona Provincial Park as well as the Mount Arrowsmith area (Trip 9).

Wildflowers thrive in shallow depressions along the ridge

Just past 8 km (5 mi), the trail runs next to a large tarn that has reliable water all summer. Another smaller tarn lies due east of here. Find a flat spot in the meadows to camp near these **two tarns**, being careful to avoid fragile vegetation.

CAMPING

There are no formal campgrounds or facilities on this trail, so choose your campsite carefully to minimize your impact on this pristine wilderness. The best place to camp is near two tarns about 8 km (5 mi) from the trailhead. However, more small tarns between the 9 and 10 km marks (5.6 and 6.2 mi) also make good campsites.

Campsites: Informal flat spots in the grassy meadows near the tarns
Toilet: None. Dig a cat hole and use Leave No Trace practices. Go down the ridge, well away from the trail and tarns, to avoid contaminating them.

Water: Collect from the tarns
Food Storage: None. Bring rope to hang your food in one of the small trees. A bear canister or Ursack is a better option.

EXTENDING YOUR TRIP

Farther along Flower Ridge: The trail continues along the ridge for approximately 5 km (3.1 mi) past the tarn camping area, to a high point at 1530 m (5020 ft). There are beautiful views of the Price Creek valley to the west. To the north, you can see the snowy summits of Mount Septimus and Mount Rosseau. The route becomes progressively rougher and fainter and has no official end point. Mountaineers follow informal cairned routes to tackle ascents of Central Crags or long-distance off-trail traverses to Della Falls (Trip 10), Bedwell Lakes (Trip 23), or Comox Glacier. Backpackers will be content to turn around and retrace their steps to camp.

FURTHER RESOURCES

Strathcona Provincial Park: info *bcparks.ca/explore/parkpgs/strath*
NTS Map: 092F12
Trail Map: Buttle Lake/Elk River Area Trail Map by Strathcona Wilderness Institute

Buttle Lake seen from the crest of the ridge

BEDWELL AND CREAM LAKES ★

BACKPACKING TRIP

Difficulty: ■/◆
Duration: 2 to 3 days
Distance: 8 to 22 km (5 to 13.7 mi) round trip

Elevation Gain: 410 to 830 m (1345 to 2723 ft)
High Point: 1380 m (4528 ft)
Best Months: July to September

Fees and Reservations: Camping fees are $10/person/night payable online or in cash at the trailhead. All campsites are first-come, first-served.

Regulations: No fires. No drones. No smoking, vaping, or cannabis. Dogs permitted on leash.

Caution: Campgrounds in this area can be very busy on weekends. Arrive early to ensure you get a spot.

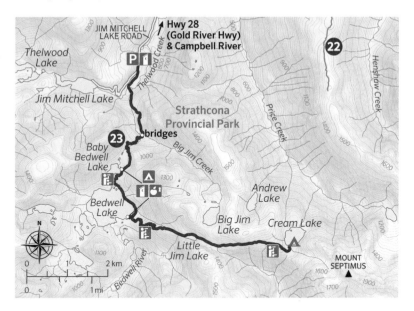

HIKE UP INTO the heart of Vancouver Island's backcountry in Strathcona Provincial Park. Follow a steep, but well-constructed, trail to beautiful campsites on rock bluffs above Baby Bedwell and Bedwell Lakes. Enjoy incredible views of Big Interior Mountain and Mount Tom Taylor from Bedwell Lake. Take a day hike on a rugged trail higher into the mountains to brilliant blue Cream Lake, where informal camping is available. The route includes stunning views of Mount Septimus, Big Interior Mountain, and Della Falls (Trip 10) in the Drinkwater valley.

GETTING THERE

From Campbell River, take Highway 28 west for 47 km (29.2 mi) into Strathcona Provincial Park. At the T-junction, continue straight onto Westmin Road and zero your odometer. Stay on Westmin for another 35 km (21.7 mi). At the south end of Buttle Lake, turn left onto Jim Mitchell Lake Road. This rough gravel road is usually graded well enough for 2WD vehicles, but sometimes AWD or 4WD is a better choice. Stay on this road for 2.6 km (1.6 mi), then take the right fork, heading steeply uphill (continuing straight will take you to a mine powerhouse). Arrive at the parking area and outhouse 3.6 km (2.2 mi) later. Find a spot on the wide shoulder, being careful not to block the road.

TRAIL

TRIP PLANNER

0 km (0 mi)	Trailhead
2.5 km (1.6 mi)	Four bridges across Big Jim Creek
4 km (2.5 mi)	Baby Bedwell Lake campground
4.4 km (2.7 mi)	Viewpoint
6 km (3.7 mi)	Bedwell Lake campground
8.5 km (5.3 mi)	Little Jim Lake
11 km (6.8 mi)	Informal camping at Cream Lake

The **trailhead** is 150 m (492 ft) up the road from the parking area. Look for the signed trail leaving the road on the left. The path descends to cross Thelwood Creek on a suspension bridge and then Big Jim Creek on a sturdy wooden bridge. Be sure to peer down through the clear turquoise water at the boulders below, worn smooth by the current. From here, the climbing begins as you wind your way uphill between rock outcroppings with the aid of many small switchbacks and stairs.

About 2 km (1.2 mi) from the trailhead, the grade eases as you traverse a bench high above the creek. The path dips through thickets of huckleberries to a set of **four bridges** across branches of Big Jim Creek at the 2.5 km (1.6 mi) mark. The terrain steepens again as you work your way uphill on more stairs and switchbacks. Near the 3 km (1.9 mi) mark, the forest opens as you reach the wet heather meadows of the Bedwell–Thelwood Divide.

Bedwell Lake from the viewpoint

Thus far, your route has followed Big Jim Creek, which drains into Thelwood Creek, and then Buttle Lake. But as you cross the divide you'll enter the Bedwell watershed, which drains into Clayoquot Sound near Tofino via the Bedwell River. The river and lakes are named after Staff Commander Edward Bedwell. He sailed on the *Plumper*, a British vessel that surveyed the Pacific Coast between 1857 and 1860. However, many locals still prefer the earlier name, Bear River, or the Nuu-chah-nulth name Oinimitis.

Scramble up a rock bluff on a ladder, then reach the turnoff to the **Baby Bedwell Lake campground** at 4 km (2.5 mi). Even if you aren't planning to overnight here, the spectacular view from the rock bluff in the campground warrants a lunch stop or at least a photo.

The route between Baby Bedwell and Bedwell Lakes is only 2 km (1.2 mi) long, but it is quite strenuous, with lots of small ups and downs. Past the campground the trail heads along a lakeside boardwalk, then negotiates a series of rock bluffs with the help of several more fixed metal ladders and staircases. Don't miss a marked spur trail at 4.4 km (2.7 mi) that leads to an outstanding **viewpoint**. Bedwell Lake is spread out in front of you, with the snowy peaks of Mount Tom Taylor and Big Interior Mountain in the background.

Mount Septimus reflected in a tiny tarn on the way to Cream Lake

From the viewpoint, the trail plunges towards Bedwell Lake on another set of metal stairs. A brief scramble across a rock step is made easier with the help of a cable handline. Take care here in wet weather. The path reaches lake level in a small bay with some picturesque rocky islands. On a warm day, this is a great place for a swim.

Follow the shoreline for a few minutes on a boardwalk. Soon you'll be climbing over rock bluffs again on the final set of stairs and ladders. Reach the **Bedwell Lake campground** on a bluff above the lake at the 6 km (3.7 mi) mark. There are excellent views down to the lake between the clumps of small cedars and gnarled mountain hemlock, dripping with witch's hair lichen.

A maze of informal trails spreads out from the information board in the centre of the campground. The rough and overgrown Bedwell Sound Trail heads south along the Bedwell River. To find the trail to Cream Lake as it heads east, follow the paths uphill beyond the outhouse. While Baby Bedwell and Bedwell Lakes are typically snow-free by late June, the route to Cream Lake holds snow until mid-July. The route steadily gains elevation as it weaves through the forest and across numerous granite outcroppings, many of which provide views of Bedwell Lake below you. The best viewpoint is about 1 km (0.6 mi) from Bedwell Lake Camp, at 1100 m (3609 ft).

After the final rocky bluff viewpoint, the trail straightens as it follows a creek bed. Follow flagging tape and markers as the route scrambles over boulders, then reaches the shore of **Little Jim Lake**, about 2.5 km (1.6 mi) from Bedwell Lake Camp. Follow a rough route along the north side of the lake. At the east end, the trail heads uphill on a rocky route that is often snow-covered, traversing a steep hillside. Watch for wildflowers like western anemone clinging to patches of soil. Keep left and continue climbing as you cross a divide, and the Drinkwater valley drops away to the right.

About 4 km (2.5 mi) from Bedwell Lake Camp, you'll arrive at the hike's high point, 1380 m (4528 ft). Follow the route as it heads downhill in a draw past several tiny meltwater tarns. Mount Septimus, named for its seven peaks, looms ahead of you. If you're up for a short diversion, scramble uphill to the right to reach a rocky bluff. You can peer down into the Drinkwater valley, which drops nearly 800 m (2625 ft) below you. If you look carefully, you can see Della Falls plunging down the right side of the valley. With a total drop of 440 m (1444 ft), it is one of the highest waterfalls in Canada. You can hike right to the base on Trip 10.

Back on the main trail, continue downhill. A rocky bluff on the left provides a great vantage point to gaze down on the blue waters of Cream Lake and the end of Flower Ridge (Trip 22) across the Price Creek valley. Continue down the steep and rocky slope to the **informal camping area** on the shores of **Cream Lake**. The turquoise waters of the lake owe their hue to fine glacial sediments suspended in the liquid. The "creamy" tint of the colour gave rise to the lake's name.

CAMPING

There are two designated campgrounds with facilities at Baby Bedwell Lake and Bedwell Lake. Random camping is also allowed in a zone to the east of Little Jim Lake, but no facilities are provided. In that area, the best camping is at Cream Lake.

BABY BEDWELL LAKE CAMPGROUND

Located on a rocky bluff above the lake, this is the first campground at the top of the ascent, so it's a good choice if you are low on energy.

Campsites: Nine wooden tent pads plus space for a few more tents on flat rocks and along the soggy shoreline
Toilet: Urine-diversion toilet on the north side of the campground
Water: Collect from the lake
Food Storage: Food locker on a spur trail north of camp

BEDWELL LAKE CAMPGROUND

On bluffs above the eastern shore of Bedwell Lake, this is the most popular campground. It makes a good base camp for a day hike to Cream Lake.

Campsites: Twelve wooden tent pads plus space for a few more tents on flat rock slabs. Do not crush the fragile vegetation to make more campsites.
Toilet: Urine-diversion toilet uphill from the info sign
Water: Collect from the lake via steep spur trails
Food Storage: Food locker near the entrance to camp

CREAM LAKE CAMPING AREA

Camping is allowed anywhere around Cream Lake. The most responsible place to pitch a tent is on the gravel flats near the trail from Bedwell Lake, where streams flow down from Mount Septimus.

Campsites: Several flat clearings in the gravel near large boulder
Toilet: None. Dig a cat hole and use Leave No Trace best practices. Go uphill, well away from the lakeshore, and be careful to stay away from the meltwater streams that feed the lake.
Water: Collect from the lake or meltwater streams
Food Storage: None. Bring a rope to hang your food in one of the trees. You may have to walk back up to the ridge to find a suitable tree. A bear canister or Ursack is a better option.

FURTHER RESOURCES

Strathcona Provincial Park: info and fees *bcparks.ca/explore/parkpgs/strath*
Trail Map: Buttle Lake/Elk River Area Trail Map, Strathcona Wilderness Institute
NTS Map: 092F12; 092F05

NATURE NOTE

SHORT GROWING SEASON IN THE ALPINE

In winter, the west coast of Vancouver Island is hit by rainstorms that blow in off the Pacific Ocean. Up in the mountains, the precipitation falls as snow, often in near-record-breaking amounts of up to 5 m (16.4 ft) each year. With such a heavy snowpack, it can be late July or even August before it melts completely, giving trees and other plants a very short growing season. As well, after the snow is gone, water is scarce since rainwater drains away into the gravelly soil. Alpine plants like western anemone take advantage of whatever moisture they can, flowering as soon as the snow leaves the ground. Mountain buttercup lives next to the fleeting streams and ponds left by snowmelt or adjacent to the drifts themselves. Look for both as you hike between Bedwell and Cream Lakes.

24

UPPER MYRA FALLS

DAY HIKE | Trail map on pp. 200–201

Difficulty: ●
Duration: 2 to 2.5 hours
Distance: 8 km (5 mi) round trip

Elevation Gain: 150 m (492 ft)
High Point: 500 m (1640 ft)
Best Months: Year-round

Fees and Reservations: None

Regulations: No fires. No drones. No smoking, vaping, or cannabis. No camping. Dogs permitted on leash.

STRETCH YOUR LEGS on an easy hike through an old-growth forest to 60-metre-high (197 ft) Upper Myra Falls. It's hidden in a deep canyon at the remote south end of Buttle Lake in Strathcona Provincial Park. Afterwards, make a quick detour to visit the dramatic cascades of Lower Myra Falls as they tumble over a series of rock ledges into Buttle Lake.

GETTING THERE

From Campbell River, take Highway 28 west for 47 km (29.2 mi) into Strathcona Provincial Park. At the T-junction, continue straight onto Westmin Road. Drive 38 km (23.6 mi) along the shores of Buttle Lake to the entrance to the Myra Falls mine. Follow the gravel road through the mine site, being careful to stay on the main road for another 1.5 km (0.9 mi). Turn right into the signed parking lot. There is an outhouse in the trees just north of the lot.

TRAIL

TRIP PLANNER

0 km (0 mi)	Trailhead
1 km (0.6 mi)	Upper Myra Falls Trail leaves road
4 km (2.5 mi)	Upper Myra Falls

Myra Creek, along with both Upper and Lower Myra Falls, were likely named after Myra Ellison, the daughter of Price Ellison, who was the minister of finance in the B.C. government. Both Ellisons were part of a 23-member government expedition to the Buttle Lake area in 1910. The party travelled up the Campbell River to Buttle Lake, then to Price Pass near Cream Lake (Trip 23).

Sturdy wooden bridges carry you across many small streams

They descended the Drinkwater valley (Trip 10) to finish in Port Alberni. They were so impressed with the scenery that Strathcona Provincial Park was created the following year.

To find the **trailhead**, cross the road you drove in on and hike down the dirt road opposite the parking lot. Walk around a yellow gate and ignore the Phillips Ridge trail (Trip 25) leaving the road on the right. About 1 km (0.6 mi) from the trailhead, watch for the signed **Upper Myra Falls Trail** on the right. (If you continue along the road to a bridge, you've gone too far.)

The trail heads north away from the road, climbing a slope in a beautiful forest of old-growth trees. Winter storms have strewn blowdown across the trail, and you may have to clamber over or under. In a few places, the trail has been re-routed around these fallen giants.

Continue along the trail as it curls around the slope, high above Myra Creek. Sword ferns, moss, queen's cup, bunchberry, and Oregon grape carpet the forest floor as you wind between big western redcedar, Douglas-fir, and western hemlock trees. Watch for huge moss-covered boulders amongst the trees. Wooden bridges carry you across small streams.

As you near the end of the trail, the falls become audible. Follow the trail as it heads into the narrow Myra Creek canyon. A wooden viewing platform provides a great perspective of **Upper Myra Falls**. When you are done admiring the cascade, retrace your steps to the parking area.

Lower Myra Falls

EXTENDING YOUR TRIP

Lower Myra Falls: Don't miss a visit to spectacular Lower Myra Falls, a few minutes' drive down the road. (You passed the parking area just before entering the mine.) It's an easy 1 km (0.6 mi) round-trip hike as you drop 30 m (98 ft) down to the falls. Be sure to take the upper branch trail to view the falls from above, then continue down the switchback to visit the pools at the bottom. From there, the falls drop in a series of cascades all the way down to Buttle Lake. Use caution on the ledges or if swimming; there have been serious accidents.

FURTHER RESOURCES

Strathcona Provincial Park: info *bcparks.ca/explore/parkpgs/strath*
Trail Map: Buttle Lake/Elk River Area Trail Map, Strathcona Wilderness Institute
NTS Map: 092F12

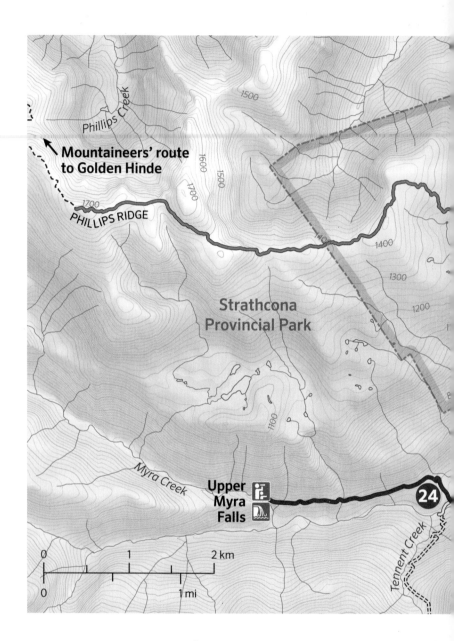

Mountaineers' route
to Golden Hinde

PHILLIPS RIDGE

Strathcona
Provincial Park

Myra Creek

Upper
Myra
Falls

Tennent Creek

24

0   1   2 km

0   1 mi

24   **UPPER MYRA FALLS** | p. 197

25   **ARNICA LAKE AND PHILLIPS RIDGE** | p. 202

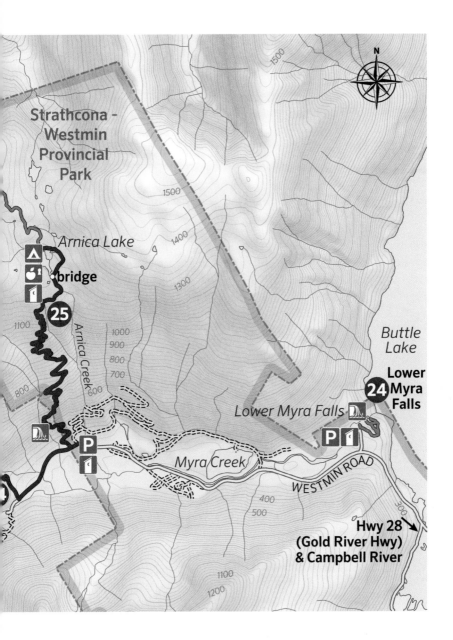

Strathcona -
Westmin
Provincial
Park

Arnica Lake

bridge

25

Arnica Creek

Buttle
Lake

**Lower
Myra
Falls**

24

Lower Myra Falls

Myra Creek

WESTMIN ROAD

**Hwy 28
(Gold River Hwy)
& Campbell River**

ARNICA LAKE AND PHILLIPS RIDGE

BACKPACKING TRIP | Trail map on pp. 200–201

Difficulty ♦

Duration: 2 to 3 days

Distance: 15 km (9.3 mi) round trip

Elevation Gain: 810 m (2657 ft)

High Point: 1200 m (3937 ft)

Best Months: July to September

Fees and Reservations: None

Regulations: No fires. No drones. No smoking, vaping, or cannabis. Dogs permitted on leash only.

CAMP AT PICTURESQUE Arnica Lake, then explore the wildflower meadows or go for a swim. Mountaineers use this trail to start a multi-day cross-country trek to the summit of the Golden Hinde, the tallest peak on Vancouver Island. Backpackers can get a taste of the area and views of the lofty mountain by tackling the rough route to the summit of Phillips Ridge on a day hike from their base camp at the lake. Although the trail to the lake gains over 800 m (2625 ft) from the valley bottom, switchbacks create a manageable grade, making this one of the easiest ways to experience the subalpine terrain above Buttle Lake in Strathcona Provincial Park.

GETTING THERE

Refer to the driving directions in Trip 24 (page 197).

TRAIL

TRIP PLANNER

0 km (0 mi)	Trailhead
0.5 km (0.3 mi)	Waterfall viewpoint
0.9 km (0.6 mi)	First water access trail
2.6 km (1.6 mi)	Second water access trail
4.4 km (2.7 mi)	Third water access trail
7 km (4.3 mi)	South end of Arnica Lake
7.5 km (4.7 mi)	Campground at north end of Arnica Lake

To find the **trailhead,** cross the road you drove in on and walk down the dirt road opposite the parking lot. Walk around a yellow gate and look for the Phillips Ridge Trail leaving the right side of the road about 50 m (164 ft) later.

The south end of Arnica Lake

The path is gentle to start, but the grade kicks up almost immediately as you climb tight and short switchbacks through an old-growth hemlock forest with lots of Oregon grape in the understorey. About 0.5 km (0.3 mi) from the trailhead, reach a small viewing platform next to a pretty little **waterfall** spilling over a cliff. A few switchbacks later, at 0.9 km (0.6 mi) and 490 m (1608 ft) elevation, the trail approaches the creek again and a marked side trail leads down to its bank. This is one of three places to fill up on **drinking water** during the hike.

As the trail continues relentlessly uphill, watch for wildflowers underfoot. Twinflower grows on mossy outcrops in delicate pale pink pairs of blooms. The pink flowers of pipsissewa, also known as prince's-pine, nod on tall stalks. The striking red and white stems of candystick thrive in clumps next to the trail. These fascinating perennial plants do not contain any chlorophyll, so they don't have any green parts. Instead, they get their nutrition from neighbouring plants through a symbiotic relationship with fungi, in particular matsutake mushrooms.

In the lower sections of the trail, breaks in the trees provide peek-a-boo views of the Myra Falls mine below and its numerous tailing ponds. Unfortunately, the hum of the mine's machinery is audible as well. However, it fades as you gain elevation.

Reach another **water access side trail** about 2.6 km (1.6 mi) from the start, at 730 m (2395 ft) elevation. The grade eases slightly for a few minutes past here, as the switchbacks stretch out a little longer. Keep an eye out for red and black huckleberry bushes lining the trail as you gain elevation. In August, these can provide a delicious trailside snack.

Globeflower (foreground) and mountain buttercup abound in the meadows

The switchbacks tighten up again as you enter the final steep section. Watch for views of Mount Myra across the valley through gaps in the trees. Reach the third **water access side trail** about 4.4 km (2.7 mi) along, at 980 m (3215 ft) elevation. Past here, climb another kilometre (0.6 mi) of tight switchbacks. The angle begins to ease and the vegetation starts to thin as the **trail enters subalpine** terrain near the 6 km (3.7 mi) mark, at 1170 m (3839 ft) elevation.

Follow the trail through small patches of pretty heather meadow for a few minutes, before it turns north to follow Arnica Creek. Descend to the **south end of Arnica Lake** at the 7 km (4.3 mi) mark. A shoreline clearing provides a great place to take a break. When you are ready to continue your hike, cross the lake outlet stream on a narrow metal bridge or hop across on rocks a few metres upstream.

The trail swings away from the lake as it weaves through patches of forest and wet meadows teeming with white globeflower, yellow buttercups, green false hellebore, and, of course, yellow arnica. Arrive at the lake inlet stream 7.5 km (4.7 mi) from the trailhead. Cross on a small wooden bridge and follow the trail up a rise to the **campground**. From here a faint trail leads left down to the lakeshore, and the Phillips Ridge Trail continues to the right, heading northwest along the ridgeline.

CAMPING

Picturesque Arnica Lake is nestled in wooded meadows. On hot days, a dip in the lake is an antidote to the hours of uphill switchbacks.

Campsites: Five wooden tent platforms at the north end of the lake. Avoid camping on the fragile vegetation near the lakeshore.
Toilet: Throne-style pit toilet on a spur trail east of the campground
Water: Collect from the lake inlet stream
Food Storage: Food locker just east of the campground

EXTENDING YOUR TRIP

Phillips Ridge: Take a day hike from Arnica Lake to explore the first section of the mountaineering route to the Golden Hinde, the highest mountain on Vancouver Island. Follow the path northwest from the campground through meadows. As the trail gains the ridge crest, it swings east and enters rockier terrain. Cairns and faint boot paths mark the route, but to be safe, bring a map and compass or GPS, because navigation can be tricky. Numerous bumps in the ridge make good turnaround points, but if you want to reach the summit of 1730 m (5676 ft) Phillips Ridge, it's a 14 km (8.7 mi) round trip with 530 m (1739 ft) of elevation gain from Arnica Lake.

FURTHER RESOURCES

Strathcona Provincial Park: info *bcparks.ca/explore/parkpgs/strath*
Trail Map: Buttle Lake/Elk River Area Trail Map, Strathcona Wilderness Institute
NTS Map: 092F12

HISTORY

MINING IN STRATHCONA PROVINCIAL PARK

In 1911, Premier Richard McBride created British Columbia's first provincial park—Strathcona. Economic pressures soon began to shape the park. Mining and logging were first permitted in 1939, and the large-scale Myra Falls mine opened in 1959, extracting zinc, copper, lead, gold, and silver. In 1987, the B.C. government announced plans to remove large areas from the park for industrial use, including proposed mines at Cream Lake (Trip 23) and Della Falls (Trip 10). After significant public outcry and protests, the government created a new Class B park named Strathcona-Westmin Provincial Park, which includes Upper and Lower Myra Falls and the trail to Arnica Lake. The Class B designation allows the Myra Falls mine to continue operating within the park indefinitely. While we may think that provincial parks protect British Columbia's natural landscapes, the history of Strathcona Provincial Park reminds us that governments view parks as economic opportunities too.

26

ELK RIVER AND LANDSLIDE LAKE ★

BACKPACKING TRIP | Trail map on p. 212

Difficulty: ■
Duration: 2 to 3 days
Distance: 12 to 18 km (7.5 to 11.2 km)
round trip

Elevation Gain: 180 to 365 m (591 to 1198 ft)
High Point: 685 m (2247 ft)
Best Months: June to October

Fees and Reservations: Camping fees are $10/person/night payable online or in cash at the trailhead. All campsites are first-come, first-served.

Regulations: No fires. No drones. No smoking, vaping, or cannabis. Dogs permitted on leash. The Elk River is open to catch-and-release fly-fishing only.

Caution: Campgrounds in this area can be very busy on weekends. Arrive early to ensure you get a spot.

HIKE THROUGH THE unlogged old-growth forest of the Elk River valley in Strathcona Provincial Park. Choose from two riverside campgrounds, then take a day hike higher into the mountains to scenic Landslide Lake. It sits at the base of Mount Colonel Foster, the fourth-highest mountain on Vancouver Island. Admire the peak's imposing 1000 m (3281 ft) cliffs and the impressive slide path from a 1946 earthquake that sent part of the mountain plummeting into the lake. If you have more energy, follow a rough and challenging route farther uphill to see chunks of glacier floating in Berg Lake, a gorgeous turquoise tarn.

GETTING THERE
From Campbell River, take Highway 28 west for 47 km (29.2 mi) into Strathcona Provincial Park. At the T-junction, turn right to stay on Highway 28 for another 23 km (14.3 mi). Watch for the entrance to the signed Elk River Trail parking lot on the left-hand side.

TRAIL

TRIP PLANNER

0 km (0 mi)	Trailhead
4.5 km (2.8 mi)	Beaver pond
5 km (3.1 mi)	Puzzle Creek and Volcano Creek
6 km (3.7 mi)	Butterwort Creek campground

The long bridge over Butterwort Creek

9 km (5.6 mi)	Gravel Flats campground
10 km (6.2 mi)	Elk River bridge
11.5 km (7.1 mi)	Landslide Lake
13 km (8.1 mi)	Berg Lake

Pass an outhouse about 0.1 km (0.1 mi) along the trail from the parking lot. The route then begins in a thick second-growth forest, then climbs a short, steep hill to cross under a power line. Look for wildflowers in the clearing, including the tall pink-purple blooms of fireweed. Back in the trees, the trail climbs steadily up several small switchbacks as it transitions into an old-growth forest. Crest a mossy shoulder at 425 m (1394 ft) elevation, having gained 100 m (328 ft) over your 0.7 km (0.4 mi) hike from the parking lot.

From here the trail heads downhill to the banks of the Elk River and follows the river as it gains elevation almost imperceptibly. There are several opportunities to take breaks on the gravel banks of the river. Watch for American dippers feeding in the water. These little songbirds dive into the rushing waters to catch aquatic larvae along the gravel river bottom.

Take time to savour the gorgeous forest in this area. Leafy salmonberry bushes tangle with thorny devil's club, drooping ferns, and cedar seedlings in the understorey. Western hemlock, western redcedar, and Douglas-fir trees tower overhead, dripping with moss. The path crosses several small creeks as they rush towards the river, some with the help of log bridges, but you'll have to rock-hop your way across most.

The forest opens into a clearing as you pass a **beaver pond** about 4.5 km (2.8 mi) from the start. Cross **Puzzle Creek** on a sturdy wooden bridge near the 5 km (3.1 mi) mark. The crossing of **Volcano Creek** a minute later is unbridged. In the early season or after heavy rain you may need to remove your boots to ford it. Shortly after the creek crossing, watch for a giant old-growth cedar next to the trail.

Reach **Butterwort Creek campground** on a gravel bench beside the river at the 6 km (3.7 mi) mark. To continue onwards, follow the brushy trail south along the river, passing the side trail to the outhouse. Cross Butterwort Creek a few minutes later on a long wooden bridge. Look upstream through the tree branches to get a glimpse of some small cascades. Past the bridge, the trail begins to climb more steeply.

Take care crossing a gully near the 7 km (4.3 mi) mark. The open brush and short trees tell the story of the avalanches that wash through each winter and spring. The valley continues to narrow as your route contours far above the river. Scramble over two rock bluffs at 7.7 km (4.8 mi) and 8.4 km (5.2 mi). Both have small, dripping waterfalls, although they may run dry later in the season. The valley widens slightly as you descend a short hill and reach **Gravel Flats campground** at 9 km (5.6 mi). Watch for the reddish-orange blooms of columbine speckled along the riverbank.

CAMPING

Camping is allowed only at Butterwort Creek and Gravel Flats. You may not camp anywhere else in the area, including at Landslide Lake and Berg Lake.

NATURE NOTE

1946 EARTHQUAKE

On June 23, 1946, a magnitude 7.3 earthquake originated in Strathcona Provincial Park near Forbidden Plateau (Trips 17, 18, and 19). To date, it is Canada's largest land-based earthquake. The shaking caused property damage in the Courtenay-Comox area, but in the Elk River valley the entire 365 m (1198 ft) North Tower of Mount Colonel Foster sheared away. Rock tumbled down the mountain into the lake below, creating a massive wave that raced up the east side of the lake as well as down into the Elk River valley. At Landslide Lake, look for the rock slabs scrubbed clean by the slide both on the approach to the lake and on its west side. East of the lake, notice the distinct line in the trees about 50 metres (164 ft) above the shoreline. The coniferous forest above predates the earthquake. The alder below has grown up where the wave scoured the shoreline when the landslide hit.

Landslide Lake and the jagged peaks of Mount Colonel Foster

BUTTERWORT CREEK CAMPGROUND

This small campground is less popular than Gravel Flats, so it is quieter. It's a good option if you got a late start. The gravel underfoot is quite coarse, so pegging out your tent can be a challenge.

Campsites: Space for 12 tents on the gravel bar. The best spots are under the trees. There are also some lumpy overflow spots near the outhouse.
Toilet: Outhouse on a spur trail to the south of camp
Water: Collect from the river
Food Storage: Food locker near the outhouse

GRAVEL FLATS CAMPGROUND

Most parties use this campground as a staging point for their day hike to Landslide Lake, so it can be crowded.

Campsites: Space for 24 tents in clearings and on gravel by the river
Toilet: Outhouse at entrance to campground
Water: Collect from the river
Food Storage: Food locker just uphill from the outhouse

EXTENDING YOUR TRIP

Landslide Lake: It's worth hiking 5 km (3.1 mi) round trip from Gravel Flats Camp and 220 m (722 ft) higher for the views from Landslide Lake. From Gravel Flats Camp, follow the river's edge for about 1 km (0.6 mi), then cross it on a large wooden bridge. Ignore a flagged mountaineers' route heading left to Elk Pass. Instead, follow cairns up rough rock slabs, keeping the river on your right. As you approach the waterfall, take a flagged route into the trees to your left. At the top, follow more cairns and flags across rock slabs to the shores of Landslide Lake and incredible views of Mount Colonel Foster and the devastation from the 1946 earthquake and landslide. A 1914 Alpine Club of Canada mountaineering expedition named the peak after Colonel William Wasbrough Foster, a politician and businessman and fellow club member.

Berg Lake: Continue above Landslide Lake to the glacial tarn known unofficially as both Berg Lake (for its icebergs) and Foster Lake (for the peak). It's 1.5 km (0.9 mi) past Landslide Lake and 70 m (230 ft) higher. Follow a rough flagged trail above the eastern shore of Landslide Lake. Work through dense alders and patches of old-growth that survived the landslide. At the south end of the lake, descend a meadowy slide path, then turn left to follow a jumbled creek bed and rock slabs marked with cairns uphill. Crest a gravel moraine to reach the lake. Admire the cliffs of Mount Colonel Foster and ice floating in the lake. Gaze behind you at Landslide Lake with Elkhorn Mountain on the horizon to the north.

FURTHER RESOURCES

Strathcona Provincial Park: info and fees *bcparks.ca/explore/parkpgs/strath*
Trail Map: Buttle Lake/Elk River Area Trail Map, Strathcona Wilderness Institute
NTS Map: 092F13

Ice floats in Berg Lake below the peaks of Mount Colonel Foster

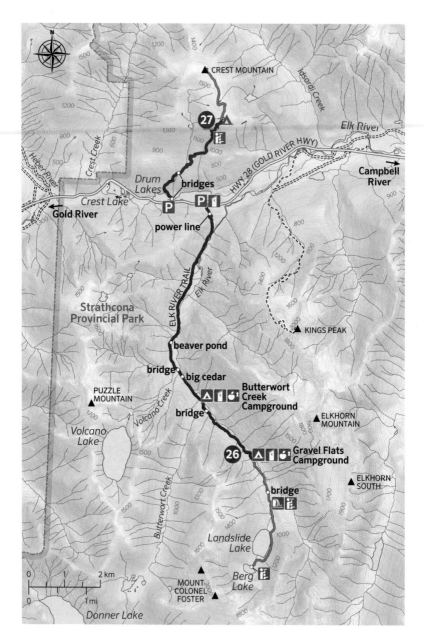

26 ELK RIVER AND LANDSLIDE LAKE | p. 206

27 CREST MOUNTAIN | p. 213

CREST MOUNTAIN

BACKPACKING TRIP | Trail map on p. 212

Difficulty: ◆
Duration: 2 days
Distance: 10 km (6.2 mi) round trip

Elevation Gain: 1130 m (3707 ft)
High Point: 1450 m (4757 ft)
Best Months: July to September

Fees and Reservations: None

Regulations: No fires. No drones. No smoking, vaping, or cannabis. Dogs permitted on leash only.

A HIKE THROUGH mature forest, numerous picturesque ponds, and panoramic views from your campsite make this trip worthwhile, though don't forget your hiking poles to help with the switchbacks on the way up (and down). Pitch your tent next to a tarn in the scenic subalpine meadows below the lofty peak of Crest Mountain in Strathcona Provincial Park. From there, enjoy incredible views of the Elk River valley and surrounding mountains. Make a day trip from your base camp to the summit, weaving through a rock garden of wildflowers and small ponds on your way.

GETTING THERE

From Campbell River, take Highway 28 west for 47 km (29.2 mi) into Strathcona Provincial Park. At the T-junction, turn right to stay on Highway 28 for another 24.5 km (15.2 mi). Keep an eye out for the signed pullout for Crest Mountain on the right-hand side, about 1.5 km (0.9 mi) after the Elk River Trail turnoff.

TRAIL

TRIP PLANNER

0 km (0 mi)	Trailhead
1.5 km (0.9 mi)	Log bridge
3 km (1.9 mi)	Gully
4 km (2.5 mi)	Viewpoint
5 km (3.1 mi)	Tarn campsites

The **trail leaves from the east side of the parking lot,** heading downhill to cross a long wooden bridge over the narrows between the two Drum Lakes.

Kings Peak (left) and Elkhorn Mountain (centre) seen from the summit of Crest Mountain

On the other side, huge wooden log rounds create makeshift steps up and over a flood control structure made of rocks in netting.

The trail begins a punishing ascent on tight switchbacks almost immediately, heading uphill through a beautiful forest with many large Douglas-fir and western hemlock trees, as well as thick mats of salal. In a few places, the trail crosses mossy bluffs. About 1.5 km (0.9 mi) from the trailhead, the path swings east briefly to cross a sturdy **log bridge** with a railing. This is the only reliable place to access drinking water on the ascent.

Past the bridge, the grade sharpens again as you work your way uphill through the mossy forest. Near the 3 km (1.9 mi) mark, the path enters a **gully** with some steep, loose sections and slightly more open forest. Watch for wildflowers like tiger lilies taking advantage of the increased sun exposure.

Once above the gully, the switchbacks begin again and you start to enter subalpine terrain. The trail can be loose and dusty here, so watch your step. The best **views** are from a bluff near the 4 km (2.5 mi) mark, at about 1330 m (4364 ft) elevation. Across the valley to the south, you can see Puzzle Mountain and Mount Colonel Foster, both of which tower above the Elk River Trail (Trip 26). The prominent points of Kings Peak stand out to the southeast.

Continue upwards on several more switchbacks through an open subalpine forest. Look for pink and white heather, magenta Davidson's penstemon, common red paintbrush, and pale purple spreading phlox along the sides of the trail. Reach a small **tarn** about 5 km (3.1 mi) from the parking lot at an elevation of 1450 m (4757 ft). There are several good **campsites** here.

CAMPING

The broad summit of Crest Mountain is a rocky meadow dotted with numerous ponds. The best camping is at the tarn at the 5 km (3.1 mi) mark.

Campsites: Several small cleared sites lie near the south end of the tarn. For spectacular views, camp atop a small bluff to the east.

Toilet: None. Dig a cat hole and use Leave No Trace best practices. Go well away from the tarn to the east or west. Be careful to stay away from the melt-water streams that feed it.

Water: Collect from the tarn

Food Storage: None. Bring rope to hang your food in one of the small trees. A bear canister or Ursack is a better option.

EXTENDING YOUR TRIP

Crest Mountain Summit: The summit of Crest Mountain is 2 km (1.2 mi) from the tarn and makes a fabulous side trip from camp. The indistinct, cairned route leaves from the southwest corner of the lake and gains 100 m (328 ft) en route to the peak, which is crowned with a radio repeater tower. Watch your step on the summit; the north side has a sharp drop-off. On the return trip, take your time exploring the extensive meadows, where you will find countless picturesque ponds and more wildflowers. Tread lightly if you venture off-trail and keep your boots on rock and dirt to protect the fragile plants.

NATURE NOTE

YESTERDAY'S VOLCANIC SEAFLOOR IS TODAY'S MOUNTAIN SUMMIT

As you explore the meadows of Crest Mountain, watch for pillow lava, the domed reddish-brown outcroppings typical on the peaks around Buttle Lake, nearby Upper Campbell Lake, and the Mount Arrowsmith massif (Trip 9). Today these rocks are mountaintops, but they originated on an ancient sea floor. When molten lava erupted from underwater volcanoes, it formed a tough crust as it met the cold water. The liquid interior remained malleable as it cooled, leading to a wide variety of bulbous shapes. Fossils indicate that these rocks were formed farther south 230 million years ago, then moved into their current location by shifting plate tectonics.

The lovely tarn near the top of Crest Mountain

FURTHER RESOURCES

Strathcona Provincial Park: info *bcparks.ca/explore/parkpgs/strath*
Trail Map: Buttle Lake/Elk River Area Trail Map, Strathcona Wilderness Institute
NTS Map: 092F13

NORTHWEST COAST TRIPS

THE RUGGED AND REMOTE northwest coast of Vancouver Island draws me back year after year. Each time I reach the end of a long, bumpy logging road or a sometimes choppy water taxi ride, I am handsomely rewarded for my journey. Deserted sandy beaches, lush rainforests, and craggy headlands abound. The northwest coast is also one of the best places to see black bears, wolves, sea otters, and whales.

Getting Around: Transportation to the trails requires time and planning. The Nootka Trail and Tatchu Peninsula can only be reached by water taxi or float-plane from Gold River, Tahsis, Zeballos, or Fair Harbour. Gold River is on paved Highway 28, but the other villages are on bumpy gravel roads. Cape Scott Provincial Park, Raft Cove Provincial Park, and Grant Bay all sit at the end of long logging roads that snake out from Port Hardy. While they may be dusty, bumpy, and often full of industrial traffic, the roads are all accessible by any passenger vehicle. The east side of Cape Scott Provincial Park can also be reached by water taxi from Port Hardy.

Indigenous Context: The west coast of Vancouver Island is the traditional territory of the Nuu-chah-nulth people, a collective of 15 nations. Gold River, Tahsis, and Nootka Island are in Mowachaht/Muchalaht Nation territory. The name *Tahsis* is a modification of a Nuu-chah-nulth word that means "way" or "passage." Nuchatlaht territory includes the village of Zeballos and the northern part of Nootka Island. Zeballos is also in Ehattesaht territory, as is the southern part of the Tatchu Peninsula. The rest of the Tatchu Peninsula and Fair Harbour are in Ka:ʼyu:ʼkʼtʼh'/Che:k:tles7etʼh territory.

The northern end of Vancouver Island is the territory of the Kwakwaka̱ʼwakw. They are divided into several subgroups, including the Tʼłatʼła̱siḵwala (Tlatlasikwala), whose territory stretches from Shushartie Bay, along the North Coast Trail, past Cape Scott to San Josef Bay. The Qwatʼsinuxw (Quatsino) have traditional territory around Winter Harbour, Grant Bay, and Raft Cove. To learn more about Kwakwaka̱ʼwakw history, art, and culture, visit the excellent Uʼmista Cultural Centre in Alert Bay.

Supplies: Campbell River is the last major centre where you can obtain groceries and outdoor supplies before heading to the northwest coast. Port Hardy has a grocery store and two gas stations. You can get gas and limited groceries at a deli in Gold River. Winter Harbour, Tahsis, and Zeballos each have a small general store with limited hours. These communities may also have gas stations but supply can be unreliable, so it's best to fuel up in Gold River or Port Hardy. Holberg has a pub but no other services. Fair Harbour has a convenience store.

Accommodations: If you are looking for a hotel, Port Hardy and Gold River are your best bets. Farther afield, Holberg, Winter Harbour, Tahsis, and Zeballos each have a few vacation rentals or fishing lodges. There are lots of camping options in the region. The Gold River Municipal Campground has first-come, first-served sites west of town. You can also camp at the Leiner River Recreation Site on the road between Gold River and Tahsis. In Zeballos, camp at first-come, first-served sites at Cevallos Campsite or at Rhodes Creek Recreation Site on the way to Fair Harbour. The Fair Harbour Marina has reservable campsites as well as cabins. Port Hardy has a few private campgrounds close to town. There are several rustic campgrounds on the logging roads northwest of Port Hardy. Nahwitti Lake Recreation Site between Port Hardy and Holberg, Kwaksistah Regional Park Campground in Winter Harbour, and the Western Forest Products San Josef Campground near the Cape Scott trailhead are the most convenient for backpackers.

The huge collection of fishing floats at Nels Bight (Trip 32)

28

UPANA CAVES

DAY HIKE

Difficulty: ●

Duration: 1 hour

Distance: 0.7 km (0.4 mi) round trip

Fees and Reservations: None

Elevation Gain: 30 m (98 ft)

High Point: 580 m (1903 ft)

Best Months: April to November

Regulations: No fires. No camping. Dogs permitted on leash.

Caution: Exploring inside the caves involves scrambling over steep, uneven, and slippery rocks. The caves are damp and chilly (7°C/45°F), even in summer, so wear warm, waterproof clothing and footwear. Watch your head on low ceilings. Bring at least two sources of light.

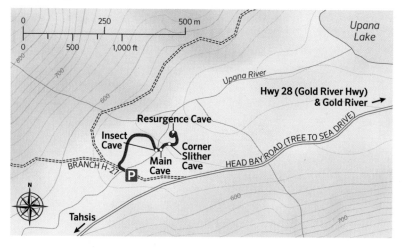

VANCOUVER ISLAND IS dotted with over 1000 caves, many of which are located near Tahsis. The Upana Caves are the easiest to reach, on a short and easy trail accessed from the main road between Tahsis and Gold River. First discovered in 1975 during road building, the caves are named for the Upana River, which flows through them. Interpretive signs explain the unique karst geology that transformed layers of shells into marble through millennia of heat and pressure, which was then eroded by rushing water to form the caves. Many of the caves have wide entrances, perfect for even the most claustrophobic cavers. Don't forget your flashlight!

Don't forget a flashlight or headlamp to explore inside the caves

GETTING THERE

From Campbell River, take Highway 28 west. At the town of Gold River, turn right onto Gold River Road and follow it for 3 km (1.9 mi). Turn left onto a bridge. On the other side, turn left onto Head Bay Road (signed for Tahsis). About 14.5 km (9 mi) later, turn right at the sign for Upana Caves onto Branch H-27. Park 0.1 km (328 ft) later, just before a bridge. There is an overflow parking area on the far side of the bridge down the right fork of the road.

TRAIL

TRIP PLANNER

0 km (0 mi)	Trailhead
0.2 km (0.1 mi)	Insect Cave
0.25 km (0.16 mi)	Main Cave
0.3 km (0.19 mi)	Corner-Slither Cave
0.35 km (0.22 mi)	Resurgence Cave

Find the **trailhead** on the north side of the bridge over the Upana River. The trail heads slightly downhill near the river through a remaining stand of old-growth forest. Watch for large western white pine, western hemlock, and yellow-cedar. A few minutes later, the trail curves left away from the river into a second-growth forest planted as part of a reforestation project in 1981. Keep an eye out for sinkholes and cracks in the rock, a signature feature of limestone karst topography.

Follow the trail down a small hill to the entrance to the first cave, **Insect Cave**. Like the other caves in the area, this one has a signboard in front with information and a diagram of the suggested route through the cave. Scramble down the slippery rocks into the cave. Be sure to look for crickets. They live in the cave between November and June.

Continue on the main trail farther downhill and around a corner to the entrance to **Main Cave** on your left. To access the cave, follow the narrow passage through The Keyhole, a weathered tube in the limestone rock. There are several passages to explore in this cave. The main route follows stairs downhill to the left, then curves into a low-ceilinged passage that leads to an opening on the edge of the Upana River. The water begins a 30 m (98 ft) underground journey here, emerging at Resurgence Cave, which you will visit later on this hike.

Retrace your steps back through The Keyhole, then turn left to continue along the main path. Take a short detour to the left to view a waterfall through the trees, best seen in the spring or after heavy rain. The trail passes through what looks like a normal second-growth forest. However, you are actually crossing the Upana River as it runs underground, about 20 m (66 ft) below you!

Another spur trail leads to **Corner-Slither Cave**. The wide, sloped entrance makes it easy to enter the cave. The path trends downhill to the right, creating a spiral pathway that soon becomes a tight squeeze as the passageway snakes downwards, so step carefully. This section is not for the claustrophobic or those who don't want to get their jackets dirty scraping against the walls. Most visitors will be content to visit the initial spiral corner and skip the slither.

Back on the main trail, head right for a few minutes. Bypass a set of stairs for now and continue to a wooden platform. Trees partially obstruct the view, but you can still gaze down at the canyon below and see the entrance to Resurgence Cave.

Retrace your steps to the staircase, then descend it to visit **Resurgence Cave**. The 10-m-high (33 ft) entrance is remarkable. Take a few minutes to admire the polished white rocks. This is marble, a limestone rock that has been transformed by heat and pressure. Watch for birds nesting in the cliffs just

The marble entrance to Resurgence Cave

inside the entrance. During periods of low water, you can explore farther into the cave along the underground portion of the Upana River. When you have finished exploring the cave, use the main trail to head back to the parking area.

FURTHER RESOURCES

Recreation Sites and Trails BC: info *sitesandtrailsbc.ca/search/search-result.aspx?site=REC3041&type=Site*

Village of Tahsis Upana Caves Self-Guided Tour: info and map *villageof tahsis.com/wp-content/uploads/2022/01/Upana-Caves-Self-Guided-Tour .pdf*

NTS Map: 92E16

Driving Map: *Vancouver Island BC Backroad Mapbook*

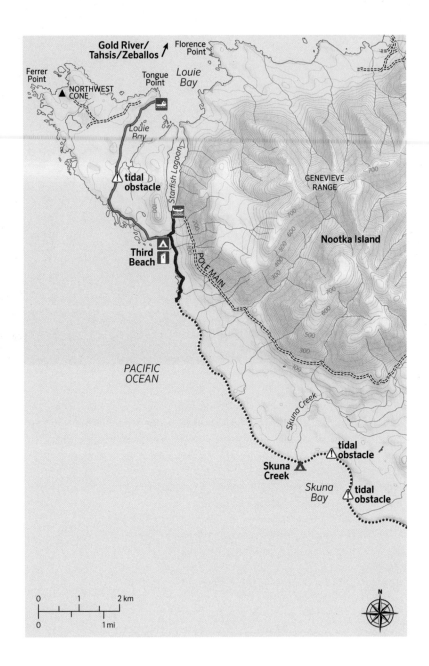

Gold River/
Tahsis/Zeballos ↗

Florence
Point

Ferrer
Point

*Louie
Bay*

Tongue
Point

▲NORTHWEST
CONE

*Louie
Bay*

⚠ **tidal
obstacle**

Starfish Lagoon

GENEVIEVE
RANGE

700

Nootka Island

700

**Third
Beach**

POLE MAIN

600

500

400

300

100

700

600

500

300

100

*PACIFIC
OCEAN*

Skuna Creek

⚠ **tidal
obstacle**

**Skuna
Creek**

*Skuna
Bay*

⚠ **tidal
obstacle**

0   1   2 km

0   1 mi

N

29

NOOTKA TRAIL ★

BACKPACKING TRIP

Difficulty: ◆
Duration: 3 to 5 days
Distance: 36 to 41.5 km (22.4 to 25.8 mi) one way

Elevation Gain: 50 m (164 ft)
High Point: 50 m (164 ft)
Best Months: May to September

Fees and Reservations: Trail fees are $50/adult and $25/child or senior. As well, each group must pay a $20 landing fee. Fees are payable to the Mowachaht/Muchalaht First Nation online, or in-person in Yuquot or at the Gold River Marina. All campsites are first-come, first-served.

Regulations: Dogs permitted but not recommended due to the high wolf population.

Caution: Nootka Island has a high wolf and black bear population, and sightings are common.

THE ISOLATED TRAIL along the west coast of Nootka Island near Gold River treats hikers to a variety of delights, including old-growth trees, sandy beaches, a waterfall, and the opportunity to see black bears and wolves. Unlike many of Vancouver Island's coastal trails, this route is almost entirely along the beach. The hike finishes in the Mowachaht/Muchalaht village of Yuquot, the site of the first contact between Indigenous Peoples and Europeans in British Columbia. Allow time at the end of your trip to visit the small museum in an old church and chat with the caretakers.

GETTING THERE

The Nootka Trail is located on Nootka Island, which can only be reached by boat or floatplane. You can access these services from the towns of Gold River, Tahsis, or Zeballos.

FROM GOLD RIVER

Gold River is the most popular departure point for transportation to the Nootka Trail by floatplane, water taxi, or freight boat. From Campbell River, take Highway 28 west through Strathcona Park to the town of Gold River. Follow Highway 28 for another 13 km (8.1 mi) to its end, at the Muchalaht Marina. Secure parking is included with your trail fees.

Air Nootka flies to Starfish Lagoon/Louie Lagoon at the north end of the trail, as well as to Friendly Cove/Yuquot at the south end. The flight follows the western shoreline of Nootka Island, which gives you a great pre-trip overview of the trail.

A floatplane gets ready to take off from Starfish Lagoon

The MV *Uchuck III* freight boat delivers supplies to remote camps in Nootka Sound from its base at the Muchalaht Marina, near Gold River. They also offer tourist cruises and transportation for hikers. With advance notice, they pick up Nootka Trail hikers from Friendly Cove (Yuquot) several days a week. Hungry hikers will be happy to hear they sell snacks onboard.

Members of the Mowachaht/Muchalaht Nation run a water taxi service from Muchalaht Marina, near Gold River, to the Nootka Trail. They pick up and drop off at Tongue Point and Yuquot (Friendly Cove).

FROM TAHSIS

Shorebird Expeditions in Tahsis offers water taxi services, with pickups and drop-offs at Tongue Point and Friendly Cove/Yuquot. To reach Tahsis, follow directions above to Gold River, then turn right onto Gold River Road and follow it for 3 km (1.9 mi). Turn left onto a bridge. On the far side, turn left onto 2WD-accessible Head Bay Road (signed for Tahsis), which is gravel. Follow this road for another 62 km (38.5 mi) into Tahsis, then take South Maquinna Drive to Westview Marina. There is pay parking at the marina.

FROM ZEBALLOS

Zeballos Expeditions offers water taxi service to and from Tongue Point and Friendly Cove/Yuquot. To get to Zeballos, go north on Highway 19 from Campbell River for 150 km (93.2 mi). Just after a bridge over Steel Creek, turn left onto Zeballos Forest Service Road (signed for Fair Harbour and Zeballos). Follow 2WD-accessible gravel roads for 42 km (26.1 mi). There are signs for Zeballos at all major junctions. There is secure pay parking at the marina.

TRIP PLANNER

–5.5 km (3.4 mi)	Tongue Point
0 km (0 mi)	Floatplane landing in Starfish Lagoon (Louie Lagoon)
1.5 km (0.9 mi)	Third Beach campground
8.5 km (5.3 mi)	Skuna Creek camping area
13 km (8.1 mi)	Calvin Falls campground
17.5 km (10.9 mi)	Bajo Point
23.5 km (14.6 mi)	Beano Creek campground
26 km (16.2 mi)	Callicum Creek
30.5 km (19 mi)	Maquinna Point
32 km (19.9 mi)	Sunrise Beach camping area
33 km (20.5 mi)	Tsa'tsil Lagoon
34 km (21.1 mi)	Sea Stack Beach camping area
35 km (21.7 mi)	Jewitt Lake
36 km (22.4 mi)	Yuquot (Friendly Cove)

In Nuu-chah-nulth, Nootka (spelled nuutkaa) means "go around" or "come around." Captain James Cook named Nootka Sound after this word in 1778, as he thought it was the name for the inlet, not a recommendation for navigation. The term was erroneously also applied to the local Indigenous people for nearly 200 years. In 1979 they chose the name Nuu-chah-nulth (also spelled nuučaan'uł), meaning "all along the mountains and sea," to represent 15 related groups. The Mowachaht/Muchalaht, who have lived on Nootka Island since time immemorial, are members of the Nuu-chah-nulth Tribal Council.

The Nootka Trail is most commonly hiked from north to south, starting with a floatplane drop-off at Starfish Lagoon (also called Louie Lagoon) and finishing at Friendly Cove (Yuquot) with a boat or floatplane pickup. You can also start the trail with a water taxi drop-off at Tongue Point at the north end of Louie Lagoon. This departure point adds an extra 5.5 km (3.4 mi) to your trip. Doing the trail from north to south allows you to explore the history at Yuquot at the end of your trip. It also means you'll be waiting for pickup at an established campground—the northern trailheads have no facilities. For ease of reference, this guide will refer to the Starfish Lagoon floatplane drop-off point as the trailhead and calculate distances from there.

If you take a water taxi from Gold River, Tahsis, or Zeballos, it will deposit you at **Tongue Point** at the northwest corner of Louie Lagoon. The boat deposits you directly onto the rocks, so you may get wet. Wear shorts and water shoes. Take a minute to explore the wreckage of the *Treis Lerarchi*, a

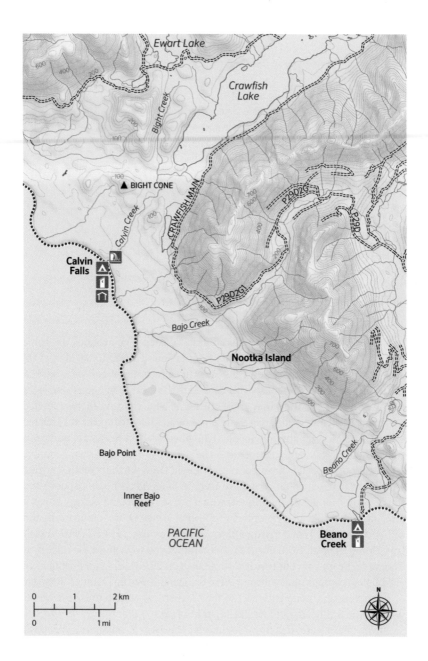

Ewart Lake

Crawfish
Lake

600 400 200

Bight Creek

200

100

▲ BIGHT CONE

100

Calvin Creek

CRAWFISH MAIN

100

P29D2G

P29D2G

P29D

700
600
400

400

Calvin
Falls

P29D2G1

100

Bajo Creek

Nootka Island

700
600
400
200
100

Bajo Point

Beano Creek

Inner Bajo
Reef

PACIFIC
OCEAN

Beano
Creek

0   1   2 km

0   1 mi

N

Evening reflections in a tide pool at Third Beach

Greek freighter. It ran aground at nearby Ferrer Point in 1969 and was towed here for salvage, but the price of scrap plummeted and the ruins remain today. Your route to the first campsite at Third Beach begins with a walk along the sand on the west side of Louie Lagoon. The route is much easier at lower tides, ideally below 1.6 m (5.2 ft), but can be completed at higher tides if you stick close to the shoreline.

About 2 km (1.2 mi) along, when the lagoon narrows, look for a path in the trees on the east side. It leads through the forest to the west coast of Nootka Island. You must take this route at higher tides, but at tides below 1.6 m (5.2 ft) you may be able to follow the lagoon out to the coast, then traverse the shoreline. From the end of the inland path, head south (left) along the shoreline on a path that scrambles across headlands and traverses pocket coves. Eventually, you'll emerge on the sands of Third Beach and connect with the main Nootka Island Trail.

Hikers arriving by floatplane will land in the eastern arm of **Louie Lagoon**, sometimes called **Starfish Lagoon** since the bottom is blanketed with starfish that are easy to see in the clear water. The plane will taxi to the southern end, where you will disembark, often in knee-deep water. Wear shorts and water shoes. There is a small, muddy beach here where you can put on your boots and gear up. It is a 1.5 km (0.9 mi) hike from here to Third Beach, one of the longest stretches of inland walking on the entire trail. It travels through a gorgeous old-growth forest with several giant trees. This section is tough going with heavy packs, thanks to lots of blowdowns, rocks, roots, and mud. Follow the square orange markers and flagging tape to stay on track.

Emerge from the forest onto the white sand of **Third Beach** and the first campground. (Confusingly, this beach is also sometimes called First Beach.) To continue along the trail, find the hanging buoys in the forest near the creek, next to the trail coming in from Starfish Lagoon. Ascend the steep slope with the help of a fixed rope. The next 0.5 km (0.3 mi) of the trail takes you through the forest around several headlands. The trail can be quite overgrown, with lots of blowdown and crisscrossing salal roots that can trip you. At very low tides, you may be able to stay on the beach for this section.

When the route rejoins the coast, you may be able to enjoy a long stretch of easy travel on rocky tidal shelves if the tides are in your favour. If not, you'll have to plod along the tops of sloped pea gravel beaches, which are often covered in drifts of seaweed and littered with driftwood. About 8.5 km (5.3 mi) from Starfish Lagoon, the trail curls east and arrives at **Skuna Creek camping area**. Cross the creek and follow the shoreline around Skuna Bay. The cliffs at the back of the bay are impassable at high tide, as is the point on the southeast side of the bay. There is no tidal bypass, so you may need to sit down and wait it out.

As you round the headland from Skuna Bay, the long sandy beach at Calvin Falls comes into view. Small aircraft from Vancouver and southern Vancouver Island often make day trips to this beach in good weather, since it is straight enough to function as a makeshift airstrip. Some of the pilots even bring surfboards to enjoy the waves. Find **Calvin Falls campground** in the middle of the beach on either side of Calvin Creek, near 13 km (8.1 mi). Calvin Creek is usually easy to rock-hop at low tide but requires wading at higher tides.

The trail continues down the beach to the south as the sand turns to gravel. At low tide, this can be an exciting place to explore the many tide pools, teeming with anemones, starfish, crabs, limpets, and other marine life. As you approach Bajo Point, the rocks become bigger and more slippery, sometimes described as "cannonballs covered in snot." It's easy to roll an ankle, so watch your step here. At low tides, you can walk on the rock shelf, which provides easier footing and the opportunity to explore more tide pools.

Bajo Point at 17.5 km (10.9 mi) is a good place to take a break. There are great views of sea stacks and an offshore reef, and you might spot whales, seals, and sea otters. In Spanish, *bajo* can mean "shoal" or "sandbank." Captain James Cook noted the offshore reef as a hazard in 1778, and a Spanish expedition gave it its name on a subsequent voyage in 1791. The forest here is the site of a Mowachaht fishing village site known as Aass. Follow a faint trail

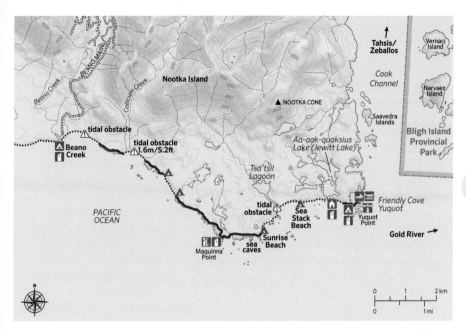

through the grass into the forest. The overgrown mounds are the remains of fallen longhouses, being reabsorbed into the forest. This is Indigenous land, so be respectful, do not disturb the site, and do not camp here.

The next section is a steady tromp across pea gravel beaches. With your feet sliding in the rocks with every step, this can be tiring at the end of a long day. Reach **Beano Creek campground** at 23.5 km (14.6 mi), on the west side of Beano Creek. The gravel bars at the mouth of Beano Creek change with each storm. In some years, crossing Beano Creek can be a challenge at high tide or after heavy rainfall. In others, winter storms push the gravel into a berm across the creek mouth and you won't even get your boots wet. The land on the east side of the creek and the beach beyond are home to a few private cabins and a lodge. The creek is named for Albert Bean, who had a cabin here in the 1920s.

The section of trail from Beano Creek around Maquinna Point is very rough and overgrown, with lots of blowdown and muddy sections. Expect slow travel times. At the west end of Beano Creek beach, the shoreline steepens into cliffs that are impassable at high tide. A rough trail through the salal marked with a buoy provides an alternate overland route. If the tide is low, continue a few minutes farther to the end of the beach in a small cove. Use the fixed line to scramble up a slippery 10 m (33 ft) rock slab that can require some tricky moves.

The trail weaves along the top of the cliff for about 2 km (1.2 mi) in dense old-growth forest dripping with moss, before rejoining the coast in a cove at **Callicum Creek**, near the 26 km (16.2 mi) mark. This is the only reliable water source between Beano Creek and Maquinna Point, so fill your bottles. The rocks at the east end of the cove are inundated at tides above 1.6 m (5.2 ft), but there is a short bypass trail. From here the route dips and weaves through pocket coves, past sea stacks, and across rough headland trails for about 4 km (2.5 mi). A few of these **pocket coves** have seasonal water sources and, depending on what winter storms have done to the beach, may also have space for a few tents above the high-tide line. On the overland trails, keep an eye out for culturally modified trees amongst the towering old-growth.

As you approach Maquinna Point, the trail follows the tops of rocky headlands that provide splendid views of the coastline ahead. After a very rough inland section that can be boggy, a marked side trail heads left to a lake, which is a good water source. A minute later, another trail heads right to the tip of **Maquinna Point**, at 30.5 km (19 mi), a great spot for a break. Maquinna is a hereditary name for Mowachaht chiefs. The point is named after the Chief Maquinna who was in power when European fur traders arrived in the late 18th century. Under his leadership, Nootka Sound became the main trading hub for the region. From the point that bears his name, look towards the Hesquiat Peninsula to the southeast, and back towards Beano Creek to the northwest. Past the point, the trail continues along the headlands to another side trail, this one leading to three sea caves that are fun to explore at low tide.

INDIGENOUS KNOWLEDGE

THE HISTORY OF YUQUOT

Yuquot translates to "the place where the wind blows in all directions" and is the centre of the Mowachaht world. Also known as Friendly Cove, Yuquot was home to a Mowachaht village that housed 13 extended family groups for thousands of years. In the 1800s, the Mowachaht were devastated by a series of epidemics. With a dwindling population, they joined with their former enemies, the Muchalaht. In the 1890s, Canadian laws stripped the Mowachaht/Muchalaht of most of their lands without their consent and confined them to a few small reserves. In 1967, the Canadian government required most of Mowachaht/Muchalaht to move from Yuquot to Ahaminaquus, near the present-day Gold River Marina. But pollution problems from the pulp mill necessitated a move inland to Tsaxana, near the town of Gold River, in 1996. Today only one family makes their home at Yuquot year-round, but members of the Mowachaht/Muchalaht First Nation spend the summer here fishing and acting as caretakers.

The rugged coastline near Maquinna Point

The trail leaves the forest and arrives on a pebble and sand beach at 32 km (19.9 mi), with a small seasonal stream fed by a circular pond behind the beach. It makes a good campsite, and hikers commonly call it **Sunrise Beach**. Past this beach, the trail resumes its pattern of alternating stretches of rough forest trail with trekking across short stretches of beach. A few of the forest entrances and exits are steep, but fixed ropes help you up and down the slopes.

At 33 km (20.5 mi), reach the mouth of the **Tsa'tsil Lagoon**. In Mowachaht the name means "where the tide comes up and goes into the lagoon." The topography here changes with storms and tides. Try to ford at low to mid tides. The best crossing is about 50 m (164 ft) inland from the mouth. The tide can rush through here as it goes out, creating a strong current, so be careful. At high tides, the crossing becomes a swim.

Continuing from the lagoon, you'll hike along pea gravel beaches scattered with driftwood and past crumbling sea stacks topped with hemlocks and salal bent by the wind. Near the 34 km (21.1 mi) mark, pass the last camping area and creek at **Sea Stack Beach**, named for the triangular sea stack just offshore. Past here, your route is on Mowachaht/Muchalaht land, and camping is not allowed on the beach.

Look for the entrance to the Yatz-mahs inland trail near 35 km (21.7 mi). (The name means "walk around.") It leads to Jewitt Lake, also known as Aa-aak-quaksius Lake. On a warm day, allow time for an end-of-trip swim. John Rodgers Jewitt was an English sailor who was captured and enslaved by

Chief Maquinna in 1803 as part of a fur-trading dispute. Jewitt lived with the Mowachaht for three years and later published his journal from the period. It was one of the first European accounts of Indigenous culture in British Columbia. The path passes several cabins and a graveyard, before arriving in the village of **Yuquot** at 36 km (22.4 mi). You can also take the gravel beach route to the village. Leave the beach when you see the carved welcome figure.

There is a campground in the grassy clearing in Yuquot. Be sure to allow time to visit the small museum inside the old church. If you didn't pay online, you can pay your trail fees here (cash only). Walk out to the lighthouse to enjoy views over the rugged shoreline. Floatplanes, water taxis, and the MV *Uchuck III* pick up from the long wharf.

CAMPING

The Nootka Trail has no designated campgrounds, but there are several frequently used areas. Most groups spend 4 nights on the trail, camping at Third Beach, Calvin Falls, Beano Creek, and either Sunrise Beach or Sea Stack Beach. But many other itineraries are possible. At the time of writing, Recreation Sites and Trails BC and the Mowachaht/Muchalaht Nation had plans to install more outhouses along the trail.

THIRD BEACH CAMPGROUND

After the hike from Starfish Lagoon or Tongue Point, Third Beach is paradise. The sandy beach and sea stacks are fun to explore at low tide.

Campsites: Lots of space on the sand above the high-tide line near the creek and at the west end of the beach
Toilet: Throne-style pit toilet behind the beach
Water: Collect from the creek on the east side of the beach. Head upstream or collect at low tide to avoid brackish water.
Food Storage: None. Hang in a tree or use a bear canister or Ursack.

SKUNA CREEK CAMPING AREA

Tucked into the mouth of the creek, this site is a good option if you don't have the tides to get around Skuna Bay. Most groups push on to Calvin Falls.

Campsites: On the sand near Skuna Creek
Toilet: None. Dig a cat hole in the forest, well away from the creek.
Water: Collect from Skuna Creek. It may be dry in very hot weather.
Food Storage: None. Hang in a tree or use a bear canister or Ursack.

CALVIN FALLS CAMPGROUND

The sandy beach and 6-m-high (19.7 ft) Calvin Falls make this the nicest place to camp on the Nootka Trail. In good weather, consider taking a rest day here to swim in the pool below the waterfall, look for fossils in the rocks next to the falls, or explore the tide pools.

Campsites: A clearing in the forest on the west side of the creek fits a few tents next to some open-sided shelters. There is also space amongst the driftwood on the beach on both sides of the creek.
Toilet: Throne-style pit toilet behind the beach, south of the creek
Water: Collect from Calvin Falls. The creek is tidal and can be brackish.
Food Storage: None. Hang in a tree or use a bear canister or Ursack.

BEANO CREEK CAMPGROUND

Beano Creek changes every year as storms and tides move the pebbles around at the mouth of the creek. There are private cabins nearby, so you may encounter non-hikers.

Campsites: There is usually space for tents in the gravel above the high-tide line. A few tents can fit in a clearing in the forest.
Toilet: Throne-style pit toilet in the forest, north of the creek
Water: Beano Creek can be brackish unless you go far upstream or collect at low tide. An alternative option is a side channel on the west side.
Food Storage: None. Hang in a tree or use a bear canister or Ursack.

HISTORY

EVENTS ON NOOTKA ISLAND NEARLY CAUSED A WAR IN EUROPE

Today Nootka Sound and the village of Yuquot are considered a quiet and remote part of British Columbia. But in the late 1700s, the area was the centre of an international conflict that nearly resulted in a European war. The Spanish navy arrived in 1774 to trade valuable sea otter furs with the Mowachaht. The British soon followed. In 1789, Spain seized several British fur-trading ships and began building a fort at Yuquot to support their claim of sovereignty over the Pacific Coast of North America. The British mobilized their navy against the Spanish in retaliation. The Spanish opted to negotiate instead of going to war, signing the First Nootka Convention in 1790. But the parties had differing interpretations of the agreement. Chief Maquinna of the Mowachaht sided with the Spanish on the condition that the area be returned to his people. Under the Third Nootka Convention, signed in 1794, Britain and Spain mutually agreed that the settlement of Yuquot should revert to the Mowachaht, who tore down the Spanish fort and other buildings.

Yuquot and the red-roofed Coast Guard station seen from the air

MAQUINNA POINT POCKET COVES CAMPING AREA

Several pocket coves between Beano Creek and Maquinna Cove make suitable campsites. Some have small, seasonal creeks.

Campsites: The coves may fit 1 or 2 tents above the high-tide line
Toilet: None in the coves. Dig a cat hole or use the throne-style pit toilet near the side trail to Maquinna Point.
Water: The creeks may be dry late in the year. It is prudent to carry water in from Callicum Creek or fill up at the lake near Maquinna Point.
Food Storage: None. Hang in a tree or use a bear canister or Ursack.

SUNRISE BEACH CAMPING AREA

This beach is a welcome sight after the rigours of the inland Maquinna Point section. However, the water source is seasonal and may be dry in hot weather.

Campsites: Room for several tents on the sand near the creek
Toilet: None. Dig a cat hole in the forest, well away from the creek.
Water: Collect from the creek
Food Storage: None. Hang in a tree or use a bear canister or Ursack.

SEA STACK BEACH CAMPING AREA

Some groups choose to spend their last night on the trail here, tucked into the driftwood on the beach behind a sea stack.

Campsites: Space on the pebble beach or at the edge of the forest
Toilets: None. Dig a cat hole in the forest, well away from the creek.
Water: A trickle of a creek runs out of the forest. It may disappear in hot weather, but you can follow the creek inland to find running water.
Food Storage: None. Hang in a tree or use a bear canister or Ursack.

YUQUOT CAMPGROUND AND CABINS

The Mowachaht/Muchalaht First Nation manages accommodations in Yuquot. Your trail fees include a night of camping in the grassy village site. Or rent one of their rustic cabins. (Ask at the church or call before your trip.)

Campsites: Room for a dozen tents in the grassy field.
Cabins: Six small cedar cabins
Toilets: Composting outhouses at the campground and on the cabin trail.
Water: Collect from Jewitt Lake, 1 km (0.6 mi) away
Food Storage: None. Hang in a tree or use a bear canister or Ursack.
Other Amenities: Picnic tables and fire pits. Cabins have platform beds, wood stoves for heat, propane stoves for cooking, and basic kitchen utensils.

EXTENDING YOUR TRIP

Tongue Point: If you flew into Starfish Lagoon, the hike along the coast and mud flats to Tongue Point and the shipwreck makes a worthwhile day trip from Third Beach. Plan to spend 5 to 6 hours on the 11 km (6.8 mi) round-trip hike. Time your visit for low tide for the easiest travel conditions.

FURTHER RESOURCES

Mowachaht/Muchalaht First Nation: online trail fee payment, Yuquot cabin info, and Gold River water taxi *yuquot.ca*
Fisheries and Oceans Canada: Saavedra Island tide table *waterlevels.gc.ca/en/stations/8645*
Air Nootka: floatplane info and reservations *airnootka.com*
Get West: passenger service on the MV *Uchuck III getwest.ca*
Shorebird Expeditions: Tahsis water taxi info and reservations *shorebird expeditions.com*
Zeballos Expeditions: water taxi info and reservations *zeballosexpeditions.com*
NTS Map: 092E10
Trail Map: Nootka Island Map, John Baldwin; Nootka Trail Topographic Hiking Map, Wild Coast Publishing
Driving Map: *Vancouver Island BC Backroad Mapbook*

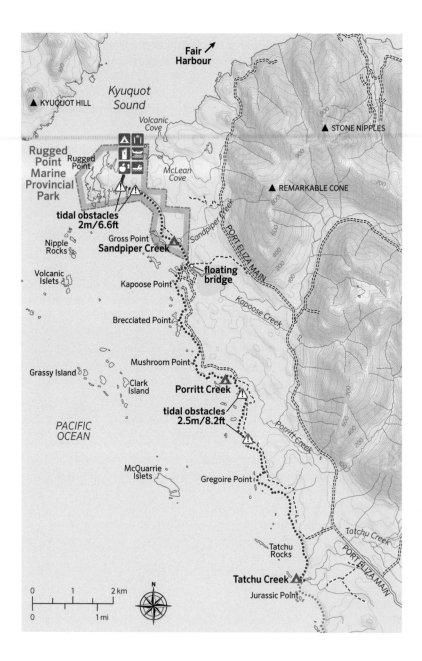

Fair Harbour ↗

▲ KYUQUOT HILL

Kyuquot Sound

Volcanic Cove

▲ STONE NIPPLES

Rugged Point Marine Provincial Park

Rugged Point

McLean Cove

▲ REMARKABLE CONE

tidal obstacles 2m/6.6ft

Nipple Rocks

Gross Point

Sandpiper Creek

Sandpiper Creek

PORT ELIZA MAIN

Volcanic Islets

floating bridge

Kapoose Point

Kapoose Creek

Brecciated Point

Grassy Island

Mushroom Point

Clark Island

Porritt Creek

PACIFIC OCEAN

tidal obstacles 2.5m/8.2ft

Porritt Creek

McQuarrie Islets

Gregoire Point

Tatchu Creek

Tatchu Rocks

PORT ELIZA MAIN

Tatchu Creek

Jurassic Point

0   1   2 km
0   1 mi

N

30

TATCHU PENINSULA

BACKPACKING TRIP

Difficulty: ◆
Duration: 2 to 4 days
Distance: 28 km (17.4 mi) round trip

Elevation Gain: 50 m (164 ft)
High Point: 50 m (164 ft)
Best Months: May to September

Fees and Reservations: None

Regulations: Dogs permitted but not recommended due to the high wolf population.

Caution: This remote area sees few hikers. A satellite messenger or other emergency device is recommended. Some areas of the trail are very rugged and require scrambling. The trail is not marked and some route-finding may be required. The Tatchu Peninsula has a high wolf and black bear population, and sightings are common.

THE ROUGH AND seldom-travelled route along the Tatchu Peninsula in Kyuquot Sound has much to offer hardy, experienced backpackers who cherish solitude and coastal exploration. The challenging trail features beautiful sandy beaches, fascinating geology, and plentiful wildlife, including endangered sea otters who thrive in kelp forests protected by offshore reefs. Several itineraries are possible, depending on hiker skill and transportation logistics. An out-and-back trip from Rugged Point to Tatchu Creek will suit most hikers. But those with experience scrambling over steep and exposed terrain can continue onward to Yellow Bluff or Port Eliza.

GETTING THERE

In general, the northern part of the trail between Rugged Point and Tatchu Creek is the most scenic and the least challenging. There are two scrambling sections between Tatchu Creek and Yellow Bluff with exposure to heights and a long, overgrown road walk section between Yellow Bluff and Port Eliza. Experienced scramblers and purists who want to complete the trail between Tatchu Creek and Yellow Bluff or Port Eliza can refer to a full description of that section at happiest outdoors.ca/tatchu-peninsula-trail, which also includes information on transportation logistics for that option.

Since most parties will choose to hike the trail as an out-and-back trip from Rugged Point to Tatchu Creek, that is what is described here. The Rugged Point trailhead can only be reached by boat from Fair Harbour or by floatplane from Gold River.

Hiking along the gravel beach near Tatchu Creek

FROM GOLD RIVER
Refer to the Gold River driving directions in Trip 29 (page 225). Air Nootka offers charter flights to Rugged Point.

FROM FAIR HARBOUR
For the first part of your journey, refer to the Zeballos driving directions in Trip 29 (page 226). Continue past the town on Zeballos Main, which curves away from the ocean and becomes Fair Harbour Main. Stay on this road for 34 km (21.1 mi), following signs for Fair Harbour at all junctions. There is paid parking at the marina. Both Voyager Water Taxi and Siiqaa Water Taxi operate out of the boat-in Indigenous community of Kyuquot but will ferry passengers between Fair Harbour and Rugged Point.

TRAIL

TRIP PLANNER

0 km (0 mi)	Rugged Point campground
3 km (1.9 mi)	Sandpiper Creek camping area
8 km (5 mi)	Porritt Creek camping area
14 km (8.7 mi)	Tatchu Creek camping area

The trail stretches along the Tatchu Peninsula from Rugged Point in the north to Port Eliza in the south. The name comes from a Nuu-chah-nulth word meaning "to chew," likely after a beach near Tatchu Point that was used for feasting and fishing by the Ehattesaht Nation. Today the Ehattesaht, members of the Nuu-chah-nulth Tribal Council, make their home on Zeballos Inlet.

Although this trail has three different access points and can be hiked as a point-to-point or out-and-back trip, the easiest and most scenic terrain is at the north end of the trail. This description covers the trail between Rugged Point and Tatchu Creek. (For a full description of the very challenging southern portion of the trail, see happiest outdoors.ca/tatchu-peninsula-trail.)

The trail begins at **Rugged Point Marine Provincial Park**, in a stunning sandy cove with a campground. If you catch a water taxi from Fair Harbour or a floatplane from Gold River, it will drop you off here. Find the trail just to the left of the covered cooking shelter. Walk past the side trail to the outhouse onto the only maintained path on the entire Tatchu Trail. It passes through an old-growth forest with several large Douglas-fir trees. Boardwalks carry you across boggy sections fringed with sword ferns, salmonberry, and salal. About 0.4 km (0.2 mi) later, emerge on the first of several gorgeous white-sand beaches in small coves.

If the tide is below 2 m (6.6 ft), you can head left on the beach around the first rocky headland. If not, look for a trail a few minutes down the beach to your left. This trail, like other overland trails on the Tatchu Peninsula, may be marked with a fishing buoy hanging in a tree. However, unlike other more popular coastal trails in this book that feature well-marked overland trails, the buoys may be missing or hard to spot.

The beach route and overland trail converge in a tiny, steep-sided cove. Follow a rugged trail uphill from the northeast corner of the cove. A fixed rope will aid your ascent. At the top of the ropes, a wooden ladder bridges a small chasm over a surge channel. After the ladder, another set of ropes helps you drop down to another sandy cove. At tides below 2 m (6.6 ft), you can walk on the beach around the next headland. At higher tides, find the trail in the northeast corner of the cove and follow it as it snakes behind a large rock outcropping.

The **overland trail** emerges on a beautiful sandy beach that stretches for over 1 km (0.6 mi) to the southeast. A stream trickles through the centre of the beach, but it is not reliable and runs dry by early summer. Follow the beach as it curves behind the rocks of **Gross Point** and dips into a smaller cove. A short, rough trail leads through the salal over the headland. Find it on the far side of the cove, just before the cliffs begin.

Once across the headland, the trail leaves the forest next to a large tree atop a rock and arrives on the shores of **Sandpiper Creek**. At lower tides, you can hop across the creek, but at higher tides, you'll need to remove your boots and

Rounding Kapoose Point at low tide

wade. There is great camping at the back of the beach, near the creek. Sandpiper Creek is the first reliable water source if you are hiking from Rugged Point.

Continue down the wide, fine-sand beach for nearly 1 km (0.6 mi) to **Kapoose Creek**. At low tide, Kapoose Creek is another good water source. You can wade the creek at lower tides. However, it is worth detouring to the edge of the forest to cross on a sturdy floating bridge. The Kapoose Creek area is private property crisscrossed with roads related to an off-grid housing development and a medicinal mushroom research facility. The ongoing construction takes away from the wilderness feel, but thankfully you will pass through the area quickly.

On the far side of the bridge, follow the grassy shoreline behind the rocks as it curves back towards the ocean. Cross a headland on a short trail through the brush and emerge on a brief stretch of sandy beach before clambering around a rocky point. A jetty juts into a tiny cove next to a small landing, the main supply point for the Kapoose Creek development. Cross the jetty onto the rocky beach and pick your way across the unique volcanic rocks at Kapoose Point. A prominent sea stack stands sentinel just offshore.

Past the point, the route returns to the sandy beach for a few minutes. You may notice openings in the forest behind the beach. These lead to the road network in the Kapoose Creek development. These roads are part of an abandoned logging road system that parallels the coast from Kapoose Creek to just before Tatchu Creek. The roads are very overgrown with salmonberry and thimbleberry, making them ideal habitat for bears. Using the road provides an alternative to coastal hiking, but is less pleasant due to the abundant vegetation and lack of views. The roads aren't marked on any maps, so a GPS app with a satellite photo overlay layer is necessary for navigation.

Continue along the coast as the route curves around **Brecciated Point**, which is made of volcanic rocks interspersed with sandy beaches. The point is named for breccia, a type of rock composed of broken fragments of other rocks cemented together. In this case, the volcanic breccia consists of blocks of lava that have solidified, broken apart, been reincorporated into the liquid magma, then solidified again.

Hiking south, you'll encounter several fine gravel beaches before arriving at **Mushroom Point**. The point has an interesting mushroom shape when viewed from the air, which led to its name. Find a rough trail through the bushes to a grassy bench behind the point. Look for paintbrush, columbine, and other wildflowers blooming here in June. Scramble southwards along the red and black jagged volcanic rocks, seeking the path of least resistance. At times you will be on a shelf high above the ocean.

Once around the point, the trail dips briefly into a small gravelly cove before traversing another rocky shelf. Watch for a short trail that cuts through thick salal behind a rocky headland. Emerge from the forest into a bay with a steep gravel beach. A few minutes along, a wider gravel terrace at the back of the beach provides a good camping area. **Porritt Creek** cascades into the ocean at the east corner of the bay. Cross the gravel beach and follow the bank

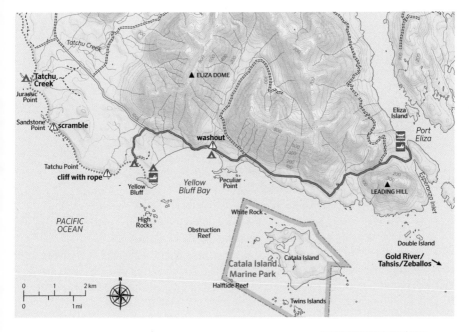

upstream to wade across Porritt Creek, best done at tides below 3 m (9.8 ft). A brief slash of deciduous trees and a set of weathered logs in the stream bed marks the location of a former logging road bridge. The water here is deep enough for a swim, a welcome cool-down on a hot day.

Heading south from Porritt Creek, round a rocky outcropping with a few careful steps across slippery seaweed-covered rocks. This area may be impassable at tides above 2.5 m (8.2 ft). After the rocks, continue along a series of gravel beaches. Arrive at a **surge channel** around 10 km (6.2 mi) from Rugged Point. You can hike through the surge channel at tides below 2.5 m (8.2 ft), picking your way across the rocks. Alternatively, look for a rough bear trail over the headland to bypass it.

Past the surge channel, find more gravel beaches and a section of sandstone shelf that makes pleasant walking at low tide. Arrive at an **unnamed creek** approximately 11 km (6.8 mi) from the northern trailhead. Follow the creek inland for a few minutes to a wide and shallow area where it is easy to wade across. The south bank is very steep and undercut in places. Scramble up to an opening in the trees, then follow a rough trail for a few metres along the top of the bank to the beach. Continue south from the creek to round **Gregoire Point** on a series of pea gravel beaches. The gravel sinks with every step, making for strenuous walking.

About 14 km (8.7 mi) from Rugged Point, arrive at **Tatchu Creek**. There is a good campsite here on the flat top of the gravel spit. Huge stumps from long-ago logging act as planters for new growth, with salal, Nootka rose, and thimbleberry growing from their tops.

NATURE NOTE

RETURN OF THE SEA OTTERS

The small coves and offshore rocks along the Tatchu Trail are home to a thriving population of sea otters. But these marine members of the weasel family were hunted almost to extinction for their thick fur coats. A 1911 treaty gave sea otters international protection, and a program reintroducing 89 animals in the 1970s has since expanded the population into the thousands. As the otters come back, the entire coastal ecosystem is in a state of recovery. When the otters were absent, sea urchins flourished, munching through underwater kelp forests, which reduced habitat for fish. Now that the otters have returned to eat the urchins, the kelp forests are expanding, providing habitat for salmon, ling cod, and rockfish. Bring binoculars to watch for sea otters as you hike.

CAMPING

Besides Rugged Point, there are no designated campgrounds or facilities anywhere along the Tatchu Trail. Theoretically, you could make camp anywhere above the high-tide line. However, there are a few ideal camping areas along the trail.

RUGGED POINT CAMPGROUND

This is the only designated campground on the Tatchu, located in Rugged Point Marine Provincial Park. It's picturesque, with a protected beach, and can be busy with kayakers and pleasure boaters.

Campsites: Three wooden tent platforms, 1 cleared spot on the dirt near the cooking shelter, and some marginal sites in the driftwood on the beach.
Toilet: Composting toilet a few metres down the trail
Water: None. Bring your own water if arriving by water taxi or floatplane. Or pack water in from Sandpiper Creek or the seasonal creek on the beach between Rugged Point and Gross Point.
Food Storage: Food locker behind the cooking shelter
Other Amenities: Open-sided cooking shelter with a picnic table, a small wooden counter, and a nearby metal fire ring.

SANDPIPER CREEK CAMPING AREA

A gorgeous camping area beside the creek on a long, white-sand beach. The only drawback is the development at Kapoose Creek, a small portion of which is visible from camp. You can also camp a few minutes away, on the beach on the north side of Gross Point.

Campsites: Lots of flat spots amongst the driftwood
Toilet: None. Dig a cat hole in the forest in the centre of the beach (avoiding both creeks) or go on the beach well below the high-tide line.
Water: Collect from Sandpiper Creek. Go upstream at high tide.
Food Storage: None. Hang in a tree or use a bear canister or Ursack.

PORRITT CREEK CAMPING AREA

A deep pool in the creek makes a good swimming spot on a hot day.

Campsites: Space for a few tents on a gravel bench above the high-tide line at the northwest corner of the bay.
Toilet: None. Dig a cat hole in the forest on the west side of the bay, or on the beach well below the high-tide line.
Water: Collect from Porritt Creek, heading upstream at high tide.
Food Storage: None. Hang in a tree or use a bear canister or Ursack.

TATCHU CREEK CAMPING AREA

This area has beautiful views and faces northwest, so you can watch the sunset over the Brooks Peninsula. However, it can be windy.

Campsites: Space for a few tents on a flat area atop the gravel spit. One cleared site in the forest along the stream bank.
Toilet: None. Dig a cat hole in the forest behind the beach to the north, or on the beach well below the high-tide line.
Water: Collect from Tatchu Creek, heading upstream at high tide
Food Storage: None. Hang in a tree or use a bear canister or Ursack.

EXTENDING YOUR TRIP

Sandstone Point: From Tatchu Creek, take a 5 km round-trip hike south along the beach to the tide pools and water-sculpted formations at Sandstone Point. Along the way, watch for fossils at Jurassic Point, which requires tides below 2.8 m (9.2 ft) to pass.

South to Yellow Bluff or Port Eliza: Experienced hikers who aren't afraid of heights can tackle the precipitous scramble around Sandstone Point and a later rope-assisted cliff descent, to continue to the water taxi pickup at Yellow Bluff, 6 km (3.7 mi) from Tatchu Creek. Purists can continue from there along overgrown logging roads to Port Eliza, 18 km (11.2 mi) from Tatchu Creek, where they can catch a water taxi or floatplane.

FURTHER RESOURCES

Fisheries and Oceans Canada: Kyuquot tide table *tides.gc.ca/en/stations/ 8710*
Rugged Point Marine Provincial Park: info *bcparks.ca/explore/parkpgs/ rugged_pt*
Happiest Outdoors: additional trail info *happiestoutdoors.ca/tatchu-peninsula-trail*
Air Nootka: Gold River floatplane info and reservations *airnootka.com*
Voyager Water Taxi: Fair Harbour water taxi info and reservations *voyager watertaxi.com*
Siiqaa Water Taxi: Fair Harbour water taxi info and reservations *siiqaawater taxi.ca*
NTS Map: 092E14
Trail Map: Tatchu Peninsula Trail Map, John Baldwin
Driving Map: *Vancouver Island BC Backroad Mapbook*

31

NORTH COAST TRAIL

BACKPACKING TRIP

Difficulty: ◆◆
Duration: 5 to 6 days
Distance: 43.1 km (26.8 mi) one way

Elevation Gain: 245 m (804 ft)
High Point: 245 m (804 ft)
Best Months: June to September

Fees and Reservations: Camping fees are $10/person/night, payable online. All campsites are first-come, first-served.

Regulations: No drones. No smoking, vaping, or cannabis. No dogs. Fires allowed below the high-tide line or in metal fire rings only.

Caution: This area has a high wolf and black bear population. Sections of the trail are very rough and technical. Expect slow travel times.

THE NORTH COAST TRAIL (NCT), completed in 2008, is one of the newest long-distance trails on Vancouver Island. It travels across rugged terrain through old-growth rainforests, coastal bogs, and remote beaches. While the route is within Cape Scott Provincial Park, be prepared for a challenging and

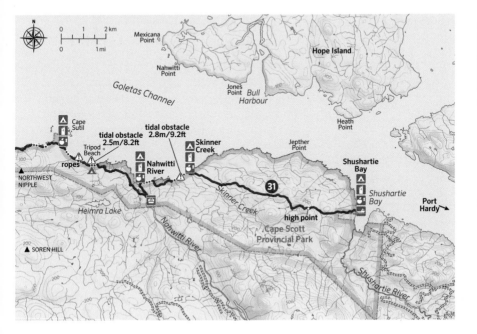

Hiking through the fog on the way to Irony Creek Camp. Photo: Greg Smolyn

exciting wilderness adventure that includes climbing near-vertical slopes using fixed ropes, riding cable cars across wide tidal rivers, and slogging through seemingly bottomless mud. The payoff is the spectacular coastal scenery and the opportunity to see lots of wildlife, including black bears, wolves, whales, and sea otters.

GETTING THERE

The west end of the NCT at Shushartie Bay can only be reached by boat. The official east end of the trail is at Nissen Bight. Most hikers opt to walk the Cape Scott Trail out to the Cape Scott parking lot, where they get a shuttle bus. Driving yourself to the Cape Scott trailhead is also an option. You can also arrange to be picked up by water taxi at Fisherman Bay, near Nissen Bight.

CAPE SCOTT WATER TAXI AND SHUTTLE BUS

The water taxi leaves from the marina in Port Hardy. From Campbell River, head north on the Island Highway (Highway 19). On the outskirts of Port Hardy, just after you cross the bridge over the Quatse River, turn right onto Hardy Bay Road. Follow this road for 1.6 km (1 mi) to the Quarterdeck Resort and Marina. The Cape Scott Water Taxi office is at the back of the parking lot, next to the inlet. They offer secure parking for a small fee.

Book ahead to arrange a water taxi drop-off at Shushartie Bay or a pickup at Fisherman Bay. Several water taxis run to Shushartie Bay each morning. Service to Fisherman Bay (and to Cape Sutil at the halfway point) is by request and depends on tides.

The same company also offers a daily shuttle bus service from the Cape Scott trailhead to its Port Hardy office.

CAPE SCOTT TRAILHEAD DRIVING DIRECTIONS

From Campbell River, head north on the Island Highway (Highway 19) for 228 km (142 mi). Just before you reach Port Hardy, turn left onto Holberg

Road. The rest of the journey is on logging roads that are 2WD accessible but can be rough and dusty. Watch for fully loaded logging trucks. All of the major intersections have signs.

From the turnoff, follow Holberg Road for 29 km (18 mi), passing Nahwitti Lake on your right. After the lake, take the left fork to continue another 16 km (10 mi) to Holberg. Stay on the main road through the village, which turns into San Josef Main Forest Service Road as it leaves town. Continue for another 19 km (11.8 mi), following signs for Cape Scott Provincial Park. Turn left at the sign into the park, and reach the gravel parking lot a few minutes later.

TRAIL

TRIP PLANNER

0 km (0 mi)	Shushartie Bay trailhead and campground
8.1 km (5 mi)	Skinner Creek campground
11 km (6.8 mi)	Nahwitti River campground
14.5 km (9 mi)	Tripod Beach tidal obstacle
16 km (9.9 mi)	Cape Sutil campground
23.8 km (14.8 mi)	Irony Creek (Shuttleworth Bight) campground
29 km (18 mi)	Wolftrack Beach
35.6 km (22.1 mi)	Laura Creek campground
43.1 km (26.8 mi)	Nissen Bight campground

The trail is most commonly hiked from east to west, beginning with a water taxi drop-off at Shushartie Bay. In Kwak'wala, the language of the Kwakwaka'wakw, Shushartie means "place to find cockles." The water taxi captain will nose the boat up against the shoreline because there is no dock. You will need to clamber off the bow onto slippery rocks covered in seaweed and barnacles. The trail begins next to a large information board and heads up the hillside immediately. You'll pass through the **Shushartie Bay campground** in the first few minutes. The first section of trail is relentlessly steep and rough as you gain 150 m (492 ft), with several muddy fixed ropes to help you up the worst bits.

The grade eases about 1 km (0.6 mi) from the start as the trail climbs through the upland bog and across grassy meadows speckled with stunted trees. Water flows everywhere, tinged red from all the cedar tannins in the soil. Weathered grey boardwalks here make for fast hiking. However, the areas between the boardwalks will have you mired in mud, sometimes to your knees. Gaiters and waterproof boots are essential to keep your feet dry. To protect the fragile ecosystem, stay on the trail, even when it's muddy, and use your trekking poles to probe for tree roots, rocks, and planks underneath the mud.

About 2.5 km (1.5 mi) from the trailhead, reach the NCT's high point, a whopping 245 m (804 ft). From here, you'll head gradually downhill towards the ocean as the path alternates between boardwalks and boot-sucking mud. A sign near 4 km (2.5 mi) marks the halfway point between Shushartie Bay and Skinner Creek. The trail gets marginally easier past here, but it is still very muddy and challenging.

The vegetation changes from inland bog to coastal forest at about 8 km (5 mi) as you head downhill on a staircase to Skinner Creek. Duck under logs as you walk along the rocky creek bed to its mouth and the **Skinner Creek campground**. After the long inland section, enjoy the ocean views across Goletas Channel to Hope Island. In Kwak'wala, the creek is called Wabetso, meaning "little river." An alternate name is Tsēɫseqā-la'alis, which means "red or thimbleberry beaches."

Leaving Skinner Creek, you can walk on the beach for 1 km (0.6 mi) if the tides are below 2.8 m (9.2 ft). At high tides, take the rough inland route that starts behind the outhouse at the campsite. At the west end of the beach, brightly coloured fishing buoys mark the start of the forest trail. Use the fixed rope to haul yourself up the steep slope to meet the high-tide bypass trail. The next kilometre (0.6 mi) of trail heads inland on an old section of settler's corduroy road, so it's a bit muddy.

Emerge on a gravel beach and head west to **Nahwitti River campground**, near the mouth of the river. This is a great place to watch for humpback whales and sea otters feeding in the kelp offshore. The estuary is also a common place to spot bears at low tide. The trail heads into the forest from the back of the campsite and parallels the Nahwitti River. Cross the river on the cable car. The river takes its name from the Nahwitti people, who had a fortified village at Cape Sutil (see boxed History text, page 254). The Kwak'wala word for the river is wuda staade, which means "having cold water."

From the cable car, the trail follows the river downstream for a few minutes before turning inland to climb up and over a 120 m (394 ft) hill. Near the 14 km (8.7 mi) mark, the trail begins to descend to the ocean on a long set of wooden stairs known as Long Leg Hill.

At the bottom, emerge on **Tripod Beach**. This small pebble beach marks the other tidal obstacle on the NCT. The rocks on the west side of the beach are passable at tides below 2.5 m (8.2 ft). There is no bypass trail, so if you arrive at high tide you'll have to wait. Despite the lack of formal facilities, some groups choose to camp in the marginal space above the high-tide line. A trickle of a creek provides drinking water. When the tide is low enough to pass, take a minute to admire the unique tripod-shaped boulder that gives the beach its name.

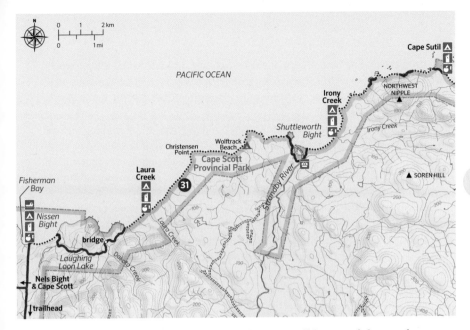

The trail between Tripod Beach and Cape Sutil is one of the toughest stretches on the North Coast Trail. The inland trail ascends several steep and slippery headlands with the help of fixed ropes. In places, the trail is nearly vertical and can challenge hikers with a fear of heights. If the tide is low enough, you may be able to bypass some of these spots by taking vague routes across the slippery cobblestone beaches. Take your time and use caution in this area.

The 0.5-km-long (0.3 mi) sandy beach at **Cape Sutil**, near the 16 km (9.9 mi) mark, is a welcome sight after the challenging rope scramble section. Walk past the campground at the west end of the beach, then follow the trail into the forest as it cuts across the neck of the cape. The cape takes its name from the *Sutil*, a Spanish ship that made a historic circumnavigation of Vancouver Island in 1792.

Over the next 5.5 km (3.4 mi), you will follow a pattern: hike along a steeply sloped gravel beach through a cove littered with driftwood, then take a muddy and rough inland trail choked with salal through the forest, before descending to another cove. The cycle repeats numerous times.

About 21.5 km (13.4 mi) from the start, you'll leave the forest behind and walk on the beach all the way to Shuttleworth Bight. Carry on across the gravel and driftwood to the wide stretches of sand and the campground at **Irony Creek**, in the centre of the bight, at 23.8 km (14.8 mi). Henry Shuttleworth built a homestead at the mouth of Strandby River in 1905. Over the years a small community formed and a school was built. Most settlers left during World War I. Today a small parcel of private land on the west side of the beach is the only legacy of the settlement. In Kwak'wala, Shuttleworth Bight is known as Kosae, Go'saa, or Kegegwis, which means "sandy beach." The lagoon to the west of the mouth of Strandby River was a T'łat'łasikwala and Qwat'sinuxw village and fishing station.

Continue along the sand for 1.5 km (0.9 mi) to the buoys marking the exit from the beach. The trail leads inland along the banks of the Strandby River to the cable car. Once across the river, it's easy walking for another 1.5 km (0.9 mi) to the coastline. Get back into the rhythm of short overland trails connecting pocket coves starting near the 27 km (16.8 mi) mark. Black bears have been active in the section of trail from Strandby River to Laura Creek over the last few years. They like to forage along the shoreline and travel the same paths between the beaches that hikers do, so make noise and stay alert.

Arrive at sandy **Wolftrack Beach**, a popular unofficial camping area about 29 km (18 mi) from the start. It has space for a few tents above the high-tide line and a small stream. Past here the path follows slanted beaches with deep gravel that can be exhausting to trudge through, especially at the end of a long day. A few short inland trails that cross headlands help provide a brief respite.

Near the 32 km (19.9 mi) mark, round Christensen Point, named for Soren Christensen, a Danish settler who built a homestead near the Strandby River in 1894. The Kwakwaka'wakw call it Yachbe, meaning "bad point." Continue slogging through the gravel to **Laura Creek** and the campground a few hundred metres farther along, 35.6 km (22.1 mi) from the trailhead.

Crossing the log bridge over Dakota Creek

From the camp, continue along the beach for another kilometre (0.6 mi), then follow fishing buoys inland up a staircase into the forest. The path follows a section of old Danish settler trail through the upland bog. About 2 km (1.2 mi) after camp, the trail crosses several branches of Dakota Creek. In Kwak'wala the creek is called Wachlalis, which means "river on beach in a bay." A massive log bridges the main channel, but a subsequent crossing is unbridged and may require a ford in times of heavy flow.

From the creek, the trail gains elevation to the plateau and Laughing Loon Lake, near 40 km (24.9 mi). The lake is very marshy, so you'll be disappointed if you were looking forward to a freshwater swim. The trail follows the lakeshore on some stretches of boardwalk punctuated by mud holes. As the trail loses elevation and heads back towards the coast, it becomes progressively more challenging, with lots of mud, roots, and slippery terrain.

Emerge on the beach at **Nissen Bight**, named for Danish settler Nels C. Nissen. The end of the North Coast Trail and the Nissen Bight campground is a kilometre (0.6 mi) farther west, at the far end of the beach, at km 43.1 (26.8 mi). While the North Coast Trail ends here, your journey doesn't. You can arrange for a water taxi to pick you up at Fisherman Bay, a few minutes along the trail. Or you can hike out to the Cape Scott trailhead, 15 km (9.3 mi) away. Follow the trail uphill from Nissen Bight for 1.9 km (1.2 mi), then turn left and follow the Trip 32 trail description to hike to the trailhead.

CAMPING

There are 7 official campgrounds on the NCT. You may camp on any of the beaches above the high-tide line, but often this isn't practical due to lack of flat space and drinking water. The most used unofficial campsites are Tripod Beach (14.5 km/9 mi) and Wolftrack Beach (29 km/18 mi). Details for those 2 sites are in the trail description above.

SHUSHARTIE BAY CAMPGROUND

This small, dark camp is set into a steep hillside above the Shushartie Bay trailhead. You could stay in an emergency or if you hike the NCT in the reverse direction and want to be ready to meet a morning water taxi.

Campsites: Three wooden tent platforms
Toilet: Outhouse next to the main trail
Water: None. Pack in water with you on the water taxi or filter from the inland bog 1.5 km (0.9 mi) up the trail. In an emergency, find a stream by heading northwest along the coast at low tide for 15 minutes to the second of 2 beaches.
Food Storage: Food locker near the outhouse

Set on the beach alongside the creek, this camp has great views across the Goletas Channel. Most hikers camp here on their first night.

Campsites: Two clearings in the forest west of the creek, or numerous sites on the beach. The nicest sites are on sandbars next to the creek.
Toilet: Outhouse accessed from a short trail west of the creek.
Water: Collect from Skinner Creek. Be sure to go above the high-tide line to avoid salt water and contamination from seagulls.
Food Storage: Food locker near the outhouse

Strong hikers with an early start aim for this camp on their first night. It is set in the forest behind the beach, which gives it good shelter from storms. Watch for wildlife at the river mouth.

Campsites: Four wooden tent platforms in the forest, plus sloped spots on the pebble beach.
Toilet: Outhouse on a spur trail near the tent platforms
Water: Collect from the Nahwitti River by following the trail upstream for a few minutes. Go at low tide to avoid salt water.
Food Storage: Food locker on the main trail

HISTORY

THE BRITISH NAVY SHELLS AN INDIGENOUS VILLAGE

Cape Sutil was the site of a T'łat'łasikwala village known as Nahwitti. During the fur trade in the 1700s and early 1800s, Nahwitti was a key port. But by the 1820s, the British had established other forts and a coal mine nearby, diminishing its importance. In 1850 the Nahwitti people were accused of killing three British men who had fled into the wilderness after deserting their posts on a Hudson's Bay Company (HBC) ship. The magistrate of the local HBC fort asked the Nahwitti to surrender the alleged murderers. The chief refused but said he was willing to pay the value of the murdered men in blankets or furs. The governor of British Columbia insisted that the Nahwitti be taught a lesson, so the British navy sailed to the village and burned it to the ground. The navy returned in 1851 with a warship and shelled the village, killing and wounding many Nahwitti people. The Nahwitti survivors later moved to Bull Harbour on Hope Island, and Cape Sutil remains uninhabited today.

CAPE SUTIL CAMPGROUND

The sandy beach at Cape Sutil is a common second-night destination. If the weather is sunny and warm, this is the best camp for swimming. The nearby cape is inside the Nahwitti First Nation Reserve and off-limits to visitors.

Campsites: Numerous spots in the sand above the high-tide line
Toilet: Outhouse off the main trail at the west end of the beach
Water: Collect from a faint creek halfway down the beach. Look for flagging tape, then follow a short trail to a collection pool.
Food Storage: Food locker on the main trail and a signed second locker set back from the beach, a few minutes west of the water source

IRONY CREEK (SHUTTLEWORTH BIGHT) CAMPGROUND

The usual third-night camp, most hikers agree that Irony Creek is the most beautiful place to camp on the NCT. Sandy Shuttleworth Bight is almost 3 km long (1.9 mi) and you'll camp right in the middle of it.

Campsites: Four wooden tent platforms in the forest just west of the creek. Numerous tent sites amongst the driftwood on the west side of the bight.
Toilet: Outhouse in the forest behind the tent platforms
Water: Collect from Irony Creek
Food Storage: Food locker near the tent pads

LAURA CREEK CAMPGROUND

Besides Shushartie Bay, this is the smallest camping area on the NCT, which can be an issue since most parties sleep here on night 4. Plan to arrive early, especially early in the season when the creek is high. The main campsite is about 0.3 km (0.2 mi) west of the creek.

Campsites: Four tent platforms in the forest. A few small tent sites in the driftwood at the mouth of Laura Creek. The high tide comes very close to these sites, so use caution. They may not be usable if Laura Creek is in flood.
Toilet: Outhouse in the forest behind the tent platforms
Water: Collect from Laura Creek
Food Storage: Food locker near the tent platforms

NISSEN BIGHT CAMPGROUND

The 1-km-long (0.6 mi) sandy beach of Nissen Bight marks the end of the NCT. Some hikers stay here before walking out to the parking lot or heading to Cape Scott (Trip 32).

Campsites: Numerous campsites in the sand above the high-tide line. Most are on the west side of the bight.
Toilet: Outhouse on the trail at the west end of the beach

Tents on the beach at Shuttleworth Bight

Water: Collect from a creek at the east end of the beach, near the North Coast Trail. Follow signs in the forest to find it. Note that the water is at the opposite end of the beach from the main camping area, so fill up before you hike to camp.

Food Storage: Food locker near the outhouse

EXTENDING YOUR TRIP

Cape Scott: Combine the North Coast Trail with a trip to Cape Scott (Trip 32). The most common way to do that is to finish the NCT, then hike another 5.6 km (3.5 mi) to camp at Nels Bight. From there, make a day trip to the Cape Scott lighthouse, then hike out to the trailhead the following day.

FURTHER RESOURCES

Cape Scott Provincial Park: info and trail fees *bcparks.ca/explore/parkpgs/cape_scott*

Happiest Outdoors: additional trail info *happiestoutdoors.ca/north-coast-trail*

Fisheries and Oceans Canada: Cape Scott tide table *tides.gc.ca/eng/station?sid=8790*

Cape Scott Water Taxi: shuttle bus and water taxi info and reservations *capescottwatertaxi.ca*

NTS Maps: 092L13; 102I16

Trail Maps: North Coast Trail/Cape Scott Marine Trail Waterproof Mapsheet, Wild Coast Publishing; North Coast Trail map, John Baldwin

Driving Map: *Vancouver Island BC Backroad Mapbook*

32

CAPE SCOTT ★

BACKPACKING TRIP | Trail map on p. 263

Difficulty: ■
Duration: 2 to 3 days
Distance: 6 to 41.4 km (3.7 to 25.7 mi) round trip

Elevation Gain: 100 m (328 ft)
High Point: 100 m (328 ft)
Best Months: May to September

Fees and Reservations: Camping fees are $10/person/night, payable online. All campsites are first-come, first-served.

Regulations: No drones. No smoking, vaping, or cannabis. No dogs. Fires allowed below the high-tide line only or in metal fire rings at Eric Lake campsite.

Caution: This area has a high wolf and black bear population. Drinking water can be hard to find at the height of summer.

WALK IN THE footsteps of Danish settlers to the northernmost tip of Vancouver Island at Cape Scott. The trail takes you through several ecosystems, including old-growth rainforest, coastal bog, and sand dunes. You'll also pass remnants of homesteads and farms. Choose from four campgrounds along the way, including the beautiful sandy beach at Nels Bight. It makes a great base camp to tackle the hike out to the Cape Scott lighthouse at the tip of Vancouver Island.

GETTING THERE

Refer to the Cape Scott trailhead driving directions in Trip 31 (page 248). Cape Scott Water Taxi runs daily shuttle bus services between Port Hardy and the trailhead.

TRAIL

TRIP PLANNER

0 km (0 mi)	Cape Scott trailhead and parking lot
1 km (0.6 mi)	San Josef junction
3 km (1.9 mi)	Eric Lake campground
9.3 km (5.8 mi)	Fisherman River campground
13.1 km (8.1 mi)	Nissen Bight junction
14.7 km (9.1 mi)	Hansen Lagoon
16.8 km (10.4 mi)	Nels Bight campground
20.7 km (12.9 mi)	Guise Bay campground

Boardwalks lead across some of the boggier sections

Find the **trailhead** next to the information board and the covered picnic area. The first few minutes of the trail are smooth crushed gravel. Watch for a huge old-growth cedar on the right (north) side of the trail. Reach a **T-junction** about 1 km (0.6 mi) from the trailhead. Turn right to continue to Cape Scott. (Turning left will take you to San Josef Bay, Trip 33.)

The trail becomes a lot rougher after you leave the junction, with lots of slippery logs, mud, and puddles. Your route to the Cape follows an old Danish settler route from the early 1900s. As you walk, look for corduroy logs underfoot and drainage ditches beside you.

Just before the 2 km (1.2 mi) marker, reach another junction. Heading straight will take you to a viewpoint at the south end of Eric Lake, once a boat dock for the Danish settlers. Turn right to continue on the main trail, which meanders through a spectacular old-growth forest on slippery boardwalks and bridges, including one made from a huge fallen log. Arrive at the **Eric Lake campground**, about 3 km (1.9 mi) from the trailhead. Follow the boardwalks through the campground to another intersection. Go left down to the lakeshore for more views and a good snack spot. Turn right to continue on the main trail.

Past the campground, the trail heads away from the lake through more old-growth forest, including a giant Sitka spruce with a diameter of over 7 m (23 ft). The trail parallels St. Mary Creek through a rocky section. Look for old telegraph wires strung through the trees. After the 8 km (5 mi) mark, the old-growth forest opens into a coastal bog ecosystem, and you begin to travel on another section of old corduroy road.

The trail gets rougher just past 9 km (5.6 mi), as you hike a re-routed section through the rainforest to a new bridge over the **Fisherman River**. On the far side, follow stairs and boardwalks towards the campground, then turn left to follow the main trail to Cape Scott. The rainforest melts away as you re-enter the bog, with small trees, tufts of grass, and tannin-rich water running everywhere. The trail is mostly on sturdy boardwalks through here, but watch out for mud holes between sections of planks.

The bog gradually turns to forest as you approach a T-junction at 13.1 km (8.1 mi). If you continue straight, you'll arrive at Nissen Bight in 1.9 km (1.2 mi), which is the terminus of the North Coast Trail (Trip 31). The main route to Cape Scott goes left. This area is a good place to take a break and absorb some local history. About 1 minute before the junction, follow an unmarked trail uphill on the right (east) side of the trail to reach a touching marble memorial for a 12-year-old Danish settler. A faint side trail on the other side of the main trail leads to more graves hidden in the salal.

Follow the main trail left from the junction as it heads downhill into the forest. In a few minutes, reach an information board at the former Spencer Farm. Look for the remains of a collapsed building on the left (south) side of the trail and an overgrown trail leading to more artifacts on the right (north) side of the trail.

The trail emerges from the forest into the open grasslands of **Hansen Lagoon** at 14.7 km (9.1 mi). A muddy trail leads through the grass to a bridge over Hansen Creek, then back into the forest. The next section of the trail is flat and easy as you hike through an old-growth forest. Pass through a huge cluster of hanging buoys and at 16.8 km (10.4 mi) emerge on the beach at **Nels Bight**, named for Danish settler Nels C. Nissen. In Kwak'wala, the language of the Kwakwa̲ka̲'wakw, it is called Tsewunchas, meaning "winter place."

To continue to Guise Bay, turn left and walk up the beach, passing several good campsites. Cross the creek where it flows across the sand, then head into the forest at the trailhead marked with an information board and a hanging buoy. The next section includes one of the only hills on the trail, gaining about 75 m (246 ft) in less than 1 km (0.6 mi). At 18.8 km (11.7 mi), reach Bowen Beach and go left, walking along the sloping sand for nearly 1 km (0.6 mi). Watch for buoys at the far end of the beach and follow them back into the trees. Walk through the dense forest for another 0.8 km (0.5 mi) along an old corduroy road, to arrive at **Guise Bay** at 20.7 km (12.9 mi). Captain John Guise commanded one of two British ships on a 1786 fur-trading expedition to the B.C. coast.

Fishing floats at Guise Bay mark the beginning of the trail to the lighthouse

From Guise Bay, you can day hike to the Cape Scott lighthouse, the north-westernmost point on Vancouver Island (see Extending Your Trip). The cape was named after David Scott, a merchant with the British East India Company who helped finance a fur-trading expedition to the area in 1786.

CAMPING

With four campgrounds along the trail, you can create an itinerary that suits your fitness level. The overwhelming majority of hikers camp at Nels Bight, then day hike to Cape Scott from there.

ERIC LAKE CAMPGROUND

This campground is popular with hikers who get a late start. It features an interconnected series of wooden tent platforms and boardwalks, surrounded by ferns and mossy trees. Some people have compared the setting to the Ewok village in the Star Wars universe.

Campsites: Eleven wooden tent platforms
Toilet: Outhouse at the north end of the camp
Water: Collect from the stream in the centre of camp or from Eric Lake
Food Storage: Food lockers in the centre of the camp
Other Amenities: A short trail leads to a small gravel beach on Eric Lake

FISHERMAN RIVER CAMPGROUND

Set in a dark, dense forest, this campground is a good option if you want to break up the long hike to Nels Bight over 2 days.

Campsites: Two wooden tent platforms
Toilet: Outhouse at the entrance to camp
Water: Collect from Fisherman River next to the bridge
Food Storage: Food locker near the outhouse

NELS BIGHT CAMPGROUND

This sandy beach stretches for over 2 km (1.6 mi). On busy summer weekends, expect to find dozens of campers here.

Campsites: Numerous clearings above the high-tide line. Most people camp at the southwestern end of the beach.
Toilets: Outhouses where the trail meets the beach, just past the ranger station, and at the start of the trail to Guise Bay
Water: Collect from the stream at the southwest end of the beach. From the Guise Bay trailhead, follow signs southeast along a spur trail to find a collection pool in the forest.
Food Storage: Food lockers behind the beach in 3 locations: next to the outhouse past the ranger station, where the trail meets the beach, and at the southwest end of the beach before the creek

GUISE BAY CAMPGROUND

This quiet campground is set amongst sand dunes in a small bay.

HISTORY

DANISH SETTLEMENTS

Hikers on the Cape Scott Trail will encounter the legacy of the area's history as a Danish-Canadian settlement. In 1894 a Danish fisherman from Seattle named Rasmus Hansen sailed into the bay and was inspired to start an agricultural settlement. Along with other Danish settlers, he built dykes in the tidal flats of Hansen Lagoon to convert them to hay fields. A trail linked the farms south of the lagoon to Fisherman Bay, next to Nissen Bight, where Nels C. Nissen ran a general store and post office. But by 1907 most of the settlers had left because without road access, the area was too remote. A second wave of American settlers arrived in 1913, but they soon encountered the same difficulties as the Danes. With the arrival of World War I, the community was abandoned for good. The area was established as a provincial park in 1973. Today you can still see the fence lines and dykes in Hansen Lagoon, along with lots of historical garbage near the junction with the Nissen Bight trail.

Campsites: Numerous sloped clearings above the high-tide line
Toilet: Outhouse on a spur trail at the southeast end of the beach
Water: Collect from the stream at the far southeast end of the beach. It often runs dry by the middle of summer.
Food Storage: Food lockers near the outhouse

EXTENDING YOUR TRIP

Cape Scott Lighthouse: From Guise Bay, make the 5.8 km (3.6 mi) round-trip hike to the lighthouse at Cape Scott. The trailhead is marked with buoys in the grassy dunes at the west end of the bay. The route follows a mossy plank road left over from World War II, when the area was home to a Royal Canadian Air Force radar station. Near the beginning, a short side trail leads left to a small beach with craggy sea stacks. The rough plank road turns to smooth gravel about 2 km (1.2 km) from Guise Bay and climbs a small hill. Keep left at the fork to arrive at the lighthouse grounds and the end of the trail. Climb the metal stairs up to the light for the best view. The lighthouse keepers, Harvey Humchitt Jr. and Todd Maliszewski, have been stationed here for over 20 years and love to chat with hikers.

North Coast Trail: Many hikers choose to add the trip to Cape Scott to their 43 km (26.7 mi) North Coast Trail hike (Trip 31). A typical itinerary starts with the NCT, detours to Nels Bight with a day hike to Cape Scott, then follows the Cape Scott Trail out to the parking lot.

San Josef Bay: The beautiful sandy beach and sea stacks at San Josef Bay make a great add-on to this trip, as either a day hike or an overnight trip (Trip 33). It's a 4 km (2.5 mi) round-trip hike from the San Josef junction to the beach.

FURTHER RESOURCES

Cape Scott Provincial Park: info and trail fees *bcparks.ca/explore/parkpgs/cape_scott*

Happiest Outdoors: additional trail info *happiestoutdoors.ca/cape-scott-trail*

Fisheries and Oceans Canada: Cape Scott tide table *tides.gc.ca/eng/station?sid=8790*

Cape Scott Water Taxi: shuttle bus and water taxi info and reservations *capescottwatertaxi.ca*

NTS Map: 102I16

Trail Maps: North Coast Trail/Cape Scott Marine Trail Waterproof Map-sheet, Wild Coast Publishing; North Coast Trail map, John Baldwin

Driving Map: *Vancouver Island BC Backroad Mapbook*

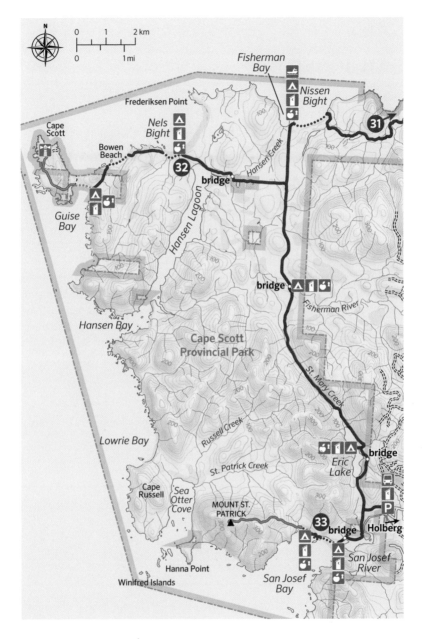

N

0   1   2 km
0   1 mi

Fisherman Bay

Frederiksen Point

Nissen Bight

Cape Scott

Nels Bight

Bowen Beach

32

bridge

Hansen Creek

31

100

Guise Bay

Hansen Lagoon

100

bridge

Fisherman River

Hansen Bay

200

200

Cape Scott Provincial Park

100

Russell Creek

St. Mary Creek

300

Lowrie Bay

200

St. Patrick Creek

Eric Lake

bridge

Cape Russell

Sea Otter Cove

MOUNT ST. PATRICK

300

33

bridge

Holberg

P

Hanna Point

Winifred Islands

San Josef Bay

San Josef River

32 CAPE SCOTT | p. 257

33 SAN JOSEF BAY | p. 264

SAN JOSEF BAY

BACKPACKING TRIP | Trail map on p. 263

Difficulty: ●
Duration: 2 days
Distance: 6 to 8 km (3.7 to 5 mi) round trip

Elevation Gain: 45 m (148 ft)
High Point: 45 m (148 ft)
Best Months: Year-round

Fees and Reservations: Camping fees are $10/person/night, payable online. All campsites are first-come, first-served.

Regulations: No drones. No smoking, vaping, or cannabis. Dogs allowed on leash at San Josef Bay. No dogs in other areas of the park. Fires allowed below the high-tide line only.

THE WIDE GRAVEL path to San Josef Bay is flat enough to push a stroller or pull a wagon, making it a wonderful destination for families and beginners. Choose from two beach campgrounds where you can wander between sea stacks, explore a river estuary, or just relax on the sand. If you crave more adventure, tackle the rugged trail to the top of nearby Mount St. Patrick for incredible views and a glimpse of a unique upland bog ecosystem.

GETTING THERE

Refer to the Cape Scott Trailhead driving directions in Trip 31 (page 248). Cape Scott Water Taxi runs a daily shuttle bus service between Port Hardy and the trailhead.

TRAIL

TRIP PLANNER

0 km (0 mi)	Cape Scott trailhead and parking lot
1 km (0.6 mi)	San Josef junction
3 km (1.9 mi)	First Beach campground
4 km (2.5 mi)	Second Beach campground

The **trailhead** is at the northwest corner of the parking lot, next to the information board and covered area. The park facility operator, 43k Wilderness Solutions, sometimes leaves wheelbarrows at the trailhead that hikers can use for hauling gear to San Josef Bay. The crushed gravel trail winds through lush rainforest and past an old-growth cedar on the north (right) side of the trail.

Walking between sea stacks at low tide

After 1 km (0.6 mi), arrive at a **junction**. Turn left to continue to San Josef Bay. (The path to the right leads to Cape Scott, Trip 32.)

The wide gravel trail heads due south, roughly paralleling the path of the San Josef River, which is out of sight to your left. There are several huge old-growth trees in this area, including a big cedar on your right (west) a few minutes past the junction. About 2 km (1.2 mi) from the start, reach an interpretive sign just before a bridge. A faint trail to the left leads to a clearing near the riverbank, which was the site of Henry Ohlsen's store and post office, in use until 1944. Today little evidence remains.

Continue across the sturdy bridge and along the trail as it curves to follow the unseen bank of the river. Watch for three trees with intertwined roots suspended above the forest floor, the product of a nurse log that has long since decayed. After crossing another bridge, it is just a few minutes to the sand of San Josef Bay. The beach stretches for nearly 1 km (0.6 miles), and the San Josef River empties into the ocean on its eastern flank. At low tide, the San Josef Estuary can be interesting to explore, but keep an eye out for foraging black bears.

You may wish to stop and camp here, at **First Beach campground**. To continue to Second Beach campground, head right (west) along the sand towards a collection of small rocky islets. At tides below 1.7 m (5.6 ft), you can continue along the beach past the islets and around a headland. Be sure to duck behind the first islet to wander through a beautiful collection of sea stacks.

At high tides, you will need to take a rough overland bypass trail that is about 0.3 km (0.2 mi) long. The start of the trail is poorly marked and partially hidden by a fallen tree, so you may need to hunt for it. It is just behind the first islet in a small gully. The first section is very steep, and you pull yourself up with the help of a fixed rope. The trail tops out about 40 m (131 ft) above sea level as it works through a brushy and often muddy section, before descending in a wet draw to the beach at the back of a surge channel. Follow the coast to the right around another rocky outcropping to arrive at **Second Beach campground** and the water source for both camps.

CAMPING

FIRST BEACH CAMPGROUND

First Beach is the easiest to reach and has lots of great campsites. However, it does not have a water source.

Campsites: Numerous clearings in the sand above the high-tide line and more in the forest behind the beach
Toilet: Outhouse on a spur trail west of where the trail meets the beach
Water: None. Bring your own or collect from the source at Second Beach.
Food Storage: Four food lockers where the trail meets the beach

SECOND BEACH CAMPGROUND

This camp offers more solitude than First Beach, since it is harder to reach. While it has a water source, it also has fewer campsites.

Campsites: Several clearings amongst the driftwood just above the high-tide line. There are also several marginal clearings in the forest.
Toilet: Throne-style pit toilet about halfway down the beach

NATURE NOTE

COASTAL UPLAND BOG ECOSYSTEM

At 416 m (1365 ft), Mount St. Patrick is the highest point in Cape Scott Provincial Park. Unlike most mountain peaks, which are craggy summits of sharp rock, the summit of Mount St. Patrick is covered in a unique upland bog ecosystem known as a blanket bog. Cape Scott sits within the wettest variant of the Coastal Western Hemlock biogeoclimatic zone. The area receives about 2.6 m (8.5 ft) of rain each year and regularly experiences winds up to 100 km (62 mi) an hour. As a result, the ground is covered in open pools of water and a thick layer of sphagnum moss, with patches of grasses, ferns, and salal. Stunted lodgepole pine, yellow-cedar, Douglas-fir, mountain hemlock, and juniper struggle to survive in small clumps. The vegetation here is similar to the upland bog section between Shushartie Bay and Skinner Creek on the North Coast Trail (Trip 31). This is a very fragile ecosystem, so take care to stay on the trail, even if that means getting muddy boots.

Sea Otter Cove and the Helen Islands seen from atop Mount St. Patrick

Water: A stream trickles through a gully at the eastern end of the beach. Later in the season, follow a rough trail steeply uphill to where the creek is still running. Alternatively, follow the Mount St. Patrick Trail for 0.2 km (0.1 mi) to reach a more reliable stream.

Food Storage: Food locker located behind the beach, midway between the outhouse and the water source

EXTENDING YOUR TRIP

Mount St. Patrick: A rough, muddy, and sometimes steep trail leads to the 416 m (1365 ft) summit. The hike is only a 6 km (3.7 mi) return trip from an unmarked trailhead at the western end of Second Beach, but expect slow travel due to technical terrain and lack of trail maintenance. The last 20 minutes before the summit are above the treeline, in a unique upland bog environment with stunted trees and lots of mud. The views from the summit are panoramic, so save this trip for a clear day. Down to the southwest you can see Sea Otter Cove and the Helen Islands. The huge turbines of the Cape Scott Wind Farm are visible to the northeast. A swath of Crown land stretches in between, pockmarked by clear-cuts.

FURTHER RESOURCES

Cape Scott Provincial Park: info and trail fees *bcparks.ca/explore/parkpgs/cape_scott*

Fisheries and Oceans Canada: Cape Scott tide table *tides.gc.ca/eng/station?sid=8790*

Cape Scott Water Taxi: shuttle bus info and reservations *capescottwatertaxi.ca*

NTS Map: 102I16

Trail Maps: North Coast Trail/Cape Scott Marine Trail Waterproof Mapsheet, Wild Coast Publishing; North Coast Trail map, John Baldwin

Driving Map: *Vancouver Island BC Backroad Mapbook*

34

RAFT COVE

BACKPACKING TRIP

Difficulty: ●

Duration: 2 days

Distance: 6 km (3.7 mi) round trip

Elevation Gain: 65 m (213 ft)

High Point: 65 m (213 ft)

Best Months: Year-round

Fees and Reservations: Camping fees are $5/person/night, payable online. All campsites are first-come, first-served.

Regulations: No drones. No smoking, vaping, or cannabis. Dogs allowed on leash. Fires allowed below the high-tide line only.

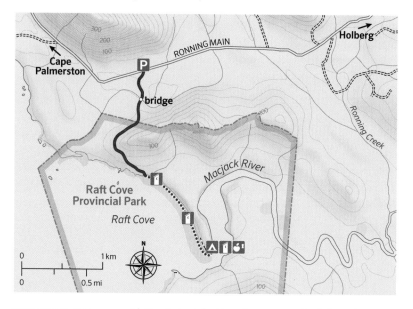

THE KILOMETRE-LONG (0.6 MI) stretch of sand at remote Raft Cove is a popular destination for surfers who brave the enormous waves rolling in off the Pacific Ocean. Hikers can explore the rugged coastline on either side of the beach to discover sea caves and pocket coves, then camp in the forest on the peninsula that divides the calm Macjack River from the rough water of the ocean. At low tide, ford the river to explore the remains of a trapper's cabin.

The windswept beach at Raft Cove

GETTING THERE

For the first part of your journey, follow the driving directions to Holberg in Trip 31 (page 248). From Holberg, continue for another 12.5 km (11.8 mi), then turn left onto Ronning Main Forest Service Road, following signs for Raft Cove. Stay on Ronning Main for 11 km (6.8 mi). Watch for a large cleared parking lot on your left.

TRAIL

TRIP PLANNER

0 km (0 mi)	Trailhead and parking lot
2 km (1.2 mi)	Trail reaches the beach
3 km (1.9 mi)	Main campground on peninsula

The **trailhead** is at the west end of the parking area and quickly heads downhill into a dark, regenerating second-growth forest. After a few minutes, emerge on an old roadbed at an information board. This was the original trailhead, before it was relocated closer to Ronning Main. The next section features board-walks and bridges that take you through wetlands around an unnamed creek.

When the boardwalk ends, the rough trail begins. Work your way through an old-growth forest of western hemlock, western redcedar, and Sitka spruce. Follow the slippery trail as it ducks under the rootballs of blowdown, wallows through mud holes, and ascends root staircases. Reach the trail's high point

The rugged trail includes lots of tree roots and mud

on the shoulder of a ridge around 1 km (0.6 mi) from the start. From there, the trail descends steadily through more rugged forest.

Reach the west end of the **beach** near the 2 km (1.2 mi) mark. The sand stretches away for another kilometre (0.6 mi) to the southeast. If you have time, the rocky coastline to the north (right) is fun to walk at low tide, when you can explore small sea caves. To get to the campground, turn left and head down the beach. Cross a trickle of a stream in the first few minutes. It dries up in the hot months, but it can be a valuable water source at other times of the year. Pass an outhouse a few minutes later. There are several small camping areas above the high-tide line or hacked out of the forest in the next section of beach.

Continue down the beach to the main **campground** at the mouth of the Macjack River, on a peninsula that separates the river from the ocean. The calm waters of the Macjack River are a great place to cool off on a hot day, and they are significantly warmer than the ocean. At low tide, you can ford the river (expect waist-high water) to fetch water from a nearby creek. The mouse-riddled remains of early settler Willie Hecht's cabin on the south bank are also worth poking around in. Follow the coastline south to explore countless pocket beaches.

CAMPING

You can camp anywhere along the beach, but the main camping area is at the southeastern end, at the mouth of the Macjack River.

Campsites: Ten dirt platforms in the forest, plus numerous spots on the beach above the high-tide line
Toilets: Two composting outhouses at the main campground, a third near where the trail hits the beach, and a fourth partway down the beach
Water: The Macjack River is brackish and undrinkable, even at low tide. You may want to pack in your own water. In spring and fall, you may be able to

collect water from an intermittent stream near where the trail hits the beach. Or ford the river at low tide to collect from a more reliable stream on the opposite side.

Food Storage: Several food lockers in the main camping area at the end of the peninsula, and 1 food locker about halfway down the beach.

EXTENDING YOUR TRIP

Canoe the Macjack River: An alternative way to access Raft Cove is by canoeing 6 km (3.7 mi) down the Macjack River. It's a long journey on bumpy backroads to the put-in. From Winter Harbour, take West Main, Topknot Main, and then a deactivated spur to the river. In summer, the river is slow-moving and flat. An advantage of arriving by boat is easy access to the water source on the east side of the river.

Cape Palmerston Recreation Area: Continue another 2 km (1.2 mi) down Ronning Main from the Raft Cove parking lot. A rough trail leads through the salal to a scenic pebble beach.

FURTHER RESOURCES

Raft Cove Provincial Park: info and trail fees *bcparks.ca/explore/parkpgs/raft_cove*

Fisheries and Oceans Canada: Cape Scott tide table *tides.gc.ca/eng/station?sid=8790*

NTS Map: 102I09

Driving Map: *Vancouver Island BC Backroad Mapbook*

NATURE NOTE

SALAL BERRIES

The beach at Raft Cove, like many others along the coast of Vancouver Island, is fringed with thick salal bushes that reach up to 3 m (9.8 ft) high. Ripening in July and August, salal berries were a very important food for coastal Indigenous Peoples. When eaten fresh, the dark purple berries are juicy with a mealy texture. The Kwakwa̱ka̱'wakw preserved the berries for winter use by mashing them, then boiling them or letting them stand until the mixture thickened into a jam. Next, they poured the jam into cedar frames set on skunk cabbage leaves and dried them over a fire. The resulting cakes were about 3 cm (1 in) thick and could measure up to 30 cm (11.8 in) wide and 90 cm (35.4 in) long. The cakes were rolled or folded in special cedar boxes for storage. When it was time to eat the cakes, they were soaked in water to rehydrate them, broken into small pieces, then mixed with eulachon oil grease.

35

GRANT BAY

BACKPACKING TRIP

Difficulty: ●
Duration: 2 days
Distance: 1 km (0.6 mi) round trip

Fees and Reservations: None

Regulations: Dogs permitted.

Elevation Gain: 40 m (131 ft)
High Point: 40 m (131 ft)
Best Months: Year-round

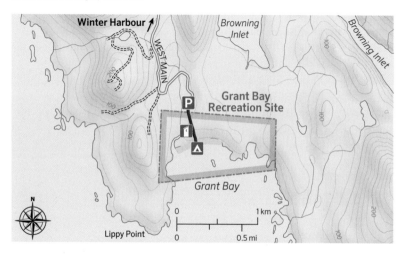

THE JOURNEY TO Grant Bay starts with a long, bumpy drive on logging roads and ends with a short and easy trail through an incredible stand of old-growth trees. Your reward is a beautiful, remote sandy beach that sees few visitors. Set up camp amongst the driftwood, then explore the rugged coastline on either side of the bay. You might even see wolf tracks disappearing into the underbrush.

GETTING THERE

For the first part of your journey to Holberg, follow the driving directions in Trip 31 (page 248). About 3.5 km (2.2 mi) after leaving Holberg, turn left onto Winter Harbour Road.

Stay on Winter Harbour Road for 4.5 km (2.8 mi), then turn left onto South 700 Main Forest Service Road, following signs for Winter Harbour. About

The beautiful white-sand beach at Grant Bay

5 km (3.1 mi) later, watch for a sign for Winter Harbour and turn right onto South Main FSR. Follow South Main for 8 km (5 mi), then turn right onto Winter Harbour Road. About 3 km (1.9 mi) later, reach a major 4-way intersection.

Your route to Grant Bay turns right onto West Main FSR. (If you want to visit the village of Winter Harbour, continue straight for 4 km/2.5 mi.) From the 4-way intersection, follow West Main to a dead end 13 km (8.1 mi) later. Parallel park on the side of the road, being careful to allow other cars enough room to turn around. A large green sign marks the trailhead.

TRAIL

TRIP PLANNER

0 km (0 mi)	Trailhead and parking
0.45 km (0.27 mi)	Side trail to toilet
0.5 km (0.31 mi)	Grant Bay Beach

The trail leaves the logging road and heads directly into a gorgeous grove of old-growth trees. Take a minute to admire the towering western hemlock and Sitka spruce trees emerging from clumps of salal and clusters of huge sword ferns. For the first few minutes, the trail is crushed gravel, which smooths out all the bumps. But soon the gravel gives way to bare soil with tree roots poking through. Shredded landscape cloth covers the trail in places, waiting for future deliveries of fresh gravel.

As light streams through the trees and you approach the beach, look for a faint trail winding through the salal to your right. It leads to a throne-style pit **toilet**, hidden from view of the main trail. As the path leaves the forest, it transitions to boardwalk across a short dune covered in grass. Follow the planks to arrive at the centre of **Grant Bay Beach**, considered one of the most beautiful beaches on northern Vancouver Island.

The fine sand stretches for 0.7 km (0.4 mi) across the back of the bay, bounded by rocky outcroppings on each side. Looking south, you'll see the jagged coastline of Cape Parkins, Lawn Point across Quatsino Sound, and, in the distance, the hills of the Brooks Peninsula jutting out into the wild Pacific Ocean. The bay takes its name from William Grant, who received a grant of Crown land in this area in 1904. Locals call it Open Bay for its shape.

CAMPING

The shallow angle of Grant Bay provides lots of sand above the high-tide line for campsites along its length. To protect the fragile dune ecosystem, camp on sand instead of in the dune grass.

Campsites: Numerous clearings amongst the driftwood above the high-tide line. The best sites are in the centre of the beach or on the east side.

NATURE NOTE

SEA WOLVES

Grant Bay, along with other remote coastal trails (including Trips 8, 14, 29, 30, 31, and 32), are the best places to see wolves on Vancouver Island. Known as sea wolves, these wolves are a subspecies of the grey wolf. Unlike most grey wolves, their diet is mostly marine-based and includes salmon, shellfish, seals, and river otters. They are also great swimmers, making their way between islands and peninsulas. Sea wolves live in small social packs of 5 to 12, led by an alpha male and an alpha female. Wolves tend to avoid humans, so spotting one is a rare treat. But you may be lucky enough to follow wolf tracks along a sandy beach. Dog tracks and wolf tracks are easy to confuse. In general, wolf tracks are longer than 9 cm (3.5 in), whereas dog tracks are (usually) smaller. As well, dogs often meander, while wolf tracks are typically found using an efficient, purposeful route.

Toilet: Throne-style pit toilet on a spur trail just before the beach

Water: The small stream at the west end of the beach is very choked with driftwood and hard to access. It is easiest to bring your own water.

Food Storage: None. Hang in a tree or use a bear canister or Ursack.

EXTENDING YOUR TRIP

Winter Harbour: The nearby village of Winter Harbour is worth a visit. It was once a bustling fishing and forestry town, but today it has two permanent residents, several summer cottages, and a small store. The main attraction is the quaint boardwalk that runs for nearly 1 km (0.6 mi) between homes and docks along the shore of Quatsino Sound.

Wolf tracks on the beach

FURTHER RESOURCES

Western Forest Products Camping and Recreation: info *wfproadinfo.com/ camping.html*

Fisheries and Oceans Canada: Winter Harbour tide table *tides.gc.ca/en/ stations/08735*

NTS Map: 102I08

Driving Map: *Vancouver Island BC Backroad Mapbook*

FACING: *Old-growth forest along
the Elk River Trail (Trip 26)*

ACKNOWLEDGEMENTS

THE LAST FEW YEARS have been a whirlwind of writing and research trips to complete this book. A Turkish proverb reminds us that no journey is long with good company... although I would argue that some are still long! I am immensely grateful for the hikers who accompanied me on research trips: Kamil Bialous, Michael Coughlin, Laurel Eyton, ilan Handelsman, Elliott Holmes, Reid Holmes, Zoe Holmes, Steve Ingold, Brooke Kinniburgh, Cynthia Lim, Urszula Lipsztajn, Geniva Liu, Tudor Oprea, Brenda Remedios, Debra Richardson, Josephine Schrott, Greg Smolyn, Katie Stafford, Georgia Temple, Shannon Thibault, Marianne Williams, Kareen Wong, and Laura Zajac. Extra thanks to Reid Holmes and Greg Smolyn, who contributed some of their photos to this book.

Lynne Stafford and Hans Hofmaier, ilan Handelsman and Katie Stafford, and Reid Holmes and Laura Zajac were kind enough to open their homes to me between trips, despite my tired and stinky state. Mike Blake of MB Guiding and Dave Wall of 43K Wilderness Solutions also deserve thanks for helping with trail conditions updates. I wouldn't have been able to finish the research on the book without Karly Dagys at Coast Range Clinic, Natalie MacLeod at Garibaldi Active Wellness, and Dr. Trisha Kivisalu at Changeways Clinic. They kept me mentally and physically healthy for long-distance hiking. I'm grateful for their encouragement and compassion.

It was a pleasure to work with the entire team at Greystone Books again. My editor Lucy Kenward was indispensable as usual. I'm thankful for her guidance, pragmatic advice, and kind reassurance. Jessica Sullivan and Fiona Siu created a beautiful design. Steve Chapman's maps illustrate the hikes perfectly. And without Merrie-Ellen Wilcox's copyediting and Alison Strobel's proofreading, you would all be painfully aware of my poor grasp of grammar.

Trails do not magically materialize. It takes lots of hard work from outdoor clubs and advocacy organizations, most of which are staffed by volunteers. The trails in this book would not exist without the following groups: Alpine Club of Canada, Vancouver Island section; Ancient Forest Alliance; Comox District Mountaineering Club; Cumberland Community Forest Society; Friends of Strathcona Park; Kludahk Outdoors Club; Maaqutusiis Hahoulthee Stewardship Society; Mowachaht/Muchalaht First Nation; Pacheedaht First Nation; Strathcona Wilderness Institute; Tla-o-qui-aht Tribal Parks Guardians; United Riders of Cumberland; Vancouver Island Trail Association; West Coast Trail Guardians; Wilderness Committee; and Wild Pacific Trail Society. If you can, give your money or time to one of these organizations.

This guidebook covers the traditional territory of many Indigenous Nations. One of the most rewarding parts of researching this book was learning about the Indigenous place names and stories connected to the trails. I'm also very grateful to Məlidas (Steven Recalma) for writing the beautiful message of welcome in the foreword of this book. I will carry with me on every journey into the backcountry his reminder to always experience the lands and waters with an open heart, mind, and eyes.

I would also like to thank my parents and in-laws for all the cat-sitting, Bruce for his reliability, Audrey for not helping at all, and Darude for writing "Sandstorm," which powered me through many writing sessions. Words aren't enough to thank my husband, Greg, for his support, patience, and love throughout this process.

And finally, I want to give thanks to you, the reader. Thank you to everyone who read my previous book, visited my website, or reached out to chat about trails. Your passion for B.C.'s backcountry fuels mine.

INDEX

Notes: Hikes indicated by page ranges in **bold**; maps indicated by page numbers in *italics*

Aa-aak-quaksius Lake (Jewitt Lake), 233–34
Ahousaht Nation, 102, 128, 129, 131, 132
Air Nootka, 225, 237, 240
Á,L̲EN̲EN̲EȻ ȽTE (W̱SÁNEĆ) (Saanich) Nation, 40, 44
Alldridge Point, 49
alpine growing season, 196
Amphitrite Point Lighthouse, 122
Ancient Cedars Trail, 124
Arnica Lake and Phillips Ridge, 200–201, **202–5**
Augerpoint Mountain, 173, 174, 177
Augerpoint Traverse, **168–77**; camping, 175–77; extending your trip, 153, 155, 167, 177; further resources, 177; getting there, 168–69; map, *160*; trail, 169–75
August Creek, 94
avalanches, 20, 168, 208
Avatar Grove (T'l'oqwxwat), *71*, **71–74**

Baby Bedwell Lake campground, 193, 195
backpacking. *See* hikes and backpacking

Bajo Point, 230–31
Bamfield, 40, 41, 76, 97. *See also* Keeha Beach; West Coast Trail
Battleship Lake, 148, 156, 170
BC Parks, 140, 155
beaches, travelling on, 20
Beano Creek campground, 231, 234, 235
Bear Beach campground, 54, 57
bear canisters, 24
bears, black, 22–23, 24, 80, 225, 243, 247, 250, 252, 257, 265
Bedwell and Cream Lakes, *191*, **191–96**
Bedwell Lake campground, 194, 195–96
Bedwell River (Bear River, Oinimitis), 193, 194
Beechey Head, 49
Berg Lake, 206, 210
Big Interior Mountain, 114, 177, 185, 191–92, 193
Big Lonely Doug (Douglas-fir), 74
Big Tree Trail, *125*, **125–27**
blackflies, 22
Blueberry Hill Cabin and campsite, 65, 67, 68
bog, coastal upland (blanket bog), 266

Bog Woodland Interpretive Loop, 123, 124
Bonilla Point campground, 81–82, 88
Botanical Beach, 52–53, 56–57
Botany Bay, 59
Boyle Point Provincial Park, 141
buses, shuttle, 15. *See also* West Coast Trail Express
Butterwort Creek campground, 208, 209
Buttle Lake, 171, 174–75, 177, 180, 185, 187–88, 215. *See also* Arnica Lake and Phillips Ridge; Augerpoint Traverse; Upper Myra Falls
Buttle Lake Campground, 181

Cabin Point, 48–49
Cable Car campground, 111, 113
cable cars, 20
Calvin Falls campground, 230, 234–35
Campbell River, 136, 180, 218
Campbell River trips: introduction, 180–81; Arnica Lake and Phillips Ridge, **202–5**; Bedwell and Cream Lakes, **191–96**; Crest Mountain, **213–16**; Elk River and Landslide Lake, **206–10**; Flower Ridge, **185–90**; Ripple Rock, **182–84**; Upper Myra Falls, **197–99**
Camper Bay campground, 83, 89
campfires, 27–28
camping, 16, 25
Canada's Gnarliest Tree (cedar), 73
Cape Beale, 99
Cape Palmerston Recreation Area, 271
Cape Scott, 256, **257–62**, 263
Cape Scott lighthouse, 256, 257, 260, 262
Cape Scott Provincial Park, 218. *See also* Cape Scott; North Coast Trail; San Josef Bay
Cape Scott Water Taxi, 248, 256, 257, 264

Cape Sutil and campground, 251, 254, 255
Carmanah Creek campground, 81, 87
Carmanah Point Lighthouse, 81
Carmanah Valley, 90, **90–94**
Carmanah Walbran Provincial Park, 91–92, 94. *See also* Carmanah Valley
Castlecrag Mountain, 150
The Cats Ears, 117
cedar, western red-, 92
Cevallos Campsite, 219
Chemainus (Stz'uminus) Nation, 40
Chez Monique restaurant (WCT), 81
China Beach campground and day-use area, 41, 52, 53, 62
China Bowls (Cumberland Potholes, Perseverance Potholes), 142, 145
Chin Beach campground, 54–55, 57, 58
Chrome Island, 141
Circlet Lake and Mount Albert Edward, **164–67**; camping, 166; extending your trip, 153, 157, 159, 167, 170; further resources, 167; getting there, 164; maps, *161, 162*; trail, 164–66
Circlet Lake campground, 166, 175
Clayoquot Sound. *See* Big Tree Trail
Coal Creek Historic Park, 142, 144
coastal travel, 20
Coast Salish peoples, 40, 136, 180
Coast Tower (Sitka spruce), 92
Cobalt Lake campsite, 115, 117, 118
cougars, 23, 69, 149
Courtenay-Comox trips: introduction, 136–37; Augerpoint Traverse, **168–77**; Circlet Lake and Mount Albert Edward, **164–67**; Cumberland Community Forest, **142–45**; Forbidden Plateau Traverse, **146–53**; Helen Mackenzie and Kwai Lakes Loop, **154–59**; Helliwell Loop, **138–41**
Cow Bay campground, 132, 133–34
Cowichan (Quw'utsun) Nation, 40, 157

Crab Shack (Nitinaht Narrows), 80, 87
Cream Lake camping area, 195, 196. *See also* Bedwell and Cream Lakes
creek crossings, 19-20
Crest Mountain, *212*, **213-16**
Creyke Point, 50
Cribs Creek campground, 81, 87
Croteau Lake campground, 148, 157
Cruickshank Canyon, 153, 157, 158, 165
Cullite Creek campground, 82-83, 89
culturally modified trees, 98, 132, 232
Cumberland, 136-37
Cumberland Campground, 137
Cumberland Community Forest, *142*, **142-45**

Danish settlements, 261
Darling River campground, 78, 85
Della Falls, **107-14**; camping, 112-13; extending your trip, 113-14; further resources, 114; getting there, 107, 109; map, *108*; mining history, 114; trail, 109-11; views from Bedwell and Cream Lakes, 192, 195
Della Falls campground, 111, 113
Della Falls Water Taxi, 107, 114
Ditidaht Comfort Camping, 80, 86-87, 89
Ditidaht Nation, 40, 78-80, 81, 91
dogs, 16, 23, 28, 128
Drabble Lakes, 150
Drinkwater Creek, 111
Drinkwater Valley, 114, 195. *See also* Della Falls
driving, backroads, 14-15

earthquake, Strathcona Provincial Park (1946), 208
East Point (Saturna Island), 45
East Sooke Coast Trail, *46*, **46-50**
Effingham River, 116

Ehattesaht Nation, 218, 241
Elk Falls Provincial Park, 180
Elkhorn Mountain, 184, 210
Elk River and Landslide Lake, **206-10**, *212*
Eric Lake campground, 258, 260

Fair Harbour, 218, 219, 240
fees, 16
5040 Peak, 102, 118-19. *See also* HišimýawiX̣ Hut and 5040 Peak
fires, 27-28
first aid, 17
First Beach campground (San Josef Bay), 265, 266
Fisherman River campground, 259, 260-61
fishing, 16, 166, 206
fitness, 13-14
floatplanes, 15. *See also* Air Nootka
Flora Islet, 140
Flores Island, 102. *See also* Wild Side Trail
Flower Ridge, **185-90**, *186*, 195
food, 17, 23-24
Forbidden Plateau Traverse, **146-53**; camping, 151-53; extending your trip, 153, 159, 177; further resources, 153; getting there, 146-47; history of, 148; maps, *161*, *162-63*; trail, 147-51
Frances Barkley, MV, 96
French Beach Provincial Park, 41
Friendly Cove (Yuquot), 225, 226, 232, 235, 237

Gem Lake, 171, 177
giant trees. *See* Big Tree Trail; Randy Stoltmann Commemorative Grove; T'l'oqwxwat (Avatar Grove)
Gibson Marine Provincial Park. *See* Wild Side Trail
Gilbert Lake, 65

Golden Hinde, 184, 202, 205
Gold River, 180, 218, 219, 225
Gold River Municipal Campground,
181, 219
Grant Bay, 218, 272, **272-75**
Gravel Flats campground, 208, 209
Great Central Lake, 109
Green Point Campground, 102
Grunts Grove, 94
Guise Bay campground, 259, 261-62
Gulf Islands National Park Reserve.
See Narvaez Bay

Hairtrigger Lake, 157, 165, 166
Halalt Nation, 40, 136
Hanging Garden Tree, 125, 127
Hansen Lagoon, 259, 261
hazards. *See* safety
Heaven Tree, 94
Helen Mackenzie and Kwai Lakes
Loop, **154-59**; camping, 158;
extending your trip, 153, 158-59,
170; further resources, 159; getting there, 154; maps, *161, 162*;
trail, 154-58
Helliwell Loop, *138*, **138-41**
Helliwell Provincial Park, 138
help, getting, 24
hemlock, western, 92
hikes and backpacking: introduction,
11-12; gear, 16-17; how to use
this book, 29-30; Leave No Trace
principles, 24-28; map, *31-33*;
overview of hikes, 34-37; safety,
17-24; trip planning, 13-17
Hišimy̓awiȴ Hut and 5040 Peak, 16,
115, **115-19**
Holberg, 218, 219, 248-49
Homalco Nation, 136, 180
Hornby Island, 136, 137, 138-39. *See
also* Helliwell Loop
Hupačasath Nation, 102
Huu-ay-aht First Nation, 40, 41, 78,
79-80, 97

hygiene, 19
hypothermia, 18, 20

ice and snow, 20
I-Hos Gallery (Courtenay), 136,
180
Indigenous Peoples. Campbell River,
180; Courtenay-Comox, 136;
culturally modified trees, 98, 132,
232; Northwest coast, 218; Port
Alberti to Tofino, 102; Southwest
Coast, 40. *See also specific Nations*
insects, 22
Iron Mine Bay, 47
Irony Creek (Shuttleworth Bight)
campground, 251-52, 255

Jack's Fell, 168, 174
Jack Shark Lake, 173-74
Jack's Trail informal camping area,
174, 177
Japantown (Cumberland), 145
Jewitt Lake (Aa-aak-quaksius Lake),
233-34
John Leesing Grove, 64
Johnston Lake, 149
Juan de Fuca Marine Trail, **51-59**;
camping, 57-59; extending your
trip, 59, 70; further resources, 59;
getting there, 52-53; map, *51*; trail,
53-57
Juan de Fuca Provincial Park, 41
Jurassic Point, 246
Jutland Mountain, 166, 171, 177

Kapoose Creek, 242
Ka:'yu:'k't'h'/Che:k:tles7et'h Nation,
218
Keeha Beach, 16, *95*, **95-99**
Kiix̣in National Historic Site, 97
Kin Beach Provincial Park, 137
Kings Peak, 214
Kitty Coleman Provincial Park, 137
Klanawa River campground, 79,
85-86

Kludahk Trail, **60–70**; camping, 67–70; extending your trip, 59, 70; further resources, 70; getting there, 61–62; map, *60–61*; trail, 62–67

K'ómoks Nation, 136, 140, 148, 180

Kutcous River campground, 131, 133

Kwai Lake campground, 149, 152, 155, 156, 157, 158, 165, 175. *See also* Helen Mackenzie and Kwai Lakes Loop

Kwaksistah Regional Park Campground, 219

Kwakwaka'wakw people, 136, 180, 218, 249, 252, 271

Kyuquot Sound. *See* Tatchu Peninsula

ladders and ropes, 20–21

Lady Rose Marine Services, 96, 99

Lake Cowichan (Ts'uubaa-asatx) Nation, 40, 136

Lake Helen Mackenzie campground, 148, 152, 155, 156, 157–58, 175. *See also* Helen Mackenzie and Kwai Lakes Loop

Landslide Lake, 209–10. *See also* Elk River and Landslide Lake

Laura Creek campground, 252, 255

lava, pillow, 215

Leave No Trace principles, 24–28

Leiner River Recreation Site, 219

Lily Loop Trail, 64

Little Jim Lake, 195

Little Kuitshe Creek campground, 56, 57, 58

Loss Creek suspension bridge, 55

lost, getting, 18

Louie Lagoon (Starfish Lagoon), 225, 227, 229

Love Lake, 114

Lower Myra Falls, 197, 199

Lyackson Nation, 40, 136

Lyme disease, 22

Macjack River, 268, 270, 271

Maquinna Point pocket coves camping area, 232, 236

Margaret Creek campground, 110–11, 112–13

Mariwood Lake, 149, 157, 158

marmot, Vancouver Island, 106, 188

Masters, Ruth, 170

Matilda Inlet: Warm Springs, 134

McKenzie Lake, 159

McKenzie Lake campground, 146, 150, 151, 152–53

McKenzie Meadows, 150

Meadow Cabin and campsite, 64, 67

Meares Island Tribal Park (Wanachus-Hilthuuis), 125. *See also* Big Tree Trail

menstruation, while backpacking, 27

Menzies Bay, 183–84

Michigan Creek campground, 78, 84–85

mining, 114, 205

The Misthorns, 114

Moat Lake, 167, 170

Monarch Head (Saturna Island), 45

mosquitos, 22

mountain lions. *See* cougars

Mount Albert Edward, 150, 167, 168, 170–71, 177. *See also* Circlet Lake and Mount Albert Edward

Mount Albert Edward camping areas, 176

Mount Arrowsmith (Judge's Route), *103*, **103–6**, 140

Mount Becher, 150–51, 152, 153

Mount Colonel Foster, 206, 208, 214

Mount Frink, 171

Mount Hall, 117

Mount Regan, 177

Mount Rosseau, 114, 190

Mount Septimus, 114, 185, 190, 192, 195

Mount St. Patrick, 264, 266, 267

Mount Tom Taylor, 191, 193

Mount Washington, 136, 137, 150

Mowachaht/Muchalaht Nation, 180, 218, 226, 227, 232, 234, 235
Mushroom Point, 243
mushrooms, 142, 149, 184, 203
Myra Creek, 197–98. *See also* Lower Myra Falls; Upper Myra Falls
Myra Falls mine, 188, 203, 205
Mystic Beach campground, 53, 57

Nahwitti Lake Recreation Site, 219
Nahwitti people, 250, 254
Nahwitti River campground, 250, 254
Narvaez Bay, 16, 42, **42–45**
navigation, 14
Nels Bight campground, 256, 259, 261
Nikkei Mountain, 145
Nim Nim Interpretive Centre (Courtenay), 136, 180
Nine Peaks, 105, 114, 177
Nissen Bight campground, 253, 255–56, 259
Nitinaht Narrows cabins, 80, 87
Nitinaht Village, 91
Nootka Sound, 227, 232, 235
Nootka Trail, **225–38**; camping, 234–37; extending your trip, 237; further resources, 237; getting there, 225–26; maps, *224*, *228*, *231*; trail, 227, 229–34
North Coast Trail, **247–56**; camping, 253–56; extending your trip, 256, 262; further resources, 256; getting there, 248–49; maps, *247*, *251*; trail, 249–53
Northwest Coast trips: introduction, 218–19; Cape Scott, **257–62**; Grant Bay, **272–75**; Nootka Trail, **225–38**; North Coast Trail, **247–56**; Raft Cove, **268–71**; San Josef Bay, **264–67**; Tatchu Peninsula, **239–46**; Upana Caves, **220–23**
Noyse Lake Cabin and campsite, 66, 67, 69
Nuchatlaht Nation, 218

Nuu-chah-nulth people, 40, 60, 102, 180, 218, 227, 240–41
Nuyumbalees Cultural Centre (Quadra Island), 136, 180
Nymphe Cove, 184

Orange Juice Creek campground, 79, 85
Owen Point, 83

Pacheedaht Campground, 41
Pacheedaht Nation, 40, 55, 57, 71, 82–84
Pachena Bay Campground, 41
Pachena Point Lighthouse, 78
Pacific Rim National Park Reserve, 102. *See also* West Coast Trail
Panther Lake, 149
Paradise Meadows, 146–47, 148, 155–56, 165, 170
Payzant Creek campground, 56, 57, 58–59
Penelakut Nation, 40, 136
Phillips Ridge, 188, 205. *See also* Arnica Lake and Phillips Ridge
plants, 156, 196
poop, disposing of, 27
Porritt Creek and camping area, 243–44, 245
Port Alberni, 40, 102
Port Alberni and Tofino trips: introduction, 102; Big Tree Trail, **125–27**; Della Falls, **107–14**; Hišimȳawiƛ Hut and 5040 Peak, **115–19**; Mount Arrowsmith (Judge's Route), **103–6**; Wild Pacific Trail, **120–24**; Wild Side Trail, **128–34**
Port Eliza, 239, 246
Port Hardy, 218, 219, 248
Port Renfrew, 40, 41, 52–53, 76
ptarmigan, Vancouver Island white-tailed, 106, 167
Puzzle Mountain, 214

Quinsam Campground, 180
Quw'utsun (Cowichan) Nation, 40,
157
Qwat'sinuxw (Quatsino) Nation, 218,
252

Raft Cove, *268*, **268-71**
Raft Cove Provincial Park, 218
Ralph Lake and River, 171
Ralph River Campground, 181, 185
Randy Stoltmann Commemorative
Grove, 94
Raven Lake, 64
regulations, 16
reservations, 16
Rhodes Creek Recreation Site, 219
Ripple Rock, *182*, **182-84**
roads, forest service, 14-15
ropes and ladders, 20-21
Rugged Point Marine Provincial Park
and campground, 241, 245. *See
also* Tatchu Peninsula
Ruth Masters Lake and camping area,
171, 172, 173, 175, 176

Saanich (Á,LE̲NENEȻ ȽTE
(W̲SÁNEȻ)) Nation, 40, 44
Saddle informal camping area, 174,
176
safety, 17-24; cable cars, ladders,
ropes, and other infrastructure,
20-21; creek crossings, 19-20;
drinking water, 18-19; first aid, 17;
getting help, 24; getting lost, 18;
hygiene, 19; hypothermia, 18, 20;
snow and ice, 20; tides and coastal
travel, 20; trailhead security, 22;
trip plan, 17-18; wildlife, 22-24
salal berries, 271
Sand Dunes campground (Second
Beach), 130, 133
Sandpiper Creek camping area, 241-
42, 245
Sandstone Point, 246

San Josef Bay, 262, *263*, **264-67**
San Juan Ridge Ecological Reserve, 64
Saturna Island, 40, 41, 44. *See also*
Narvaez Bay
Saw Blades campground, 111, 113
scəwaθenaʔɬtəməxʷ (Tsawwassen)
Nation, 40
Scout Camp Recreation Site, 109
Sea Lion Rocks, 78
sea otters, 218, 230, 244, 250
seasons, 13
Sea Stack Beach camping area, 233,
234, 236-37
Second Beach (Sand Dunes camp-
ground), 130, 133
Second Beach campground (San Josef
Bay), 266-67
Semiahmoo Nation, 40
shark, bluntnose sixgill, 140
Shepherd Peak, 188
Shorebird Expeditions, 226, 237
Shushartie Bay campground, 249, 253
shuttle buses, 15. *See also* West Coast
Trail Express
Shuttleworth Bight (Irony Creek)
campground, 251-52, 255
Siiqaa Water Taxi, 240, 246
Skinner Creek campground, 250, 254
Skuna Creek camping area, 230, 234
Slingshot Meadows, 150
snow and ice, 20
Sombrio Beach campground, 55-56,
57, 58
Sooke, 40. *See also* East Sooke Coast
Trail
Southwest Coast trips: introduction,
40-41; Carmanah Valley, **90-94**;
East Sooke Coast Trail, **46-50**;
Juan de Fuca Marine Trail, **51-59**;
Keeha Beach, **95-99**; Kludahk
Trail, 59, **60-70**; Narvaez Bay,
42-45; T'l'oqwxwat (Avatar
Grove), **71-74**; West Coast Trail,
75-89

Sproat Lake Provincial Park, 102
spruce, Sitka, 92
Square Lake, 66
Squeaky Point, 49
Starfish Lagoon (Louie Lagoon), 225, 227, 229
St. John's Point, 140
Strathcona Park Lodge, 180
Strathcona Provincial Park, 136, 170, 180, 198, 205, 208. See also Arnica Lake and Phillips Ridge; Augerpoint Traverse; Bedwell and Cream Lakes; Circlet Lake and Mount Albert Edward; Crest Mountain; Della Falls; Elk River and Landslide Lake; Flower Ridge; Forbidden Plateau Traverse; Helen Mackenzie and Kwai Lakes Loop; Upper Myra Falls
Strathcona-Westmin Provincial Park, 205
Stz'uminus (Chemainus) Nation, 40
Sunrise Beach camping area, 233, 234, 236
Swim Cove, 49
swimming, 27

Tahsis, 218, 219, 220, 226. See also Upana Caves
Tatchu Creek camping area, 244, 246
Tatchu Peninsula, **239–46**; camping, 245–46; extending your trip, 246; further resources, 246; getting there, 239–40; maps, *238, 243*; trail, 240–44
Tea Hut day-use cabin and campsite, 64, 67, 68
Ten Essentials, 16–17
Tent Lake Cabin and campsite, 66, 67, 69–70
Terrace Beach, 122, 124
Third Beach campground (Nootka Trail), 230, 234
Thrasher Cove campground, 84, 89

Three Sisters (Sitka spruce), 92–93
ticks, 22, 182
tides, 20
Tla'amin/Sliammon Nation, 136
Tla-o-qui-aht (ƛaʔuukwiʔatḥ) Nation, 102, 119, 127
T'łat'łasikwala (Tlatlaoikwala) Nation, 218, 252
T'l'oqwxwat (Avatar Grove), *71*, **71–74**
Tofino, 102. *See also* Port Alberni and Tofino trips
Tongue Point, 226, 227, 237
Toquaht Nation, 102, 119
Tower Cabin and campsite, 64, 68
trail conditions, 14
trailhead security, 22
TrailRider, 156
trees: culturally modified, 98, 132, 232; identifying, 92. *See also* Big Tree Trail; Randy Stoltmann Commemorative Grove; T'l'oqwxwat (Avatar Grove)
Tribune Bay Provincial Park, 141
Triple Peak, 116, 117, 118, 119
Tripod Beach camping area, 250, 253
trip planning, 13–17, 24–25
Tsa'tsil Lagoon, 233
Tsawwassen (sc̓əwaθenaʔɬtəməxʷ) Nation, 40
Tseshaht Nation, 102
Tsocowis Creek campground, 79, 85
Tsusiat Falls campground, 79–80, 86
Ts'uubaa-asatx (Lake Cowichan) Nation, 40, 136

Uchuck III, MV, 226, 234, 237
Uchucklesaht Nation, 102
Ucluelet, 102. *See also* Wild Pacific Trail
Ucluelet (Yuułuʔiłʔatḥ) Nation, 102, 115, 119
U'mista Cultural Centre (Alert Bay), 136, 180, 218

Upana Caves, 220, **220-23**
Upper Campbell Reservoir Campground, 181
Upper Myra Falls, **197-99**, *200-201*
Ursack, 24

Valencia Bluffs, 79
Victoria, 40, 41
Victoria Peak, 184
Voyager Water Taxi, 240, 246

Walbran Creek campground, 82, 88
Wanachus-Hilthuuis (Meares Island Tribal Park), 125. *See also* Big Tree Trail
Warm Springs (Matilda Inlet), 134
wasps, 22
waste disposal, 26-27
water, drinking, 18-19
water taxis: introduction, 15-16; Cape Scott Water Taxi, 248, 256, 257, 264; Della Falls Water Taxi, 107, 114; Shorebird Expeditions, 226, 237; Siiqaa Water Taxi, 240, 246; Voyager Water Taxi, 240, 246; Zeballos Expeditions, 226, 237
weather, 13
West Coast Trail, **75-89**; camping and cabins, 84-89; further resources, 89; getting there, 76-77; history, 88; maps, *75, 79, 81, 82*; reservations, 16; trail, 77-84
West Coast Trail Express, 52, 59, 62, 76, 96

Western Forest Products San Josef Campground, 219
We Wai Kai Nation, 136, 180
We Wai Kum House of Treasures (Campbell River), 136, 180
We Wai Kum Nation, 136, 180
whales: grey, 78, 129; humpback, 250; orca (killer whale), 44
wildlife, 22-24, 28
Wild Pacific Trail, *120*, **120-24**, *123*
Wild Side Trail, **128-34**; camping, 132-34; extending your trip, 134; further resources, 134; getting there, 129; map, *128*; trail, 129-32
Winter Harbour, 218, 219, 272-73, 275. *See also* Grant Bay
Wolftrack Beach camping area, 252, 253
wolves, 23, 128, 132, 225, 239, 247, 257, 274
W̱SÁNEĆ (Á,LEṈENEȻ ȽTE) (Saanich) Nation, 40, 44
Wye Lake, 63-64, 67, 70

Yellow Bluff, 239, 246
Yuquot (Friendly Cove), 225, 226, 232, 235, 237
Yuułuʔiłʔatḥ (Ucluelet) Nation, 102, 115, 119

Zeballos, 218, 219, 226
Zeballos Expeditions, 226, 237

ABOUT THE AUTHOR

TARYN EYTON is a born-and-raised Vancouverite who now calls Squamish, B.C., home. She has been hiking all her life and backpacking for 20 years. Eyton runs an all-things-outdoors website, happiestoutdoors.ca, and works as a freelance outdoor and adventure travel writer.

She is a certified Leave No Trace Master Educator and has been volunteering with Leave No Trace Canada to teach awareness workshops for the last 15 years. Eyton is a Fellow of the Royal Canadian Geographical Society, a member of the Board of Directors for the Vancouver International Mountain Film Festival, and President of the Friends of Garibaldi Park Society. Her first book, *Backpacking in Southwestern British Columbia: The Essential Guide to Overnight Hiking Trips*, was published in 2021.

Facebook.com/HappiestOutdoors

@happiestoutdoors

Taryn@HappiestOutdoors.ca

HappiestOutdoors.ca/BackpackingonVI